GREAT
MIRRORS
SHATTERED

IDEOLOGIES OF DESIRE

David M. Halperin
Series Editor

GREAT MIRRORS SHATTERED

Homosexuality, Orientalism, and Japan

John Whittier Treat

New York · Oxford
Oxford University Press
1999

Oxford University Press

Oxford   New York
Athens   Auckland   Bangkok   Bogotá
Buenos Aires   Calcutta   Cape Town   Chennai   Dar es Salaam
Delhi   Florence   Hong Kong   Istanbul   Karachi
Kuala Lumpur   Madrid   Melbourne   Mexico City
Mumbai   Nairobi   Paris   São Paulo   Singapore
Taipei   Tokyo   Toronto   Warsaw

and associated companies in
Berlin   Ibadan

Copyright © 1999 by John Whittier Treat

Published by Oxford University Press, Inc.
198 Madison Avenue, New York, New York 10016

Oxford is a registered trademark of Oxford University Press, Inc.

Library of Congress Cataloging-in-Publication Data

Treat, John Whittier.
Great mirrors shattered : homosexuality, orientalism, and Japan
/ John Whittier Treat.
p.   cm.—(Ideologies of desire)
Includes index.
ISBN 0-19-510923-6
1. Homosexuality—Japan.   2. AIDS (Disease)—Japan.   3. Gay men—
Japan—Sexual behavior.   4. Homosexuality—Japan—Public opinion.
5. Public opinion—Japan.   I. Title.   II. Series.
HQ76.3.J3T74   1999
306.76'6'0952—dc21   98-20609

Material from *Mikakunin biko buttai* (Unidentified Shadowing Object) by Masahiko Shimada (Bungei Shunju,
1986) is reprinted courtesy of the author.

1 3 5 7 9 8 6 4 2

Printed in the United States of America
on acid-free paper

In memory of Jesusa B. Palaruan
(1966–1987)
Bahala na ang Diyos

CONTENTS

PREFACE

This is a small book about a large number of things. I would like to tell you about Japan, and why my obsession with it, akin to a romance, made the later disappointments so acute. I would also like to explain how those disappointments were, in turn, made insights into my own prides and prejudices. Then there were the romances themselves. I know something about the gay people born in Japan and those who enlist there later in life, and that is part of this story as well. I have a theory to tell you about why Americans go there, and why some stay. Finally, I have my own little tale about why I left, only to return again and again.

This is also a book about something old but only recently of general note: Orientalism, which I can define without irony as the Western study of everywhere else. Much has been said about this, especially in the last twenty years, but perhaps my particular take on it is original. It is certainly unabashedly personal. This book is also about something very new—AIDS—and how it changed "everywhere else." That too is personal. Like many short books nowadays, it is about a full life halfway through its natural course, compressed into the brevity of a few pages. I know there are other books such as this of course, but this one is mine.

A memoir of a life as plain as this one would certainly be vain, were it not for an epidemic none of us could have predicted but that has made many of us prematurely retrospective. In part, this is one of our strategies for surviving a catastrophe that otherwise threatens to end our lives without the old age we all hope for. As a genre, the memoir is also how a certain kind of knowledge, however local, is often secured nowadays in lieu of broader or sturdier registers for our late twentieth-century experiences. Mine is told as an account of a little over one year in my life, age thirty-four, spent abroad and now, over a decade in the past, receding far in memory as well as geography. I had no choice, I now realize, in waiting this long to publish this book. Not only my profession but my mortality required, in a word, "perspective": time enough to know what I intuited, and sometimes feared, was not served so much by confession as by reflection.

The student of another culture who travels there goes thinking: I will watch how those people live, or work, or write, and then bring their lessons home. But he goes abroad as a man, or woman, and so with his intellectual intents goes too a sexual body. His desire for knowledge is easily confused with his desire to possess or be possessed by other things: passion. The body becomes his methodology, and his desire for union an epistemology. Many of us, if male and heterosexual, will bring back wives—the souvenirs of a place where we also left a part of ourselves. Others might return home alone, but we were all in those distant lands lovers of a kind.

But what about today? When the body of even the most well-meaning interloper, and his desires, are quarantined out of fear of death? Suddenly the body as instrument, either for knowledge or for pleasure, is rendered impotent. That student of another culture is made aware of his material intransitivity, by which I mean his physical body's new-found opaqueness as a carrier of ruin. In place of its former utility as a convenient conduit for learning, the dangerous flesh itself in peril now looms as an ironic object of study. If "knowledge is power," as Orientalism teaches, then to ask after AIDS just who is known and what is ruled may yield surprising answers.

Unfortunately this book is still not a polished work, and my answers to those questions still inarticulate. More years would not have remedied *that*. The book is about "me," but only as a venue to trace the conjuncture of life and death, America and Japan, sense and the inexplicable, desire and hatred, that has singularly focused my mind on what I have come to see as shared and effectively inseparable among all those things. You are invited, therefore, to read this as more a comedy than a tragedy.

I have not written a scholarly work. There was not much of an archive to consult, and I freely invented names for other people and tinkered with memories of my own when my greater purpose was served. This book throws together with admittedly little design, hopelessly tiny pieces of people and shards of time past and present into a story without a plot—or, to put it another way, into what once would have been a very Japanese kind of book in its willful meanderings. Much of what is said here are not my words, but quotes from other people cited with either admiration or contempt. (I can only hope it is always clear which.) There is a general narrative driven by the calendar; but there are also many detours dictated by the caprice of association in which I have learned, in search of understanding, to trust. I would have preferred to have given you something more readable. But to the extent that this is real history, that was not possible. Real history, as we know, seldom obeys what we believed were its promises.

Roland Barthes, one of the more important characters in this book, wrote that Japan afforded him "a situation of writing." There is a long tradition of writers, East and West, who needed to travel far to see, or admit to, things close at hand. But in my case it would be more accurate to argue the opposite: that writing is how I have come to tell you about Japan. My experiences are hardly unique, on the one hand, and certainly not pertinent or even interesting to most people on the other. But when I traveled to Japan in the late 1980s to write a long overdue study of the literature of Hiroshima and Nagasaki and then found myself in the midst of a sudden national panic over a virus I thought I could leave behind, I realized that the cruel fates modern times hand us may be random, but apparently evenly distributed. Neighborhoods infected, no less than cities annihilated, are our contemporary truth. In that sense, this is the book that my earlier *Writing Ground Zero: Japanese Literature and the Atomic Bomb* made me write, not least of all in order to make the world, where no one is safe from contingencies of our own manufacture, clear in all its implications.

This book started out as an essay in *positions: east asian cultures critique*, in which I thanked Tani Barlow and August Miller for, in the first instance, the chance to put down on paper things important to the way we scholars of Asia work, but heretofore only talked in private about; and in the second, for help with gathering material about AIDS in Japan after I had returned to the United States. Now I have to acknowledge their successors: my friends David Halperin (who recruited this expanded manuscript when it was only an e-mail apparition) and Dennis Altman, a mentor of mine for years who also, if for reasons other than David's, thought this kind of book a good idea and whose own great joy in writing, on even the most serious problems we face, proved contagious.

Lastly, thanks for this and that to Kate Cummings, Ed Kamens, Amy Robinson, Laura Driussi, Susan Hanley, Earl Jackson, Jr., Edward Baron Turk, Oxford University Press, the Stanford Humanities Center, and especially Ellen Neskar for lucky room thirteen.

John Treat

Seoul, July 1998

GREAT
MIRRORS
SHATTERED

It soon became evident that the foreign "barbarians" were not to be driven away. Hundreds had come, from the East as well as from the West; and all possible measures for their protection had been taken; and they had built queer cities of their own upon Japanese soil.

—Lafcadio Hearn, 1896

SEPTEMBER

Certain Details

My doctor says he'll take a chest X ray. "Yes, that's how it often starts." "It" is pneumonia, and "how" is the bronchitis that has been with me all summer. Now, only two weeks before I go to Tokyo for a year, I cannot wait any longer to see my doctor. Unless I am willing to go to Japanese doctors later.

One other summer in the near future, when I will not get through a day without feeling an adrenaline surge of terror; when oral fungi will march down my throat and rashes on my back creep around to my stomach; when conjunctivitis will confound my eye doctor and my regular doctor gently tells me there is only one test left, Dan (not sick, but now infected with my fear) and I will go to the "small and dreary" King County Public Health building staffed with counselors who have already passed (some only to fail) through the tiny portal where the paths of our generation of gay men converge. There, ordered to separate cubicles, we will give up between us less than a thimbleful of blood. Of the next two weeks I will not remember much other than some cryptic phone calls to people I thought I might never call again, and a visit to my parents both to distract myself and to show them, just in case, "how he looked back then." For two weeks I will wait to discover for certain what I was afraid that September X ray would augur. For two weeks I will, in a familiar pattern, abandon my lover to face his own dread without me.

I will pass that test, but that is another story and not this one. This book is about Acquired Immunity Deficiency Syndrome in Japan, and the panic that erupted over it there in the late 1980s when I was living in Tokyo. But with each successive rewrite of these thirteen chapters, I find myself telling more about myself and my quarter-century involvement with Japan, the same two and a half decades in which I and my kind in America rose to the challenge of our desires and, now, to the body's newer challenge. This book is about how we find ourselves so unalike or similar at the most unexpected times, in the most unanticipated places; how both our affinities and differences play tricks before our eyes whenever we look closely at ourselves and those friends or strangers standing beside us. It is also about the work of memory, where all our serial selves exist at once, collapsed atop each other in a heap of uncannily congruent experiences, compressed into a thin and delicate wafer we call, for lack of a more accurate term, one's own life.

The doctor sends me down the hall. "Two lefts and a right," then into the lab, where I soon have my chest x-rayed. I am told to wait in the small lobby while the image is developed. Handed a big manila envelope, I am retracing my steps back to the doctor when I am intercepted by his nurse, who takes the envelope from me. I reenter the examination room, sit on the edge of the table, and stare at the supplies neatly lined up on the small desk and the shelf above it. Everything antiseptically enclosed in smooth and cool paper sheaths, ready to be disposed as soon as any part touches my saliva, my rectum, my blood.

In September I do not have pneumonia. It is only bronchitis. The doctor smiles at me, and promises it will get better. But not, as it turns out, until it gets worse.

Do you remember? The *New York Times* on July 3, 1981? Is it only in hindsight that you think you do? Two days later, in the first mention in Japan of what did not yet have a name, the daily *Asahi* newspaper features a headline that translates as "Bad News for Homos." (Years later, when the bad news would be worse, an English-language pamphlet distributed to foreigners arriving at the New Tokyo International Airport will still speak of the special dangers faced by "homos.") "The United States, said to be a homo heaven," reported the *Asahi*, "has seen the outbreak among homos of an extremely rare cancer called Kaposi's sarcoma."

By July 20 the *Asahi*'s competitor, the *Mainichi*, was carrying the news from the United Homo Heaven of America that while "almost all the victims are young male homosexuals, it is beginning to spread to frequent drug abusers and hemophiliacs." Two years later to the day, the Japanese press would admit in a double-negative circumlocution that a Japanese hemophiliac has now died of AIDS, despite earlier denials by the Ministry of Health and Welfare.

November 23, 1981. At the Ninth Congress of the Tokyo Hemophiliac Association, hemophiliac "Mr. K" asks Professor Kazama of Teikyo University about the reported relationship between AIDS and hemophilia in the United States. It is "a homo disease," he reassures the audience, "with nothing to do with hemophiliacs."

I have given up my studio apartment near the corner of John Street and Summit Avenue since I will be gone for an entire year. All my belongings were moved into the back of Dan's garage last weekend, when I rented a truck and got my friend Jack to help carry the heavier things. I arranged everything perfectly in the small corridor between the wall and Dan's Toyota, my boxes stacked like stones in a Mayan pyramid. Everything rises to an apex only inches from the garage's unfinished ceiling. I drape them in sheets. My boxes would look like an immense ghost, were it not for all the little pink roses on the top sheet and the faded blue stripes on the bottom.

Dan and I have been lovers for less than a year—not long enough to be living together by our cautious calculations. We usually spend one night at his place, the next at mine. But since the first of the month, because I've given up my apartment and because it will not be long before I leave for Japan, I have been sharing his small bungalow with him every day. It is the kind of house once built for families, but now, in our more affluent and less fertile age, the perfect size for one gay man and maybe one other. There are many of these bungalows in Seattle, whole neighborhoods of them. Dan's sits two-thirds of the way up a steep hill overlooking the ship canal that connects Lake Washington to Puget Sound. It is one of the nicer houses on the street, newly painted, with two young saplings planted in front. But inside it looks deserted, or perhaps only very recently moved into. In fact, Dan has been there for years.

A scientist at the university where I teach Japanese, Dan has installed only those things he absolutely needs: one sofa, one table, four chairs, a color TV, a VCR, a microwave, a hot-air popcorn popper, a bed, a desk, a stereo, one bookcase. There are no paintings or pictures on the wall, no knickknacks, no high school trophies (but a college-era bowling ball props one door open) or any useless, or precious, things. All the windows are nailed shut, never opened even in the hottest summer heat. Dan is impervious to changes in the body. He registers only the ideal world of equations and formulas. When I came into his life, it was as a welcome diversion: a reason to depart from a routine of work, frozen dinners, and television reruns. And he for me: a reason to stop my frantic search, my serial monogamy, my nighttime hours of anxious sleeplessness.

For a short time, Dan's house is also my house. More than a guest, less than an occupant, I make myself at home by filling the closets, piling my books in a room usually closed off, putting my half-full jars of indeterminate Oriental condiments into an otherwise empty refrigerator. But I move nothing of Dan's. I disturb none of his careful order, introduce none—well, little— of my trademark chaos. In less than a week's time, I and my few personal effects not under the sheets with either be thrown away or relocated to a foreign country. And Dan's life will be back to its single, measured rhythm once more. That, anyway, is the plan.

Seven years later Dr. Abe Takeshi, chair of the Ministry of Health and Welfare's AIDS Surveillance Committee, would explain why the clinical testing of blood products for use by hemophiliacs was delayed for more than two years:

> When one company is ahead of the others in the research and development of a new drug, the duty of a research council is to coordinate things among the companies to make them even, for the drug inspection by the Ministry of Health and Welfare. At least two or three companies should be bound together. . . . We needed to give patients the impression that all pharmaceutical companies are reliable to the same degree. . . . All companies must compete fairly. . . . It was for the sake of the patients. Those who complain don't understand things.[1]

They say it was first noted among the Japanese in 1982. We noticed it first. We saw the signs in young Japanese men we passed on San Francisco streets or sat across from in New York restaurants. And in the homes of young Japanese men we personally knew: "Ken" and "Shu" and the others with their proudly truncated, Americanized names: the dancers and the waiters, the lovers of antique dealers and the students at our universities. Who were born Japanese but had escaped to make their lives in America. Who grew thin and wasted away here, or who died of brain fevers so suddenly there was no time, even if they had wanted, to get on the flights that did take a few back "home" to little towns up and down the long, northeast Asian archipelago.

March 22, 1985.   The Ministry of Health and Welfare acknowledges that a Japanese national, an artist residing in San Francisco, has contracted AIDS. The *Asahi* alerts the nation: "Real AIDS in Japan, Too." (What editor could resist that "Too"?) Sick, he goes home, and Dr. Abe's committee dubs him Japan's first victim—their very own Patient Zero.

Why this irrepressible desire in us to seek out origins? To know the first before which was naught? When for viruses as well as all other forms of life, there is only a circle? Perhaps our obsession is one for the dream of "conception," that moment when a fornicating father or fate or the hand of a god had to have intervened, made a choice, determined history. This is the obsession of memory, too, as I flip through old appointment calendars and address books only to see faces like apparitions before me. Memory had to have been handed to us on our way out of the garden, to haunt us with the knowledge that once, before the body was shattered, we remember a whole body. A Famous Greek put out his own eyes not to be blind, but in the vain attempt to forget.

Report.   Randy Shilts says that soon after the publication of *The Band Played On*, "We were offered $1 million by a Japanese company to do the Patient Zero story." What might have interested Japanese investors in Air Canada steward Gaetan Dugas, whose sexual history has passed into popular lore as proof of our pathology?

Could that particular desire we name voyeurism serve the rationale of entire nations? There is an old word in the Japanese language: *kaimami*, a view stolen through a screen. Ancient court aristocrats did it, and so did young medieval lovers. Today, however, it is a nation of voyeurs who are at work. Japan itself watches the sweep of history from the far rim of the widest ocean, only occasionally forced or inspired to participate in the events of other places. From islands that ships seldom found, the Japanese look from a distance at wars and revolutions and now diseases that creep across the continents, poised to make a leap across the water. Why should they not think themselves different, apart, immune? Why should they not believe themselves unique—yet, for that same reason, remain enslaved to an incessant curiosity about the rest of us? A desire to *be us*? This nation has defined itself as remote, peripheral, and so is joined to the very object with which it identifies but cannot embrace. Even if the object of that gaze is a body in torment.

Japan wants to be the first to broadcast the story of Patient Zero, but it is a want predicated on a denial. Shilts tells of "one prominent Japanese scientist" who said to visiting Americans, "Isn't it a shame you have the problem in San Francisco. . . . It's because you have homosexuals. Of course, we don't have homosexuals here."[2]

Homosexuality, it is reported by Japanese researchers, is practiced by six percent of Japanese college students and is "latent among one-third of high-school boys."[3]

Dan sits at the dining room table as I fill the suitcases that are laid out in the middle of the living room floor. He cannot believe that I am going away for a year and yet will need only these two pieces of luggage. He marvels even more once he realizes that the larger of the two is going to be entirely filled with books, papers, and note cards. *"What about dress shirts?"* I'm thinking to myself: I'm glad I'm going away. *"I've got the one, you know, to wear with a tie."* A year will give me a chance to think about whether this relationship has been a good idea or not. *"I don't see any pants."* Has it only been his comfort that I've sought? Because it is so terrifying to be alone now? *"Look, they're there."* I look at Dan and feel ashamed for thinking these things. *"Three." "One sweater?" "One."* He feels nothing but love for me, and I use that fact to satisfy my other needs. *"Don't you need, um, a winter coat or something?"* My many needs. *"I'm going to buy one there."* Why would anyone have a relationship with me? *"I don't see too many socks."* When I am this calculating? *"If I do laundry once a week, all I need are seven pairs."* Why are you, I say to myself in an effort to end this little drama in my head, so bent on screwing this up before it's even started? I need to go to Japan now. I am an assistant professor of Japanese literature who has to write a book, make his mark, impress his colleagues back home by leaving them to go live a year on someone else's money. Plus, there are my own, private reasons. I'd like to turn back the clock, if only a few years' time, and pick up where I left off. *"You're amazing."*

Dan is surprised that I can travel without what would be, for him, the utter necessities of a hair dryer, multiple vitamins, ear plugs, a steam iron, and two office rolodexes. But I mean to travel light, and in fact this is exceptionally economical packing even for me. I want to hit the ground running, not be burdened with things I do not need, even with those I do need. I am trying, though I cannot tell Dan this, to strip my life for just this one year down to the barest essentials. I want to feel free, I would say: not of him so much, but then he is part of what I want to leave behind. AIDS is here in Seattle now. Mike is dead, and Josh, too. Others are close, and still others just beginning. And so I remember Japan: the last place I was before this second war in my life was declared, the last place I was before they threatened to draft me against my will once again.

The suitcases close easily—they are not even full. There will be one more bag, a small knapsack that I will carry onto the plane. In it will be my ticket, the passport, money, things to keep me occupied for ten hours over water. These are things I do not trust the airlines with, and they include my address book from the last time I lived in Japan. That was only five years ago, but now far enough gone to feel like another life altogether.

May 1981.   Tetsuji and I were in the departure lounge at the Tokyo airport, waiting to go to Hong Kong for the Golden Week holiday. Japanese seldom have real vacations, but recently the first days of May have become one. I surprised Tetsuji: all I told him is that we were traveling abroad (so bring your passport) and to a warmer place (only summer clothes). This cost me plenty, but Tetsuji, who worked as a poorly paid picture framer, was clearly enjoying this little treat already. He discovered our destination as soon as we checked in at the airport, but the rest of the long weekend ahead of us was a mystery that he wanted to savor.

In the departure lounge Tetsuji nudged me, and discreetly pointed out a handsome Japanese man waiting to board a flight to the United States. He looked gay the way that American men look gay, not the way Japanese men look gay. Tetsuji told me he was a famous printmaker who lives and works in San Francisco. Later Tetsuji would show me the catalog from one of his shows. I would think I remembered a cough, an unnatural gauntness, a pair of sunken eyes—those lonely eyes that still insisted on seeing even after disease ravages them: the damnation of remembering.

"We just do not have as many homos here as in America," will write one Japanese expert in an article on Japan's coming AIDS hysteria in this, my sabbatical year. "Certain aspects of our youth culture do seem homosexual, but there aren't many of what you would call real homos."[4]

By the summer of 1983, *Barazoku*, Japan's gay "Rose Tribe" magazine, does its first special report on *eizu*, the Japanese pronunciation of "AIDS." Two years later in another *Barazoku* piece, editor Itō Bungaku—the self-appointed leader of Japan's male homosexuals, the self-professed heterosexual guide to what is best for us—tells his readership not to worry. "There are few in Japan who use drugs, and no one here has hardcore sex like in America. So what happened there can't happen here."

> Interviewer: What did you think was the cause of AIDS, before the discovery of the virus?
> Dr. Matsuda: Well, since it was a homosexual disease, we had the idea that the cause laid in their peculiar sexual practices.
> Interviewer: A disease borne of anal intercourse! (Laughter)[5]

October 1979.   My first weekend in Japan since 1974. I made efficient use of it. A Japanese man, my acquaintance with him limited to a few hours, was whimpering something over and over again softly into the mattress, but I could not make out the words. I turned him over onto his back and asked him if anything was wrong. His eyes riveted into mine, he lifted his head off the bed and asked me in unidiomatic but perfectly plain English to use my hand.

As I prepare to start my sabbatical year in Japan, everything I read about AIDS in Japan concerns *yakugai eizu*, or AIDS that results from contaminated blood products. Eventually we would learn that those contaminated products, in Japan as in so many places, were knowingly distributed.

Dr. Abe Takeshi, Japan's expert on hemophilia, says he has "no fear that hemophiliacs with AIDS may unknowingly infect sexual partners because of the intimate doctor-patient relationship. 'I have all the information on their behavior. Hemophiliacs keep their life very nice,' he said."[6]

It is only a small step from talk of bad blood to talk of bad people. Blood may be a bodily fluid, but it is also our romantic trope for the fragile purity of the nation-state, both of which now stand threatened by many messy "social" diseases. Any mention of "blood" panics a society nervous about its health or ethnicity, and Japan is more nervous than most. Racial purity is important to Japan, but it seems impossible to preserve these days. Wealth is attracting migrant labor, and not only from poorer Asian neighbors. In the late 1980s, Tokyo, Osaka, and Nagoya are increasingly peopled with young go-getters from America, Britain, or Australia, all ready to make their fortunes if not their lives in a country that, until their arrival, had always considered itself a place that exported and never imported human beings. Only a few of us, after all, are the true immigrants here.

With a Japan no longer just Japanese come the new unnerving anxieties: clumsy interlopers who do not know the rules, who will not obey the careful restraints, who cannot know how subtlely lives here are choreographed. The greatest fear will always be our sexuality, a power that fills our larger bodies, more masculine if male, more feminine if female, and threatens to spill over into the calm pools of Japanese good sense and foul their pure waters. So "blood," at least some of ours, must become "gay blood," which must become "promiscuous semen" if we—they—are to be inoculated against the plague of undisciplined desires.

> The women's movement aside, Japan has not yet seen any group organized around its differing sexual practices. Homosexuality is not thought of except as an eccentric penchant, and heterosexual activity with multiple partners is considered profligate, immoral. So there has been from the start a limit to how far AIDS can spread in Japan.
>
> AIDS is not an epidemic in Japan for the same reasons that sexual promiscuity and anti-family ideas do not exist here.[7]

The Japan that it thinks it is, is not always the Japan that we think it is. *The Free Lovers*. Hollywood films, pornographic woodblock prints, and anecdotes heard at Thanksgiving from uncles who were stationed there during the Occupation make us imagine a Japan devoid of our American constraints. *In Japan's large cities there is a class of girls who are essentially sensualist-minded in their outlook on life*. Black market fortunes, sex in exchange for nylons, cheap beer at the PX, and lots of drugs on the street. *To most, this means simply sexual pleasure in all its ramifications*. An American man's paradise. *They are gay, in a cynical way, and very daring when drinking*. Japan is the only real place that Gulliver ever visits. *As in the case with most Japanese intellectuals, these girls also go through a foreign phase in which they try to extend their research to foreigners*.[8] I go to Japan this year to extend my research, too.

FIVE MORE AIDS VICTIMS REPORTED

> The Health and Welfare Ministry Friday determined that five more persons, one of them a foreign male homosexual, are victims of AIDS (Acquired Immune Deficiency Syndrome).
>
> The foreign male and a Japanese man, among the five designated as AIDS victims, have already left Japan.[9]

September.   Arriving on the last day of the month, I resume the excitement
of five years ago. The air, the light, the sounds, the smells are as exhilarating
to me as they were when I lived in Japan in the early 1980s, when my life
in both Japan and America was less encumbered. I had half a dozen good
years once, from the end of an Asian war that threatened to make me kill to
the start of an epidemic that now threatens to kill me. More of us Americans
are dead today of AIDS than died in Vietnam. But there is a vital difference.
The class and color that exempted so many white middle-class males from
becoming government property for two years back then are now the same
class and color that put us at a higher risk. Nothing bad is ever supposed to
happen to us crackerjack college grads, we always pass our tests, we are
destined for success. It won't happen to me. That's for other people, the less
privileged or perhaps just the unlucky. But this is not what I am thinking
just now, as I wait for the limousine arranged by my sponsors, the Japan
Foundation, to take me from the airport into the city.

The War of the Worlds
>   Pierson: Mr. Phillips, I cannot account for it.
>   Phillips: By the way, Professor, for the benefit of our listeners, how far is
>   Mars from the earth?
>   Pierson: Approximately forty million miles.
>   Phillips: Well, that seems a safe enough distance.[10]

The Japan Foundation has been around since the early 1970s, when it was
established by a government concerned with Japan's suspect reputation
around the world. It has offices in Bangkok, Canberra, Los Angeles, New
York, Paris, São Paolo and other places where Japanese products, capital,
and tourists flow. It is effectively run by Tokyo's Foreign Ministry, whose
investment in people like myself is presumably considered a wise wager in
future public relations. They flew me here business class.

I *am* a good bet, I suppose, despite my bookish line of work. I am an
Ivy League graduate in my early thirties, of mixed European stock but with
an impeccably Anglo-Saxon name: potentially, one might even think, a future
opinion-maker in my country. Many of us who have come here on these
stipends no doubt are. Not just college professors, but bankers and diplomats
as well as a potter or two. I am being "recruited," if one wants to put it that
cynically. I will research some suitably academic topic, write my findings up
in a book that thanks the Foundation in its acknowledgments, move a notch
(maybe two) up the career ladder, and thus become (if I know enough to be

grateful) suitably *shinnichi*, "pro-Japanese," a so-called Japanophile. Of course, I am already. It is the Japan Foundation's mistake to think it takes money to attract me and my kind to this place. We have been coming to these islands since boats would take us; since there has been a way to eke out a living, however meager, in a country that nonetheless affords us other kinds of compensation.

The Japan Foundation makes other, related errors. It never stops to consider (How do I know this? Because, I think to myself, I wouldn't be here if it were otherwise) just who we are who want to come to this crowded, expensive place. The Foundation knows my name and my pedigree, and it thinks it knows the extent of my desires: to be in Japan, the place I study.

But there is more. What I want are not the facts I will cull from the books I read here this year, because that I could have done back home. There is something else I want, and I am not alone in this. We putative all-American types drawn to this far country are hardly typical of our countrymen, and if we *are* future leaders in our respective fields, those fields hardly matter much. We are, after all, so different at home, so why not come to this most different of nations? Perhaps the Japan Foundation *does* know this. For while most Japanese themselves travel to America to be close to the center of the world, there are a few who go to my reputedly empty and lawless country to be as different *there* as I am here now. But I, in the fall of 1986 and with a year's worth of Seattle debts paid in advance, get to travel in style. The black limousine is waiting for me at the curb.

The route to Shigeo and Ayako's home takes me through the center of Tokyo. I scan the late-afternoon streets for what I remember and what might be new. I wind down the window of the air-conditioned car to smell the familiar moist, sickly-sweet smells of Tokyo that, in just a few hours, I will no longer notice as different from where I have just come.

Last time here, only a few years ago, we believed Tokyo existed solely for us. We were young and hip; if foreign or gay as well as young, hipper still; if foreign and gay and young all at once, then just too damn hip. If we had money, all the better: but in those days many things were negotiable currency. We had the style and the nerve to act up in a faraway place that granted us the freedom of the foreigner and that made hedonism heroic. That thin slice of years, spent in the company of friends with a bounty of good taste and bravado, was when we ricocheted between the bars and clubs and restaurants and parties of a Tokyo that we arrogantly thought had only entered the International Homosexual Grand Tour with our lucky, belated arrival.

Eros Unbound: we ruled in a city beyond the borders of a repressive Christian West, but well within the empire of desires ruled by what we were sure was the triumphantly queer Tide of History. When I left Tokyo in 1982 to return to New York, I was leaving my gay white mischief to go back to where the very idea of us was being reinvented and improved on daily. I was going home to where, if no longer the god that every American homosexual might be in Japan, I was nonetheless welcome at the Saint.

By the fall of 1986 the provinces had a new appeal. Tokyo is now where I will get away from it all. I will not read the *New York Times*, I will not get phone calls from worried friends or, what is worse, not *not* get phone calls from worried friends. Eros Bound: there will be no party here, but also fewer funerals. My energies will be sublimated in my work, I will practice my Japanese, I will write those things I need for tenure. I will live as if nothing is wrong. But this is not what I am thinking about in the backseat of the Japan Foundation car, enjoying my long-anticipated return: maybe, just maybe, the party would be on again, the *ancien régime* restored. I am back.

"In those days," wrote Saikaku in his seventeenth-century *The Great Mirror of Male Love*, "having fun was easy."[11]

I have this year off to do research for a history of atomic-bomb literature. I'll read books about the real atomic bombs, the two that blew up here, and not about the ones American science fiction postulates for our intergalactic future. It is the middle of the 1980s, and no book like mine has yet been written in English. This is a subject that, in fact, even the Japanese themselves have not had much to say about. My research, therefore, is straightforward: read those testimonies, poems, stories, and novels left behind by writers irradiated and eventually killed by our two fission devices, Fat Man and Little Boy. There are many of these things to read, but not an impossible number. Working steadily every day, I can eke my way through all of it. My method also has the advantage of any planned activity: it provides me with a useful distraction, something to chip away at daily and meanwhile keep other concerns at bay.

Some of the writers I am studying left either Hiroshima or Nagasaki for new places. Many went to Tokyo, but others traveled as far as America. What they tell me, though, in their stories and novels, is that you never really leave your city, or its terrors. Go away, their lesson is, and what you fled becomes your constant companion: in time, it may even be your friend, if only because it is so familiar and constant.

*   *   *

Shigeo and Ayako are waiting for me. My driver had to phone them to get exact directions to their home, and Ayako is standing outside in the street to signal us. The three of us had become good friends in the mid-seventies in New York, when Shigeo was stationed there by his company.

Ayako is Shigeo's second wife, and much younger than he. She worked in the same firm as he did, but quit once their romance began. Now Shigeo was being not so gently eased out of the company himself; his worries about what he would do in his early retirement would dominate our conversations during my stay at their home. But Ayako's problems were the more serious, even if they did not always get equal billing around the dinner table. A history of depression was that family's big secret. I say family, but there were no children, a rare thing in Japan but surely the reason why I was just this kind of good friend with them. All three of us are, in Japan, odd—which made our friendship all the more important.

As I am flying to Japan, a Japanese professor of philosophy publishes an essay that declares: "The greatest irony of Western civilization is that it requires both war and incurable diseases to sustain itself."[12] AIDS is his prime and most current example; but nuclear weapons are another. His argument is a familiar one, and not just to me. Modern capitalist societies are held to require disruptions on the order of world conflagrations and epidemics to disrupt the relations of production and consumption, thereby stimulating new growth. I would prefer to believe otherwise, as every odd rumble of my stomach or ache in a muscle raises the inevitable fear; and as every reference to the great war of my own gay generation makes me, if ever so slightly, sweat and replay my lucky survival. As I am flying to Japan I think: this professor writes as if Japan is somehow spared this cruel calculus of modern life. But it is only September now.

Ayako had enjoyed New York immensely, and that was also, I could guess, why they had returned home a bit earlier than expected. Years later she would tell me how bizarre the sidewalks in Tokyo still looked to her, with everyone's hair the same shade of black. Maybe I am a visible reminder of her own difference, my hair and my eyes the sign of something that within her was, for Japan, odder still.

But I have my own secrets. My stay at their home included excited talk about America and, albeit to a lesser extent, my plans for the coming year. Shigeo and I would share a beer before dinner, and maybe one more afterward. But much later at night those first two weeks of October, after my

Japanese friends had gone to bed thinking I had too; after the house in which I was staying until I could find my own place to stay was totally silent, I would creep quietly into the parlor, open the glass front to the liquor cabinet, and siphon off an inch (or was it two?) from Shigeo's decanter. (How much longer could I go on doing this before they notice?) It worked like medicine, deadening the burning sore in my lungs that was already returning (blame it on the Tokyo air!) and was worse at night, robbing me of the sleep that might also have anesthetized. The warm sting of the liquor would coat my esophagus, meander across my chest, and caress my senses. *Click*. One more night I escape the clutch of the dull anxieties and sharp fears that have stolen away with me to Japan.

Lafcadio Hearn is the first of my forebears I want to tell you about. *Hearn's early career, then, conforms to at least one picture of the fin de siècle artist.* He was not the first foreign gentleman in Japan, nor the most important, and certainly not the most like myself. *He is not addicted to drugs or excited by homosexuality, but he treats his life as an experiment; he pledges himself "to the worship of the Odd, the Queer, the Strange, the Exotic, the Monstrous."*[13] But Hearn is, in my imaginary, the best friend I have among my professional ancestors, all the adventurers, castaways, missionaries, diplomats, scholars and conquerors. Why?

On the eve of my departure for Tokyo, Dan and I had said good-bye to each other our usual way, with a dinner that was basically an excuse for heavy drinking. That night, only hours before I would board the plane, I awoke to find him sprawled atop me, asleep and immoveable. Great efforts finally dislodged him; explanations the next morning held the stupor to be the compounded effect of booze and Halcyon, a combination prompted by Dan's unspoken distress at my imminent departure. Just as when I left Tetsuji behind in Tokyo a few years earlier, it was easy for me. It always is easy for the one who goes and leaves an empty space for the one who stays behind to stare at. I had before me a reprieve: a year in Japan, twelve months without reading of false hopes or hearing of sudden turns for the worse. For Dan there would be only the terror of facing those things and his own private conjectures alone. Neither of us would, those first few months of my sabbatical, speak the fullness of our fears to the other. Even today we avoid certain details. And each of us still knows things the other does not.

We went out to a favorite place of his and had salmon, the most ritual of our Northwest meals. It was a gay restaurant, so the food was wanting, but it was where Dan felt the most relaxed. The waiter that evening was an acquaintance of ours. Or rather, of Dan's: his lover before me. Perhaps due to embarrassment, or simple awkwardness, Dan neglected to introduce us. Throughout the meal there was an odd silence whenever the waiter approached. When he did speak, it was always to Dan and never to me. He did not so much as cast a glance my way. It was only during the car ride home that I asked Dan his name. Dan said he had drawn a complete blank. Why this waiter, on this particular night? Could he be why we passed, so willingly, into a stupor that night? What other things will I never know?

Dan told me the relationship had never been successful, that from the start it had been all wrong. There was talk of a stolen wallet. Perhaps he meant to reassure me with this, but a lover's confession of failure must, in turn, raise its own doubts. We have not been together long enough for me, on this eve of my departure, to leave Seattle for Tokyo now without new worries. Worries about just whom I will have to depend on, and for so many things, at such a great distance. But such worries are among the things I will need to keep to myself. Worries become another worry. And thus yet another thing to keep to myself.

It does not take me long to find a place to live. No matter how much I enjoy Shigeo and Ayako's company, I am concerned about overstaying my welcome. And there was always the chance that Ayako's secret would erupt into the open and shatter the careful international decorum we observe each evening. My last morning there, as Ayako is helping me load her car with my things, she tells me about a dream. We were back in New York, but Shigeo is not there. Ayako is living alone in the old apartment and I visit one Friday night for dinner. We have a long talk about nothing in particular. I begin to realize that Ayako is flirting with me by telling this dream. Why now? Each of us knows things the other does not, but we do not mention them.

I remember a real dinner with Ayako. It was not unlike her dream, and not unlike my farewell dinner with Dan. We met at a small sushi restaurant in the middle of Tokyo that Shigeo was fond of, and everyone there knew Ayako well, too. *We were at our favorite place. We had salmon.* But the conversation was as private as the one she had dreamt: she told me so much that my male lovers never have, just what she thought and just what she felt. But what she told me, of course, was not quite everything. Could others at the long counter have overheard us? *The waiter seemed to know Ayako.* If so, no one cast a glance our way. *The waiter never cast a glance at me.* Surely they thought we were lovers and thus entitled to our confidences. *I wonder if he and Ayako had been lovers*. As the years go by, those confidences can grow in number, but they need to be guarded just as jealously.

1992.   Someone in Seattle has had "HIV+" tatooed on his forearm. No secrets there anymore. His employer balks, fires him, and he becomes a five o'clock news story on the local TV stations for thirty-nine seconds. Now the whole world knows. *Everyone casts glances at him*. But I can imagine that, in lieu of what most people would think his deepest truth, etched in ink forever, he has others.

OCTOBER

Stray Dogs, Ready Cash

I have moved into a small, newly built studio apartment in Nakano, a neighborhood far from anyone I know or any place I think I would want to go. But as I soon learn and remember, too, this spot has a familiar history.

One of our histories, I suppose, starts with Marco Polo. *Chipangu is an island toward the east in the high seas.* He was only seventeen when he left Venice for the East in the thirteenth century, two years younger than I was when I made my first trip. *Fifteen hundred miles distant from the continent.* Some people wonder if he really ever made it to the Far East. On his death bed, when a priest urged him to admit his stories had been lies, he replied "I did not tell half of what I saw." *And a very great island it is.*[1]

Tokyo was an obscure fishing village until Ōta Dōkan built his little fort there in the middle of our fifteenth century. By Japanese standards Tokyo is not very old. *Dōkan was fifty-four when he began work.* But its population now is so great it no longer counts as a city at all. *He wondered to himself: will I live as long as my father did?* For more than half a century now it has had the status of a prefecture, a region of boroughs and suburbs and towns where dwell more than twelve million of us. *Not only a builder of castles, he was a poet who lived in a violent time when it was difficult to tell one's friends from enemies.* Ōta Dōkan would be lost here today, not one "of us" at all. *He was, in fact, eventually killed by one of his rivals in love.*

Marco Polo never made it to Chipangu, we know that for certain. The Chinese called it a land of dwarfs, and never thought too much about it. Perhaps his hosts told him not to bother. But for other Westerners, those who went east in Polo's wake, Japan's allure would be irresistable. Some would make the journey and then stay forever: precisely because it was so far away, and so impossibly unreal a place.

In the twentieth century Nakano, along with Shinjuku, was part of the higher ground where survivors of the Great Kantō earthquake of 1923 rebuilt their homes. They thought it would be safer. For a while, we now know for certain, it was.

From the perspective of a map of the entire Tokyo plain, Nakano lies close to the old center of Edo, which is what Tokyo was called before it was made the capital with the arrival of the boy emperor Mutsuhito in the mid-nineteenth century. But from the point of view of either a homosexual or an expatriate who lives in the tight cluster of neighborhoods collected near the city's heart, Nakano is far enough away.

1980.   On Sundays I would visit Tetsuji at his little shop on the upper floor of the old mall. The stairway up to the top had the rancid smells of both industrial-strength linoleum cleaner and stale cooking oil. I seldom passed anyone else headed anywhere this high up in the Broadway, which must once have been someone's good idea of modern marketing.

It wasn't really Tetsuji's shop, of course. He was merely the employee of an absentee owner whom I never met but heard much about, none of it good. Tetsuji worked there alone every day save Wednesdays, from ten in the morning to eight at night, putting bad reproductions of art into cheap frames. It had to have been the loneliest job in the city, working in an almost un-discoverable shop in a mall that, had it been in the United States, would certainly have been long out of business. One Christmas I splurged and bought him a combination radio-cassette tape player, something rather pricey for me but absolutely impossible for Tetsuji, even when purchased at one of the discount outlets in Akihabara. When I next visited him at the shop, he had it on, but at a volume so low it hardly seemed worth it. Who could have overheard it? Tetsuji was not frightened of his employer, but he knew who was the boss and how necessary his salary, half what I received from the

Japanese government to be a student, was. He knew that however few his fellow tradespeople were atop the Broadway, none would think their business helped by the musical choices of a young Japanese homosexual with a special foreign friend.

It only takes seven minutes to ride the Central Line train from Shinjuku to the main station in Nakano, but like the sense of geography in Tokyo in general, and like still other things in particular, actual distance has nothing to do with perception.

For a Japanese, an address in Nakano might be desirable. Once it had been a hunting reserve for the shoguns. Today it is where Shigeo and Ayako have their house, and though Ayako muses aloud to her husband about trading it for a downtown condominium, this neighborhood started having fine homes when the earthquake inspired wealthy victims of it to build new residences further from the crowded lanes of the old city. I read all this in a guidebook I find one day in a small bookstore near my own new home and I think: yes, this is a good place for you, too. Safer.

The name "Nakano," of uncertain etymology, is attested to in records a millennium old. One hundred archaeological finds scattered throughout means that people lived here before people had history. In more recent centuries it is where the Tokugawa shoguns kept their hawks for falconry; and where one of them, the seventeenth-century Tsunayoshi, began to enforce Buddhism's injunction against killing any living thing. It was in Nakano that he established one of his several refuges for the city's stray or mistreated dogs.

Tetsuji may have complained about his employer, but never the job itself. Perhaps he enjoyed the solitude. In any case, he was left both to his labors and his thoughts at the shop, and was shielded from a society that no doubt expected greater ambition from a graduate of Waseda University.

Tetsuji had plans naturally, but none that he pursued at work at the Broadway. Japan as well as predisposition had made him a private person, indistinguishable perhaps from millions of others in a country where shyness is a virtue, not a condition. But it was also his desires that drove him to the relative refuge of a tiny dark shop in a decrepit mall in a nondescript neighborhood of the city. Back then Tetsuji was an internal exile in his own country, with rights as curtailed as any American expatriate's were multiplied.

Saikaku, a contemporary of Tsunayoshi, wrote in *The Great Mirror of Male Love*: "There is in present-day society a glut of both stray puppy dogs and ready cash, a state that results in widespread ostentation and wasteful spend-ing."[2]

One of the rituals of being a Westerner in Tokyo is going to the Sunday *nomi no ichi*, the literal Japanese translation of "flea market." Spread out on mats or tarpaulins across the grounds of a neighborhood temple or shrine, there are several such bazaars. Each boasts a slightly different inventory and cli-entele. None is much older than the history of foreigners living in Western-style apartments but with a hankering for the authentic Japan. Small pieces of furniture, sets of china plates, and piles of used kimonos predominate. Sometimes there are more interesting things: either older, like scrolls of cal-ligraphy, or "newer," 45-rpm records of big band music from the American Occupation period. By the late 1980s, it all looks like picked-over junk—not like the good stuff I got back in the seventies, such as when Tetsuji and I found the lacquered lantern with the original Meiji-period paper still intact on its shade. But what I saw back then must itself have looked like picked-over junk to the foreigners who had been going since the 1960s, or earlier.

One of the markets—the one every second Sunday—is near Roppongi; another, on the first and fourth, in Harajuku. Easy walking distance, at most a subway stop or two, for the expatriate businessmen and their wives living nearby. The languages one hears from the browsers are fluent English, or sometimes French, German, or Spanish, and always broken Japanese. *Furui desu ka? Ikura furui?* Is it old? How old? *Ikura? Takai ne.* How much? Hmm, expensive. *Kau.* I buy.

The exceptions are the Japanese who come to shop at the market. Their Japanese is perfectly fluent, but other than that they never seem really very Japanese. Maybe they live in luxury apartments, too, like my most affluent friends do. Maybe they are also husbands and wives looking for native knick-knacks to accent sleek tables designed in Milan or brushed steel shelves lit with tiny halcyon spot lights. These Japanese look at the Imari bowl, the tiny netsuke, or the Meiji bamboo basket as things as exotic as might the Citibank executive: it is Japan re-imported, quaintly Oriental now that foreigners want them, too. The only real difference between them and us foreigners is that they, as a rule, are still Japanese enough to have retained some modicum of good taste. They leave the piles of old and soiled kimonos alone.

Or they are Japanese homosexuals, either alone or in the company of foreign lovers. For them an appreciation of the neo-Japonesque is ironic proof of their Westernness and, therefore, their difference. They will sometimes speak broken English (the other flea market *lingua franca*) to their fellow

Japanese merchants, perhaps because that is what they have just been speaking with their lovers and have forgotten to switch back; or because they would just as soon be mistaken for *gaijin*, "foreigners" themselves, and discard their Japaneseness without having to discard Japan. To be, in other words, expatriates at home. In internal exile.

Both these Japanese and the more knowledgeable foreigners can be found at the one monthly *nomi no ichi* that requires a somewhat longer train ride, if only by a bit. Near my new home in Nakano, it is a market I and others have been coming to for years. The first Sunday of the month is the one day that many people I know do come to this former neighborhood of hawks and dogs. In Arai, a part of Nakano only a few minutes on foot from my studio apartment, is the Yakushi temple. Built to the Buddha Bhêchad-jaguru, the Physician of Souls, Japanese came here in the past to seek cures for blindness and other eye afflictions. Today, they, like we, come looking for bargains in antiques and curios. "Old Japan," as Professor Chamberlain wrote a century ago, "was to us a delicate little wonder-world of sylphs and fairies."[3]

The Yakushi temple market generally has the best things and attracts the more serious shoppers. We tend to recognize each other. Some of us are expatriates working at the same firms, all here for only a year or two or three, and thus under some pressure to assemble our booty before reassignment back to New York or London. Others are homosexuals, usually here for a longer tour of duty. A few months from now, when I am no longer living in Nakano, I will come back here one bright cold Sunday morning in the company of half a dozen American, European, and Japanese homosexuals, buy not much of anything, and while the early afternoon away in a little restaurant that kindly tolerates our kind, as we obligingly run up a very large tab drinking beer and *sake*. As Saikaku noted, there is much widespread ostentation and wasteful spending, here where once lucky dogs ruled.

Marco Polo spent twenty-five years at the court of the great Kublai Khan, where he heard his marvelous stories about far Chipangu. *The people are white, civilized, and well-favored.* I had an uncle who was in Japan after the war, and told me his own stories. *They are idolaters, and are dependent on nobody.* About what happened in back of the PX, and outside the enlisted men's clubs, too. *And I can tell you the quantity of gold they have is endless; for they find it in their own country. . . . few merchants visit the country because it is so far from the main land, and thus it comes to pass that their gold is abundant beyond all measure.*[4] About what a young man, far from home and in a vanquished nation, could get in exchange not only for what he possessed, but what he was.

Sometimes I would visit Tetsuji at work on Sundays, a day off for me (as if every day wasn't) but his busiest (if any day was). I remember one. It was also cold and sunny. I thought I'd go see him for a while in the shop, but first take advantage of the long trip on the Tōzai (meaning, appropriately enough, "East-West") subway line from my place to visit the flea market at Yakushi temple as well.

It was early in the day, and few stores in the long covered arcade that began outside the main entrance of Nakano station and ended at the far northern end of the Broadway were open. I emerged into the bright light, zigzagged and kept walking along the street leading to the temple. The air was dry and fresh. I was in a good mood and prepared to spend a little money. At the temple I found a porcelain hibachi, once used indoors to heat with smoldering charcoal, but nowadays more likely a planter or, if elegant enough, displayed for its own beauty.

This hibachi was nice, but not what any connoisseur would want. It was only 10,000 yen. By the fall of 1986, the numbers of foreigners living in Tokyo would make such things five, six times as much: beyond my grasp, and not worth it anyway.

But in 1980 I was able to buy it, and did. I hauled it like felled game up to the fourth floor of the Broadway, proud of my acumen. The florescent lights in the stairwell flickered unpleasantly. Like the main floors themselves, they had not been polished or even swept in a very long time.

Tetsuji was at work when I interrupted to show him my trophy. Ten thousand yen would have been one-seventh his monthly paycheck. He joined me in the pleasure of my victory, and marveled both at how lucky I was and at the strange ways of foreigners.

Solitude guarantees a certain rhythm. Work does get done in my little Nakano studio. Distance and a meager stipend mean that evenings are spent at home, where the closeness of the walls inspires its own sort of melancholy cadences. The schedule late at night is this, dictated by lungs that would not heal: first, a long bath in my tiny tub, whose steam eases my breathing. Second, a large tumbler of some sort of alcohol balanced precariously on the rim of the tub, which makes the hurt recede even further. Once or twice a week, careful to dial before I get too drunk but no sooner than my voice has lost its bronchial raspiness (afterwards I'll be free to drink as much as I want), I call Dan in

Seattle. I tell him I miss him and that I am fine. ("Oh, that? No, been over it for weeks.") What point would there be to say that I am sick and getting sicker? It could only frighten him, and myself too, to hear those words said aloud and made real. He might demand I see a doctor: impossible for a gay American male in Japan with an upper-respiratory infection in the fall of 1986. So I lie, or talk about things I did not really care about, things to fill the chasm that threatens to open up between us.

October.   Eager to acclimate myself to my new neighborhood, I walk around a lot. I see that today, a dreary Sunday, a public gym near Nakano station is holding the Mister Nakano Body-Building Contest. Why not go in, I think. My bronchitis has turned me from a gym-goer into a gym-observer. I climb the grimy staircase lit only by a flickering florescent light, and enter a room already filled with young men, many armed with cameras, awaiting the start of the competition. Equipment and mats that had been pushed to the edges of the room suggested that this gym might also be where many of the contestants trained.

I stay for the first two or three men, but become uneasy at being the only foreigner there. Is my voyeurism too obvious? *Kaimami*. Am I allowed, as a American, to make my desires this plain? I get up and slip out, but, at the very last moment, another of the spectators spins around and takes my picture.

Seattle.   I went to his office, but though his door was ajar, he was not there. I scribbled a note on his blackboard, otherwise covered with formulae, to let him know I had been by.

Half an hour later the phone in my office rings. *"Hi, John? It's Dan. I'd just gone down to the mail room for a second."* We make a date to go to the movies that night. *"Yeah, well, I was on my way to . . ."* After I hang up the phone, I start to think: you know you're going away. Is this a good idea? *"Lunch would be fine. I've already . . ."* You're not really attracted to him, are you? *"Yeah, me too."* But there is something about him that makes you like him already. *"How about tomorrow?"* And just what is that?

Later I would find out that Dan had just the week before broken off with his boyfriend and was not contemplating another relationship any time soon. I myself was going out with someone else, a recent arrival from Montana, who was visiting his family outside of Bozeman when I had met Dan at the birthday party for a mutual friend we'd both been invited to. Sex with my cowboy was leaving something to be desired: whether it was his taste in such things or a more recent shyness inspired by fear, I did not know. But it was easy to stop seeing him.

For the first couple months Dan always came to my house, never I to his. I suspected that he had someone living there with him, and that he meant to keep us apart. Then, suddenly, the sex stopped, too. First, the confession of an old venereal disease; then, the real confession of a lingering pain over the loss of the younger man. I think: brother, this has been a mistake from the start. A chasm opens up, but I later I will remember back and think: just where did my own newfound shyness come from?

Halloween is one American custom not yet imported here. *Ladies and gentlemen, we interrupt our program of dance music to bring you a special bulletin from the Intercontinental Radio News.*[5] In another year or two, young foreigners, mostly gay, will dress up in costumes and board, from whatever station is closest, the head car in the Yamamote trains that run in a circle around the central wards of the city. *Ladies and gentlemen, I have a grave announcement to make.* What could ordinary Japanese have thought? Would those old enough have recalled what we, too young, did not? That during the Occupation, Americans (aliens with bodies too large to be real) also had their private car on this same train to ride? *Incredible as it may seem, both the observations of science and the evidence of our eyes lead to the inescapable assumption that those strange beings who landed in the Jersey farmlands tonight are the vanguard of an invading army from the planet Mars.*[6] Scores of tall men and women, in outrageous dress and makeup, swarming into the typically undisturbed silence of a commuter's train ride home. Urban terrorism, acting up: the combination of a festival of the dead and a exhibitionist display of a queer imperative. Why, on second thought, do foreigners have to dress up at all to masquerade? Or to frighten strangers? We are already aliens, and already inspire fear.

October 31, 1986.   This year I stay home in my studio apartment, from whose little sleeping loft I look out at the lights of the Shinjuku skyscrapers. *All that happened before the arrival of these monstrous creatures in the world now seems part of another life . . . a life that has no continuity with the present, furtive existence of the lonely derelict who pencils these words.*[7] The English-language Armed Forces Radio broadcasts that perennial thriller, Orson Welles reading *The War of the Worlds.* Martians have landed, they're killing everything and taking over. Aliens with strange bodies. *There, I can see the thing's body. It's large as a bear and it glistens like wet leather. But that face.*[8] Destroying our way of life. Humanity is finally saved only thanks to the stealthy work of viruses their odd bodies cannot withstand. *Later when their bodies were examined in laboratories, it was found that they were killed by the putre-factive and disease bacteria against which their systems were unprepared.*[9] We all learned this as children. But listening to Welles this particular night, for the first time I do not know which side to cheer for.

Julia Kristeva, a Bulgarian in Paris, writes:

> Eventually, the shattering of repression is what leads one to cross a border and find oneself in a foreign country. Tearing oneself away from family, language, and country in order to settle down elsewhere is a daring action accompanied by sexual frenzy: no more prohibition, everything is possible. It matters little whether the crossing of the border is followed by debauchery or, on the contrary, by fearful withdrawal. Exile always involves a shattering of the former body.[10]

Any gay American not in America knows this to be true. For years we insolent persons were a sought-after nationality, our New World sexuality the stuff of homosexual legend. Jack has told me what it was like in Germany, back when Americans were idolized as supremely, singularly sexual. Few Germans could hope to compete with a chiseled Californian or Texan boy with a toothy grin, big shoulders, a legendary libido, and the wantonness to act on it. Not that that was Jack's look, or mine: still, we were Americans too, and paid-up members of a special race.

In the late summer of 1979, just a week after having moved from New York to Tokyo for the first time, I took the train into Shinjuku Friday night to go to a gay bar I knew foreign men and their Japanese admirers frequented. I walked out the east exit of the station, down the broad street lined with department stores, across another busy boulevard, and into the suddenly smaller-scale, less crowded neighborhood. This is Ni-chōme, the Second Block, that part of Shinjuku set aside during the Occupation for Japanese prostitutes to service American personnel relatively discreetly, but now the principal center of Tokyo gay nightlife. "Ni-chōme has ordinary shops, temples and shrines mixed in with its cafés and sex establishments," says the local atlas. I climbed the stairs to a crowded room, damp with human breath despite the air conditioner going full blast. A bartender intercepted me, quick to take my drink order before I disappeared into the restless herd. Beer in hand, I stood in the middle of the room and made sure not to look at anyone in particular.

Boye De Mente, in his book *Bachelor's Japan*, briefly tells readers about this neighborhood:

> Many of the former houses in Tokyo's well-known Shinjuku 2-chome district are now "nude studios." Each "studio" has from two to six very pretty young girls who stand in the doorway or lined up in front of the studio. The girls attempt to attract business by calling to passing men, occasionally taking them by the arm or some other appendage to press home their point.[11]

It was still early. I was there at this hour because I did not yet know the local protocol and because I knew I would have to catch the last train home. Almost at once I saw Hank sitting on a narrow stool at the bar nursing his own beer. He was one of a dozen white men in the bar, along with twice as many Japanese men. Given the time of night, each camp was still caucusing.

Hank was my type, my type still being what I had had in New York until last week: stocky, square-jawed, moustached, blond, a little shorter than me. White.

We made conversation. I was oblivious of the Japanese around me. Later I would find out that Hank was always oblivious of the Japanese. Despite his long residence in Tokyo, which was to end soon, he had never developed the attraction to Japanese men that most of us, after a few months, do. Later I would find out why. In any case, he invited me home.

I would not have noticed at the time, but I am sure our joint, premature departure was remarked upon. Japanese *gaisen* (an acronym for "specialists in foreigners") do not care for it when two foreigners go home together. Scarce resources should not be hoarded.

Outside the bar we linger a bit in the cool evening air. Two policemen eye us warily as they slowly pass by. As we walk toward the main street, where Hank had parked his motor scooter, we walk by two more policemen, who study us as I, provocatively and stupidly, study them. Hank made room on his Honda for me, and we speed down another busy street to a place he assured me was not far. Nakano. I had to take his word for it. I was new to Tokyo. I had no idea where I was. But racing down the Ōme Kaidō road, with Japanese pedestrians caught in the crosswalks scurrying out of our way and my arms wrapped around Hank's solid torso in the one kind of close embrace American men are allowed, I felt I was home and on display all at the same time.

June 1986.   Shiokawa Yūichi, chair of the Ministry of Health's AIDS Surveillance Committee, tells a Paris conference that Japan has a low HIV infection rate because it has a low incidence of homosexuality and that those homosexuals it does have are less promiscuous.[12]

As I continue my walks in my new home of Nakano, each day extending the territory covered a little further, I eventually make it to the little neighborhood of Nogata. This, I remember, is where Hank lived. It was, as I now appreciate, a rather nice apartment—big enough for a Western-style bed and a full size kitchen table, private with its own entranceway down an alley landscaped with exotic plants in terra cotta pots. He was some kind of highly paid English teacher. I won't be living in Nakano long enough to ever visit this neighborhood again and actually try to find his place—that's a tired old game for me anyway. But I do begin to realize that Nakano and I have other things in common.

We got down to business fast. Hank took out the poppers and told me he wanted me to fuck him. Hank had a thick dick, and a chest and belly completely covered with soft blond fur. He was what many Japanese men who want white men want. Hank was a foreigner reeking of butter and beef for the locals; an astronaut, a marine, a baseball player, a secret agent for me. All my fantasies. But Hank was a bottom in a country full of them.

The room was completely dark. I started to laugh. Somehow we'd been trying to do too many things at once, and the amyl nitrate ended up getting poured down his right ear. Hank started to cry out, then scream in pain. *Shit, what should I do?* It must have been around midnight. *Call the ambulance!* I dialed 110, got emergency services. "Where are you located?" Fuck if I know. Hank can't speak Japanese. *Hank, what's the address here?* "Nogata. Nakano." *Nogata desu ka? Nogata no doko desu ka?* "Where in Nakano?" I tell them something based on what Hank, on the floor curled up in a ball and still moaning, can manage to tell me.

The dispatcher told me to go aside and stand in the street: the ambulance would eventually see me and so know which house was Hank's. I pulled on my pants and shirt and went out into the deserted dark streets barefoot. There were no streetlights, I could have been anywhere. It was almost cool now, and I could see all the stars. The smells of the plants in the neighbor's yards were lush, almost tropical when mixed in with the piquant stink of the Tokyo sewers. Then a couple blocks away I spotted an ambulance, silent but flashing its colored lights, as it drove past on a perpendicular road. They must have seen me, too, because the ambulance soon circled around and came to a stop by the front of Hank's alleyway.

Hank was almost normal again when I led the two medics into the apartment. What must they have thought? In fact, Hank didn't want any help now and told them everything was fine, but the medics not only insisted on looking into his ear, but on taking him to a small emergency clinic and a real doctor.

Of course we didn't mention the amyl nitrate. I mumbled something about Hank having had a bad earache for some time. The medics, as they led him to the van, asked me for my name and address. I had to pretend to be a old friend of Hank's, and thus a long-time resident of Japan. Some years later my friend Glen would get into a traffic accident driving one of his Japanese tricks back from Ni-chōme to his apartment in Daikanyama. He told the police his passenger was a "friend." When the officer asked Greg what the friend's name was, Greg couldn't say.

So somewhere in Nakano, I now recall, must be the clinic that the ambulance took Hank and me to. An elderly doctor listened to my now well rehearsed story of the suddenly worsened earache and did his cursory exam. All evidence of the real cause must have disappeared, because he seemed to have been satisfied by this account. The doctor told Hank to come back in a day or two for a proper visit, and we were free to go. The medics took us back to the apartment. We took off our clothes and got into bed. It had to be nearly dawn. But Hank asked me to pick up where I had left off.

"The foreigner who imagines himself to be free of borders," Kristeva goes on to say, "by the same token challenges any sexual limit. Often, but not entirely. For a narcissistic wound—insult, betrayal—can disturb his economy of boundless expenditure, which he had thought for a moment to be unshake-able, and invert it into a destruction of psychic and corporeal identity."[13]

Late the next morning, the two of us still in bed, Hank talked on the phone to an American while he sat on my dick and slowly fucked himself. He was making arrangements to meet this friend that afternoon at the Isetan department store and go shopping for a dress shirt. So they do that here, too, I thought to myself. I came inside of him while he was still discussing what entrance they'd meet at.

*   *   *

"Today, sexual permissiveness favors erotic experiences and, even with the fear of AIDS, foreigners continue to be those for whom sexual taboos are most easily disregarded, along with linguistic and familial shackles. The eighteenth-century cosmopolitan was a libertine—and today still the foreigner, although without the ostentation, affluence, or luxury of the Enlightenment, remains that insolent person who, secretly or openly, first challenges the morality of his own country and then causes scandalous excesses in the host country."[14]

Kristeva, otherwise one of us, writes without the terror I now feel as a fellow stranger abroad. "Even with . . . ," she writes: such an ordinary concessive for her, such a powerful conjunction for me. How can we compare our "scandalous excesses," once of desire, now of death? Then again, how can we not?

If Japan is the "host," then I am either a guest or a parasite. One night I go to Ni-chōme, where even "guests" feel comfortable. It may be where years ago I went and met Hank that first night of my Tokyo education, but here, like everywhere, things have changed. That bar was still there, but the ghetto is now crowded by dozens of newer and larger ones. I go into one with a promising exterior, but realize once I am through the door that the crowd is too young for me. I've aged and Japanese adolescents are bolder than they once were. But before I leave I meet Chan, a Taiwanese student at a fashion design school in Kichijōji. We fall into the familiar patter. He tells me it's "virtually public knowledge" that Calvin married Kelly because "he's dying and he wants someone to take care of him." He gives me his card.

Summer 1980.   I played extended hookey from my studies in Tokyo and went back to New York for a week to help Japanese television film a documentary about Second Avenue. While there I ran into Hank in the East Village. He told me that he lives nearby and teaches English to Japanese exchange students at a university in the neighborhood. He looked great. We didn't talk long, because his boyfriend was coming over to the apartment in a few minutes. Hank told me with great excitement that the guy really fucks the shit out of him. He was glad to be in New York; he's got everything he wants. I have never seen him since.

The next day I take the card out of my wallet and look at it. In America, Chan would be the foreigner, I the host. In Tokyo, there is still a difference

between us, he the postcolonial bottom and I the postcolonial top. Taiwan
was a Japanese colony for the first half of the twentieth century and the
Taiwanese still seem more Japanese in many ways than do other Chinese.
Japan was an American colony for only seven years, but I still retain some
modicum of the prestige of the conqueror. But we are also both guests here,
with our fingerprints on file with the local authorities and neighbors who keep
a watchful eye on us. Japan makes us similar, as does our mutual, eccentric
penchant: here we are two gay men, members of Cocteau's lost tribe in a
diaspora ruled over by our Eros, if someone else's Logos.

Years ago in Beijing I remember seeing in the crowds of people all
dressed in the same drab suits one bold, exceptional splash of color—a young
man's kerchief tied with special flair about his neck. Everywhere there is that
laugh, that look, that surfeit of irony, that proud badge of an outlaw distinction. Later, when I thought I saw him again leaning on the rail on the bridge,
I also thought he was trying to attract my attention. Dangerous at the time—
maybe now, too—to make love to a man in a repressive police state. And also
especially attractive. How insolent and so very very hot of us, I will later think.

Chan is no one I would go to bed with: too young and too purposefully
effeminate. He seems somewhat more interested in me. I am, after all, higher
up on the food chain. The reasons are entirely historical. I am white and
American; he is Asian and Chinese. We meet in Japan, a kind of neutral
ground not neutral at all.

There is definitely a Top and a Bottom to the colonial order of things.
The penis and its corresponding orifices have their geography. A white body
strewn atop a darker one, making love and at the same time reenacting the
imperial nature of things. But just remember that our hierarchies are meant
to be inverted, and the darker skin impressing its weight onto the lighter
below is also part of history's inexorable logic, one of the ways our special
passion survives. "Why can't we be friends now?" Fielding says to Aziz. "It's
what I want. It's what you want."[15]

I leave young Chan and the big bar behind and find my way to little Xenos,
an old favorite. Writers hang out here, as well as veteran Japan hands too.
The Master is very funny and treats me like I belong there. It is always easy
to strike up a conversation at Xenos. Master will make introductions and call
me "Professor." I took Tetsuji there once years ago, but he did not seem to
like it very much.

Tonight it is crowded, and I have to wait for one of the stools along the bar to become free. I don't know anyone, but soon Master has me chattering away. Eventually, perhaps on my fourth or fifth drink, I start to control the conversation at the bar, or at least speak in the loudest, most insistent voice. Everyone is listening to me. Now I am the Master.

Wareware, the grandest word in the Japanese language for "we," usually means "we Japanese" and so not me. But it is our tradition to steal words from others and hurl them back, either lightly or like stones. Sometimes, late at night and sitting at a counter in some tiny club, the lights low, the bartender at his wittiest, my Japanese at its most fluent (or so the booze makes me think), and my bar mates their most attentive, I can murmur *wareware* like a mantra and believe it includes me, too.

Tsunayoshi the Dog Shogun is also remembered for another excess, beyond that of fondness for animals: that for young men. Like his father and great-grandfather before him, a taste for boys was cause for little comment. "The ruler," tersely states one historical record, "liked sex with males."[16] But Tsunayoshi had the unsettling habit of favoring them in his court, and even made a dozen or more of them daimyō. "The ruler liked youths. They were promoted, for the most part, because of sex."[17] It is also reported that Tsunayoshi's example inspired men all over the country ambitious for power to take boys as lovers.

The last full year of Tsunayoshi's reign, 1708, was a year of disasters. In addition to floods, fires, volcanic eruptions, and typhoons, there was an epidemic. In the first days of 1709, the Fifth Shogun was dead of a pox he had tried to treat himself, refusing his doctors' advice and using instead herbal remedies of his own design.

Marco Polo saw many strange and marvelous sights on his way east: not only pepper and silk, salt and jade, but eyeglasses, ice cream, and spaghetti. He had been looking for unicorns, which he was sure he'd found when he saw the rhinoceroses of Java.

Do not forget the great cities he saw, too, some of which floated in the air over deserts and others which were carved out of pure crystal. What would he write about Tokyo, were he to discover it today? He would see streets lined with leafy *keyaki* trees, a hill with cobblestoned sidewalks leading up to where the old geisha have retired, thin expressways that lace the nighttime sky like ribbons of light, fortune tellers busy with hands of unmarried women, and foreigners as odd as any Turks in the Great Khan's capital, here to trade their goods along our century's very own Silk Road.

> His palace was the scene of moral depravity, the ruler intent on strange sexual pleasures, entertainments, and banqueting, with a mania for performing dances in front of his retainers. He was driven by superstition, and he was under the influence of a woman. He was extravagant, wasting the substance of the realm on lavish gifts to unworthy favorites and Buddhist monks, for whom he built great temples. He adulterated the coinage. During the final years of his rule, heaven condemned his lack of virtue by causing strange natural phenomena and by visiting disasters upon the country.[18]

By the fall of 1986, Tetsuji does not work at the frame shop anymore, or anywhere in the Broadway. He is long gone from the Tokyo scene, but I am the one who is back. When I left him in the summer of 1981, he was in tears, stupified at the ease with which I left him.

Unlike Hank, Tetsuji is someone I will continue to see over the years. I seek him out. I know he is healthy, which only means I have no evidence to the contrary. Hank I have surrendered to my own American past, and to that time and place that I, if only a little earlier than he, left behind.

There is no Dog Shogun ruling over us now, but instead another tyranny. Sent into exile, as Tsunayoshi did his own enemies, Tetsuji in his home, I in mine, and Hank wherever he is, keep quiet tally of the crimes we are accused of, and of the time we have served.

NOVEMBER

New Words

This is the month when everything changes. My sabbatical will not be what I had predicted. My scholarly work will continue, but vain hopes for a year away from my America will disappear and my fears about dying a premature death will revive. November is the month when, in fact, nothing changes. This month my sabbatical ends only to begin all over again.

In Seattle, November is the first of the two dark months, and I am glad to be elsewhere when I imagine Dan's days. By January the afternoon light in the northwest will linger longer, and early flowers will bloom before it becomes February: but at this time of year, only short, rain-filled days briefly punctuate a cool, and then cold, train of deep black nights.

In Tokyo, November is the second of the two autumn months. The days shorten, but are not yet short. It is the first of the dry months, when the air starts to crackle and the trees display colors that Seattle's weather only rarely allows.

Tourists often come to Japan in the fall. You see them on the big luxury buses or walking the Ginza in small packs. Fewer now, perhaps, given the now costly yen: but it is that same valuable currency that draws others of us to Japan.

*   *   *

Imagine, for example, that you are Jesusa B. Palaruan, a twenty-one-year-old native of the Philippines. You entered Japan in September this year on a fifteen-day tourist visa issued to you under a false name. The Japanese syndicate that recruited you in Northern Luzon takes you (but not your four-year-old son) to Matsumoto in Nagano prefecture, a city well known for a sex industry all out of proportion to its size. Two hundred Filipina entertainers are already there legally. Hundreds more of *Japayuki*, or foreign sex workers (referred to in the press as "hostesses"), are there in the underground. Once largely Korean and Taiwanese, now you and your countrywomen are the majority. You work in a "discotheque" under the name of Suzie. The papers will report that between your arrival and your deportation less than two months later, you had sexual intercourse with fifty men.

1974.   I returned to the United States to finish college. Bartending skills I learned that summer in Japan were put to use when I found employment a couple of nights a week at Prince Rashid's.

Rashid's was located in a strip mall along Highway 9. In the fall of 1974 this rural stretch of New England, populated with tens of thousands of college students, had only Rashid's as a "discotheque" as urban America was rife with them. I worked there sporadically, though my schedule was of some importance. It mattered what nights you were assigned to work. As the one dance bar in the area that had to cater to several distinct constituencies, one night was Black Night, another was Puerto Rican Night, and Wednesday was Gay Night. That did not mean that the black bartenders wanted to work black night, or gay bartenders on gay night. Rather, it was all a cooly calculated matter of tips. Blacks ordered a lot of drinks, but were lousy tippers; gays tipped okay, but didn't booze up. Best of all were the Puerto Ricans, who both drank plenty and rewarded us well, too. I had sexual intercourse with one person.

Jesusa.   They say that you knew before you came to Japan; the Philippine government will tell the Japanese government that you tested positive during a "routine" check-up. But maybe all you knew is what I worry is my own fate: that those coughs and headaches and stubborn rashes and night sweats never went away and finally made you go, so feverish you are ready to accept whatever comes, to the Immigration Bureau and beg to be sent home. You are sick not only of being sick, but of being poked every night by strange men—unlike some of us, who would find we enjoyed it, and would even pay for the privilege of being violated.

Immigration is only too happy to comply with your wishes. You go back to the Philippines where you die soon thereafter. (What happened to your little boy?) But not without leaving your mark on Japan, where the "Matsumoto Japayuki Incident" incites a national panic. Hundreds of men seek medical advice, and galvanized police across Japan lead raids against illegal foreign workers not only in bars but at construction sites and truck stops. Nightclubs across the country hang out signs that say "No Foreign Items Work Here," or "The Contents Are Completely Domestically Produced, No Imports Are Sold At All." And near where I choose to play: "This Establishment Has Refused Foreign Customers Ever Since It Opened. . . . Please Come In And Indulge Yourself Without Worry."

Death in Venice

> At the street corners placards were stuck up, in which the city authorities warned the population against the danger of certain infections of the gastric system, prevalent during the heated season; advising them not to eat oysters or other shell-fish and not to use the canal waters. The ordinance showed every sign of minimizing an existing situation. Little groups of people stood about silently in the squares and on the bridges; the traveler moved among them, watched and listened and thought.[1]

History. During the Occupation period there were signs in Tokyo that read: "Fraternization with the Indigenous Personnel Is Forbidden." Did they mean for their rules to be taken seriously? That young American men would not discover their freedom in the country they had come to occupy? In yet another of our modern ironies?

I don't remember ever getting picked up by anyone while I worked at Rashid's, or picking anyone else up. But some nights I'd go on my own as a customer, and especially whenever Sarah wanted a ride. Sarah was a black girl I somehow had gotten to know, probably because she was a regular at Rashid's whatever kind of a night it was. A friend who was away for the year had left his Volkswagen Beetle with me, and so I could get us from town out to the strip mall. She would show up around my empty frat house at night and talk me into going to Rashid's, which meant giving her a ride.

Sarah never had to work very hard to talk me into joining her. I liked her. Sarah was not particularly attractive, but she was sexy: back then her color made her sexy to a young man ready for the lessons I assumed she could teach. I was at that stage many gay men go through on their way to being gay, drawn to one sort of the forbidden before embracing another. A black woman for me, Asian or older women for others of us: all a stepping-stone into the difference where we would eventually, inevitably, seek what we are now.

It did not take much to talk Sarah into going home with me one night. A lonely person, she often drank too much. I took advantage of her, as I suppose I did of other people back then. I never knew for sure, because Sarah never shared her story with me. Could I have been a stepping-stone for her? On her own way into difference? Toward what was, for Sarah, her own forbidden?

Jesusa.   They say that you "were infected with AIDS through an American soldier when [you were] working in a sauna in Manila." They always seem to know when and where the virus made its invisible way and turned an innocent party into a guilty one. You were a victim, they say, who then victimized others who then. . . . On November 21 you and your Tita Aida were already back in the Philippines, but I read in the papers that Japan has twenty-one AIDS patients, ten of whom are male homosexuals and "caught the disease through sexual contact with foreigners"; the rest are hemophiliacs who were likewise "infected from imported blood products." Jesusa, you come from one place very different from where I come, but we are very similar. I worry that I will be deported, too, hustled onto a plane by officials wearing latex gloves, barred from the country where I, too, came to work. The difference between you and me is that I am not sick enough to go to a doctor or to Immigration and to hell with what they do with me after the test. But that is only a difference of degree between us, not of kind.

Aside from hemophiliacs infected by blood products, it appears that the route of the AIDS invasion into Japan is at present limited to sexual traffic with HIV+ foreigners. . . . The fact of AIDS in Japan today is that an alien substance is invading us from the outside.[2]

Lafcadio Hearn would marry Mattie Foley when he lived in the United States, a former slave whom he loved but who would come, one day, to hate him. Was it because Mattie realized Lafcadio used her to travel further? From what the world told him he was, the bastard son of an Irishman and a Greek woman? To what he finally awoke to be, on the rugged coast of another island in the furthest place of all.

Hearn was one of the most famous foreigners in late-nineteenth-century Japan, the country where he finally felt the most at home, and where he died in 1904.

"The Venetian authorities published in reply," Thomas Mann writes, "a statement to the effect that the state of the city's health had never been better; at the same time instituting the most necessary precautions."[3]

Report. The words that Japanese high school students most associate with AIDS: (1) homosexuality, (2) death, and (3) foreigners.[4]

In 1981 Glen and I went to the Philippines for a two-week vacation.

Glen was my best friend in Tokyo those years and if I wasn't spending my time with Tetsuji, I was with him. We had met at a bar shortly after the Canadian Ministry of External Affairs had posted him to Japan after a long stint in Paris. It was New Year's Eve, a very crowded night in Ni-chōme's little bars. Glen was new in the country and not yet the famous figure among us he was destined to become. So he gravitated to me quickly that night, as I had only months earlier gravitated to Hank. Despite the packed small room crowded with gay revelers Japanese and foreign, he made his way to me.

There was the obligatory, but this time especially laughable, attempt at sex. Another great gay friendship begins.

Some years in the future I would learn that Glen would, in turn, play host to a Jerry then himself new in Tokyo. Jerry got a very expert tour of Ni-chōme. But back in 1979 I was the tutor despite my own relatively recent arrival and I took my duties seriously. Glen had a car—diplomats were allowed to buy them from each other at cheap prices unlike the rest of us— and I knew my way around. So the city became ours. The elevated expressways above Tokyo that laced the city like twisted ribbons of candy took us in minutes from one neighborhood to another, from one club or bathhouse to the next. Glen was good-looking, and next to his car that was his greatest utility to me. Anywhere we went we attracted attention, which is to say, men.

Our favorite place was Senga. Years later, when I was long gone and Glen was soon headed to the embassy in Islamabad, that was where he gave himself his own going-away party. I even thought of flying to Japan for the weekend to attend it. By that time he knew almost as many people as knew him. He was nearly an institution, a Living National Treasure of faggotry. It really was time for him to go, come to think of it. But at first he was the young ingenue, and I the equally young impresario.

Senga was perfect for us. Down a narrow street at the top of Dōgen-zaka—you knew what alley to turn down by the futon store on one corner, Snack Captain on the other—it was the closest thing Tokyo had to an American-style gay sex club in those days. Twenty years later, the city would have scores, and in neighborhoods everywhere, but back then it was quite a find. Glen and I, but mostly Glen, made it famous among Tokyo's white boys.

The name "Senga" meant something like a Thousand Elegances, and it was a rather grand place for those of us accustomed to the cramped piano bars of Ni-chōme. There were lockers, private rooms, a sauna, cruisy showers, and a small bar on the premises. Everything, in a concession to local taste, was piss elegant (if not exactly as numerous as a thousand). There were fake plastic flowers, shag carpeting, cheap reproductions of Western art in gaudy frames. The hired help was oh-so nelly. And in another concession to Japanese custom, most of the action took place in what could only be called orgy rooms, except that there were no orgies. The action was definitely one-on-one, unless one counted voyeurs as participants. On a floor strewn with mattresses and boxes of tissue, men in couples drew themselves together under the privacy of blankets, where they joined bodies in all the ways anatomy permits. It took us a while to get used to mounting each other in semi-public as if it were private; but not all that long a while. We soon became welcome regulars. Eventually Glen and I would be let in for free.

My tours for Glen's edification were international as well as domestic, and that is why in early 1981 we went to the Philippines. I had gotten seats on a jumbo jet to Manila otherwise filled with working-class Japanese men on their way there for nothing but sex. But then again, despite a smug contempt for our fellow passengers, so were we.

The typical restraint we, or at least I, had to observe in spending money in Japan was needless in the Philippines, where the value of the yen allowed us to stay in a luxury hotel, take taxis even for just a couple of blocks, and eat at the best restaurants. Every night we made the scene at Coco Banana in Ermita, not far from trendy Remedios. Coco was then the most famous gay bar in what is still Asia's gayest city. It's gone now, replaced with newer clubs, but none retain the Coco's flair. This was during the Marcos years, but despite the curfew imposed on the city, homosexuals seemed exempt from the strictures of his martial law. Rumor had it that a foreigner, gay but owner of one of the Philippines' largest plantations, was a very close friend of Ferdinand's and so his government tolerated us. Another rumor had it that Imelda adored gay men and so gave us her special dispensation.

In any case, Coco Banana was flourishing in the early 1980s, along with the rest of the gay world. The Coco was famous for closing periodically and then reopening with an entirely new interior decor. The owner, we had heard, had been impressed with Studio 54 when he visited New York. When Glen and I were there, the theme was white. White feathers, white balloons, white curtains. And Glen and I were, among the Mestizos, the Chinese, and the Filipinos, the *Kanos*. The White People.

Not everyone was gay. There were obvious *bakla*, and even a few *lits go*. But, true to its New York model, this was the Beautiful People place. Glen headed straight for a young man sitting on the bleachers that rose high on one side of the dance floor. Outside, in an enclosed garden, I made small talk with another American I recognized from the pool at our hotel. He told me he comes to the Philippines several times a year. Loves it. As his eyes follow a half-naked Filipino walk across the deck, he tells me he's an arms trader.

Summer 1980.   That summer in New York, while visiting briefly from Tokyo, I ran into Hank. I have told you about that already. But there was more to our reunion than a simple surprised hello. It is so hard and so easy to find old friends in a place like that. Before Hank had to go meet his new lover, there was time for us to go back to his place and, for old times' sake as well as today's fun, put our bodies together in a remembered coupling. His apartment was small and very hot. The unmade bed was alongside a wall with an open window by its head. Soot from the dirty August air peppered the white sheets. They smelled just as Hank always had, with some cologne I cannot identify but which I often noticed on other men of my generation, something in retrospect as definitively 1970s as the music. Before Polo and Calvin, but after Old Spice and Aqua Velvet. *Pierre Cardin*.

I laid him down on his back, ran my tongue over his chest damp with midday sweat; when I got down to his crotch, his legs moved apart and up. I chewed on his balls and his ass, his attentive cock. When he wiggled himself into position, I took the cue, grabbed his ankles and made his legs go high over his head. I leaned into him with my hips as he opened up for me. Real gay sex. I listened to him squeal and moan and tell me how to move.

Soon enough I come. *Sarah, I'm gonna come.* I thought: here is sperm made up of nutrients I had ingested a world away, things from fish and soybeans and seaweed that my body had turned into my own salty spunk.

Are you gonna come, too? Things from the country where he once lived, and I still do: an *omiyage*, a little Japanese souvenir for him. *Sarah, I love you!* Here was something I brought Hank these thousands of miles like a gift, something from the place we shared as aliens thrown together by our sameness (to each other) and our difference (from them). *Com'on, com'on! Do it!* Not so many years later I would wonder if some small part of my sperm, so generously coating the insides of his bowels, had not come from other continents, too. *Oh baby, you're fucking good.* Deepest Hank. *Oh, Sarah baby.* Darkest Africa. *Saaarah.*

I shared a cab with Brodie the arms dealer back to our hotel. He had a suite at the top. He took a shower and then lay naked atop the bedspread on the huge bed. The curtains were not drawn, and I could see the lights of Manila in the mirror on the opposite wall. After sex, I showered myself. As I was drying myself, I noticed the brand names of all the fixtures in the spacious room. Everything had been imported from Japan or America. Even Brodie and me.

Bored with my reading, and still feeling claustrophobic on account of both my small studio and the bronchitis, I take walks in my Nakano neighborhood. I discover one day a ramen shop with spectacularly high prices. The fine print on the menu cards tells me that each dish is infused with a unique mixture of Chinese medicines. Oh, I think, what a find. What ails me of course is not listed as any of the ailments promised a cure: I opt for the "cancer" noodles and figure, well, sooner or later.

"SHIITAKE" SUBSTANCE MIGHT DETER AIDS

A substance contained in hypha extracts from "shiitake" mushrooms . . . is denaturalized lignin, according to a research team at the University of Tokyo's Agriculture Department.

It has also been confirmed that lignin deters the propagation of the AIDS virus, the team said.[5]

Godzilla was awoken from his ancient slumber by America's promiscuous A-bomb tests, but he could only be defeated by the ingenuity and resourcefulness of Japanese scientists. We all learned this, too, as children.

*   *   *

"This is Orson Welles, ladies and gentlemen, out of character to assure you that the *War of the Worlds* has no further significance than as the holiday offering it was intended to be. . . . We annihilated the world before your very ears."[6]

Glen and I were in Manila long enough to each have a mini-affair. He met a young man cruising in one of the city's malls and started seeing him every day. The cost for this fraternization to Glen was another article of his clothing each day. A pair of jeans ("for my cousin," was the pleaded refrain) one day, a windbreaker the next. By the end of our stay, I think Glen must have been down to one pair of shorts, his underwear, and one T-shirt that either he thought he would need to wear to get back into Japan or, more likely, that no Filipino *bakla* wanted.

Glen and his escort ended up going off to an island resort popular with Manila's world-weary gay boys and their foreign boyfriends for a week. I tagged along. It was a long bus and then ferry ride followed by a breezy commute in a dugout canoe, but well worth it. Many people had done it before us. There's even a novel about the place.

The Singalong Tribe

Underway at last, they skimmed glassy waters, jagged coral passing beneath. Vegetation was thick on all shores. Klaus, whose youth had been partly spent in Brazil with his parents, thought he was on an Asian delta of Amazonian proportions. Actually, it was an illusion created by a confusion of islands and shore line. The craft beached in a sandy cove. Bongbong paid the boatman, rejoining Klaus already ashore.

Here was a perfect coral-filled laguna where everyone slept in charmingly rustic bungalows, but ate in a quite good restaurant that was a branch of a famous Manila eatery exclusively staffed by dwarfs. Our only hardship came at cocktail hour, when all the guests would have to line up for their daily ration of ice cubes outside the bungalow inhabited by the Swede who owned the resort and therefore its only refrigerator.

The Singalong Tribe

He led his companion up a rise through coconut palms. Then Klaus saw their destination through a clearing: a line of elevated, native-style huts of bamboo and grass weave. All had criss-cross verandahs. At a glance, the

European knew he had arrived at a place as close to paradise as he would ever get in this world.

We would not have known of this resort without the help of Glen's young friend, now wearing all sorts of North American-sized clothes that did not fit him. As it turned out, he and Glen did not need this clothing in the first place: the largely gay clientele in this laguna walked around nude in the daytime and lounged around bonfires on the beach at night wrapped in sarongs.

The Singalong Tribe

Here, for a short span of their lives the two would find a peace that they would always remember as long as they drew breath. There would be days of sun and sparkling water; nights of conversations under kerosene lanterns and bed matting under mosquito nets. They would forget air-conditioning, television, hot showers, cinemas, ice cream, telephones, newspapers and all the paraphernalia of civilisation.[7]

One of the guests was a famous American jazz musician, here for a few days before his concert in Manila. Other foreigners were mostly European, and mostly in the Philippines for its bounty of young men. The Filipinos often knew each other: leading gay tourists from the city to this remote resort was an itinerary repeated over and over. For their part, the foreigners often exchanged information among themselves while sunning on the beach about similar accommodations in Thailand, Indonesia, and other southeast Asian sexual ports of call. A Portugese journalist told me that Mozambique has the best beaches—pure white sand, he reports. "And very dark men." At night, they would dispatch their *bakla* lovers to each other's cabanas.

It was not until I returned to Manila, however, that I had my own encounter with a Filipino. I left Glen and his friend early to tour Manila on my own and see things he was not particularly interested in. But one night, feeling both lonely and adventuresome, I visited a branch of the Club Bath chain. In the United States the Club Baths had established itself as a franchise as familiar to gay men as Holiday Inn was to the rest of America; but finding one in Manila still came as something of a surprise.

Inside, it was just like its American cousins. There was a reception room where they checked your I.D., took your money, and issued you a towel and a key; rows of lockers that lead, variously, to showers, a steam room, a lounge, several group-grope rooms and, most spectacularly, corridors of small cubicles where Filipinos, like their equivalents across America, lay one side or other up on small beds under lights carefully adjusted to illuminate, or hide, physiques their owners hoped would intice visitors.

It was in one of the darker corners of the Manila Club Baths that I met a man whose long, muscular legs first made me think I'd found another foreigner, but who turned out to be a bona fide Filipino, albeit from the very south of the archipelago and a Moslem. We made very comfortable love on a rug in a dark corner of the maze and then went to the lounge to talk. We sat on a sofa beside an aquarium with a florescent lamp that made him look bad and me even worse. He was in Manila to attend medical school, and was not shy to speak out about what he thought were the abuses of the Marcos regime. As I stroked his hard thighs, he spoke with much confidence about the destruction of his country at the hands of its leaders; as I tried to arouse him a second time, he went on to remind me of what America had contributed to the tragedy that was, and is, the Philippines. We went back to the rug in the dark corner and screwed again, America fucking the Philippines once more with gusto, or so it must have appeared; but in fact it was two men who, despite history, took temporary refuge for one moment in a mutual and voluntary desire.

I cannot now remember this medical student's name, but if he were not a Moslem I would want him to be called Jesus. A sibling of Jesusa's, a relative of the women who, without the hopeful future that awaited her brother, could not afford his macho politics; had to go to Japan and spread her legs too, but to any man who wanted it; who had to endure dirty talk rather than initiate it; and in a language she could not always understand, but whose meaning was clear. *But she wanted to go. And he wanted you.* What is the difference between the desires we think are our own and those willed us by history?

A joke.   The Japanese Prime Minister tells a meeting of his party colleagues: "American G.I.'s are getting AIDS—the Japanese yen has gotten so expensive, they have to fuck each other instead of Japanese whores."

Sarah always had a blank look in her eyes, as if she were perpetually high. Maybe she was. I knew nothing of her except her life at Rashid's. I did not even know where she lived—she never invited me to her place. It was always in my room at Beta Theta Pi where we had sex. There was nothing improvised or even much fun about it. I was driven by something not quite desire, or curiosity; she did it as if it were for money. Which is to say: lifeless, she lay there, only a few sounds that almost seemed words when, I could only guess, she climaxed. If she had been a man, I never would have been content. But, as it was, fucking her as if she were not much more than the old mattress beneath us, I was plowing ahead, through her to get past her, toward what her skin and hair foretold for me: *that clear expanse of a foreign land*. That place where I would be as different from what I then was as Sarah herself was and always would be. I looked beyond her, to my self as I was then fashioning it. But she looked nowhere. How much of this, too, was our history?

November.   I have to leave my studio and go to a conference, where I speak to several hundred people on an academic topic. Never a good public speaker—I stutter and stammer in English, do even worse in Japanese—I have a temperature as I make my way to the conference site. Drenched in sweat, or so I think, I get through my talk sounding, surely, like a perfect idiot. At the reception that follows I meet two American women and, eager for their conversation, I invite them out for a drink. I will never see them again, but my time pleasantly spent in their company lets me forget that I am sick—now that probably several hundred people now know it. (Did I look flush? A little gaunt? During the break: "Haven't you lost some weight, Treat-*san*?") I can also almost forget that I am in Japan. Why didn't I realize that escape would mean being left alone with thoughts I cannot escape?

> Recoveries were rare. Eighty out of every hundred died, and horribly, for the onslaught was of the extremest violence, and not infrequently of the "dry" type, the most malignant form of the contagion. In this form the victim's body loses power to expel water secreted by the blood vessels, it shrivels up, he passes with hoarse cries from convulsion to convulsion, his blood grows thick like pitch, and he suffocates in a few hours.[8]

Why did I become a professor of Japanese literature? My parents were neither American missionaries nor Japanese immigrants. In fact, I chose my profession precisely because it was so remote from where life was meant to take me; a choice like a farm boy growing up to be a choreographer, a high-school dropout who becomes a silver appraiser for Sotheby's, the heartthrob confirmed as a Catholic priest: an intuition that different places can also be the safe ones.

Jack, my friend who teaches German literature, tells a story similar to mine. We grew up in moribund Northeast industrial towns, and we grew up gay. Which is to say, against gray and level landscapes unrelieved by color or beauty, we decorated the horizon with our own bodily daring. Jack could have gone into Japanese, or I into German. What mattered is that we needed escape routes, ways out of the dull places that fettered us and ways into the realm of possibility. This kind of homosexuality is only in part an attraction for same, only in the most rarified way an identity of who desires with the desired; nor is it simply a variant heterosexuality defined by the mutual lure of the younger and the older, the paler and the darker. It is all those things and none of them; it is neither a division nor a unity. Instead, out of an exuberantly confused act of being emerges not self or other but something our ponderous ontologies do not concede—a flash of bliss, a swirl of help-lessness, a tower of omnipotence, a leap of faith, a chance for the sublime, a rush for the clear expanse of a foreign land.

> Yet the source of the unexpected contagion was known to him only too well. This yearning for new and distant scenes, this craving for freedom, release, forgetfulness—they were, he admitted to himself, an impulse to-wards flight, flight from the spot which was the daily theatre of a rigid, cold, and passionate service.[9]

Sartre, a heterosexual who knew all this better than the famously homosexual Frenchmen to follow, wrote:

> A person is not born homosexual. He becomes one or the other, according to the accidents of history and to his own reaction to these accidents. I maintain that inversion is the effect of neither a prenatal choice nor an endocrinian malformation nor even the passive and determined result of complexes. It is an outlet that a child discovers when he is suffocating.[10]

So I come to Japan, where I hope to choose what I am between those two unalterable, existential terminals of my birth and death; where I can jettison the same things that Jack did on his way to the land that slaughtered his race; that my gay Japanese friends in Seattle did when they elected to endure the national contempt for yellow men in order to stay in America. Where we each end up is so different, and of course not different at all.

Kikanshien. I learn the word for bronchitis that fall. We learn lots of new words that year, even if we never say them out loud but only read them in the papers. *Kansen*, *yōsei*, *densenbyō*, *mansei*, *karini-haien*: infection, positive, contagious disease, chronic, pneumocystis carinii. And place names, too: Komagome.

One night Sarah was menstruating, and my penis smeared the sheets with her blood. Warm, thick, it was both novel and sensual. This was before the idea of blood, rather than being the fluid that makes us human beings all the same, became the register of our final difference. We used to think that race was the ultimate test of our loving resolve, but now we have other binaries dividing us, as well as other tests to take.

November.   I decide to write my doctor back home. I ask him plaintively: What should I do? Submit to Japanese medicine? And risk the consequences? Am I going to get better? It's been months now. Two weeks later he writes back. But he tells me there's really very little he can do for me thousands of miles away. This is his way of telling me to be brave and go see the doctors who are close.

One day I call Barbara, an American friend who, married to a Japanese, has lived in Tokyo for years. Barbara knows many doctors. She is a hypochondriac. I decide one especially distraught day to ask her for a reference. Of course I made up some excuse about why. But she cannot help me anyway—all her doctors are gynecologists, or homeopaths, or are private and won't take my insurance. I am relieved at this latest reprieve.

Later that week, on one of my neighborhood walks, I pass a small clinic. My lungs are particularly bad today. I think, grow up and see a doctor. Confess. Ask for help. Say nothing, hope he guesses, does the right thing. Which is what?

Dr. Yamada of the Yamada Clinic, a one-man operation, turns out to be a woman. Immense relief: not only are the odds of my new doctor being competent now enormously improved, but I know that the chances of that steely-eyed, male-to-male fear of me will be less. Who am I kidding.

Dr. Yamada is surprised to see a foreigner lumber into her surgery, but she quickly recovers. A good sign. The room is relatively spacious, but crowded with all sorts of lab equipment. The X-ray machine behind Dr. Yamada's desk looms ominously over both her and the little stool she asks me to sit down on. At the same time, I look down at my feet ridiculously crammed into tiny plastic slippers. I feel like a child whose wild hormones have made some of him gargantuan, other parts miniature: I am Gulliver on his travels.

But Dr. Yamada's sphinx-like expression suggests that nothing at all is out of the ordinary.

After a little small talk—"How long have you been in Japan?" "Do you live in the neighborhood?"—I briefly summarize the history of my bronchitis, at the conclusion of which Dr. Yamada nods. She asks me to take off my shirt, and calls her assistant in. I am about to be examined. A cold stethoscope is placed against my back; my arm is wrapped tightly by the blood pressure device; a tiny pointed thing with lights probes my ears, throat and nostrils. I am asked to breathe deep, I am asked to breathe out. Prompted for a cough, I comply. The doctor's commands are curt but not unfriendly. She and her assistant pass the clipboard back and forth noting figures in the blanks of the form. It is all entirely businesslike.

Sarah's genitals stood out in bold relief. The labia were bright pink and shiny-moist against the black color of her skin and tight pubic curls; the inner labia brighter and pinker still. Her erect clitoris curved slightly to one side and seemed to pulsate. Her vagina was slightly open and oozing a clear liquid. Even today, I could draw a picture. I desired her sex at the time, but for reasons I only now understand. Very clinical, it was all entirely businesslike.

Dr. Yamada takes another X ray. While the assistant goes off to put it through the developing machine, she lets me put my shirt back on and asks me a few more questions about my health, both in general and about my bronchitis specifically. No question even begins to hint at AIDS or my sexual orientation. She has a sister in New York, she tells me, and then, distracted by the returning assistant, drops this topic and reaches for the film.

Dr. Yamada examines my X ray carefully, for a longer time than I find reassuring. I feel like this image of me, passed from doctor to assistant and now back to doctor again, is an odd kind of fetish. I feel that some natural order has been inverted, that what I am here to look at is now looking at me. No, not quite me, but a representative of me, all blurry streaks of black and white and gray that will, eventually, lead to some conclusion. Like my own research. Like my own little essays, passing judgment not over bodies, but entire histories.

Dr. Yamada says it's still there but isn't particularly bad. She passes the X ray once again to the assistant, who inserts it in an envelope and then clips it to my freshly prepared file. I am both pleased and a little depressed: nothing new to worry about, but still a lingering problem. She doesn't ask for either a sample of my urine or blood: more relief. Now in quick succession, she sells me the canonical three sets of mystery pills that all Japanese doctors—who are their own pharmacologists—have at the ready. She tells me I'll eventually get better and blandly sends me on my way.

Ruth Benedict, the famous American anthropologist, was the author of a famous examination of Japan. But she did it during the war, and so never went to Japan. *Japanese men and women who had been born or educated in Japan and who were living in the United States during the war years were placed in a most difficult position.* She had Japanese and Japanese-Americans in the United States for her informants, from whom she no doubt learned many useful and true things about the enemy. *They were distrusted by many Americans.* But she must have thought: What is this like, writing a study of a culture I only know from a distance, by proxy, with all the problems that have to intervene? *I take special pleasure, therefore, in testifying to their help and kindness during the time when I was gathering material for this book.*[11] What Japanese person's shirt did she take off, what young Japanese person's legs did she spread apart to learn what she learned?

I go home from the Yamada Clinic relieved. But for some reason, that night I go through more than a liter of cheap sake, a record even for me.

Report. "The government said Friday there are no minorities in Japan."[12]

I have a confession to make about Sarah; I mean about sex with her. I was Sarah; I mean I wanted to be her. Sex then was already homosexual. She was female and heterosexual, I was male and homosexual, but my desire for her was a desire to be her. To Be A Black Woman.

There are other gay men who, like me, want to be black women. We listen to them sing, borrow their sassiness, rely on their pain. They are women, and so we can half identify with their gender; they are black, so we can half identify with their strength and their style. A couple of years before I met Sarah, I went to a party at my all-male college done up like Diana Ross, though I had to tell everyone who it was I was pretending to be. I do not look like a Motown diva. But I have always wanted to be one.

Making love to Sarah would be like the love I made in the years to come with her perfect opposite: lean, moustached white men with hard muscles and stiff cocks who make me lie still. Just as I wanted to steal their masculinity by burying my genitals inside them, or theirs in me, I used my penis to scoop up the pigment of Sarah's Africa and paint my skin with it;

take her cleverness and wit and her perfect deep stare into the confessed Truth: as much part of what makes me queer as the beautiful hard lines of the man that I also caress, in desire if not deed, to possess.

If narcissism is love of the same, then what do we call my love for Sarah? If I *am* her, despite all proof to the contrary? History is, finally, only part of the story. What do we call my love of men, who have things I never will? History is not just the record of what went before, but what we wish might have. What makes my embraces heterosexual, or homosexual? History: our gay invention. What part of me is it that desires, what part of others that I dare to make mine? But only if it remains forever different?

DECEMBER

The Common Good

At the time my reason was high rent; in retrospect, it was loneliness. To be apart from one's lover five years after the news broke is to be alone when the news finally sinks in. Now with a test available, all of us who did not know are both comforted and frightened by our deliberate ignorance. I move in with Ben to create a purposeful static, background noise to drown out the constant low rumbling I hear in the distance.

Death in Venice
> The beginning was fear; fear and desire, with a shuddering curiosity. Night reigned, and his senses were on the alert; he heard loud, confused noises from far away, clamor and hubbub. There was a rattling, a crashing, a low dull thunder; shrill halloos and a kind of howl with a long-drawn *u*-sound at the end. And with all of these, dominating them all, flute-notes of the cruellest sweetness, deep and cooing, keeping shamelessly on until the listener felt his very entrails bewitched.[1]

Ben lives in a two-bedroom house down a long, twisting alley not far from Mejiro station. Mejiro means "the whites of the eyes," and there are any number of stories of how this neighborhood along the north bank of the Kanda River got its name. Maybe it was once where white stallions were bred.

53

Or one of its temples was once so popular that the crowds of worshipers were so great that even "the whites of their eyes" could not move.

But for me, Mejiro means that I am closer to the center of the city. I can easily get anywhere. I can, if I wish, walk home to Mejiro from the Shinjuku bars if I do not mind the hour it takes. But Tokyo in the early morning hours is wonderfully silent and still, and I enjoy having it all to myself without the stares of others.   .

In fact this house is actually located just within the boundaries of the borough of Shinjuku, in a little section called Shimo-Ochiai, or the Lower Confluence, so named because here is where the Kanda and Igusa waters once met. Ben's multinational employer had found the house for him, and he had intended to stay there by himself. But to make a little money, and ease his loneliness, he ran a classified ad in the *Japan Times*. After I called him, he invited me to come over to see it.

The house is old and poorly built. The rent, however, is low and Ben, at first aloof, turns out to be just what I need. And I am what he needs. Ben is one of those foreigners who has drifted to Japan, a country he does not much care for but for which he can imagine no alternative. There is a long history of people like Ben in Japan, people who have chosen to come here not because of what it is, but what it is not, which is wherever it was that they came from. In Ben's case, that place is not so much his native northern California as it is a wildly dysfunctional family, complete with an indifferent father, a divorced manic mother, and a drug-using catatonic younger brother. After college Ben was predictably at a loss over what to do next. I say "predictably" because his family, his father in particular, had made it abundantly clear to him again and again that he would never amount to much—a lesson he took to heart.

Someone once must have casually mentioned Japan, and the opportunities for English teaching there, to Ben. The idea took hold because it sounded at least halfway respectable and because it would mean being out of the easy reach of his relatives. Do those Japanese paying all that money for English conversation lessons know what motivates their teachers? Less a love of the subject and more a refusal to have the conversations they should have. Ironic, isn't it? I, though armed with an eminently more prestigious rationale, have also come to this very farthest place. What I am escaping is, in kind and in contrast, a family I love, but nonetheless a family. My parents did nothing but love me, but the kind of love I now think of is not one with which I can repay them. Funny: Ben, though he does not realize it, has an understanding of all this. We will be perfect friends.

Ben is *nonke*, "straight." He has a girlfriend back in America, but she visits in the spring and that is the end of that. Ben is shy and has trouble meeting women. His few encounters while I live with him will not be the stuff of romance. He admires me, which is to say both my life in America with Dan and my many friends in Tokyo. But he also knows that I have secrets as deep as his own, and that I am at least as vulnerable as he. He chose me over a number of roommates ostensibly better suited to him, some straight guys and a couple who were Jewish to boot. When I got the call from him that he'd like me to be his housemate, I knew the reasons why.

There is also a long history of my living with straight men with whom I have intense and long-lived friendships. Having been a student for as long as I was, and therefore in need of rent-paying housemates, is only part of the reason why. I am interested, as I long have been, in studying unstudied masculinity close up. How does Ben do it? Every gesture, and every word, declare both his love of and indifference to women. Whereas any perceptive glimpse of me says out loud: he is not interested in women and so of course he pays them close attention. And from Ben's point of view: here is a new housemate with the usual male anatomy and so much of what goes along with it. But he loves my own kind, for reasons I cannot begin to fathom. What is it about our maleness that makes it so important to all of us? For such impossibly different causes? And different fates?

Ben, like the others before him, will over the course of the months to follow meet friends who have spent the night with me, and have to endure the sounds of our lovemaking and then the typical awkward banter the next morning. He will hear me on the phone talking talk to friends unlike anything he has ever heard other men say to each other. He will see me disappear for weekends away that I do not, cannot, invite him to go along on. What he will get is someone who will listen carefully to his story, someone who will take an interest in him unlike that any heterosexual friend of his ever has.

The world often thinks that straight men hate gay men, and some do, but there also can be a strange attraction between the two. Outside the company of women, but with a sexual energy there that can never be acted on or wholly repressed, there is now one more way to discern something true about ourselves.

It makes sense that this latest chapter in my life with men takes place in Japan, where my difference as an American from the Japanese is replicated at home in Mejiro, even while Ben and I look to all the world like copies of each other. His sexuality and mine are entirely opposite, but our personalities are oddly akin. How similar his is to the way I live with Japan: a place so different from my own, but also a place where I feel I can be myself in a way impossible at home. There are all kinds of attractions that are simultaneously between opposites and synonyms, and they can be sexual, racial, or cultural. They can be other things, too.

"Are the sexes really races?"[2] Are we really so different after all? Then again, perhaps a white gay man is even more inscrutable to a white man oblivious to his sex's desire than is he to a black man who understands how strange our loves can be. Or even more so to a black woman in America, for whom sex with me cannot be possible without the complications of a history rich with the ironies of impossibility.

In another odd twist, Ben is sicker than I. Prone to the flu, bad headaches, exhaustion, and, most dramatically, attacks of hyperventilation, Ben provides me with the perfect distraction—someone more vulnerable than myself. He makes me think about someone other than myself; and I find I enjoy being responsible for one part of his well-being.

His Japanese is rudimentary, so I accompany him to his doctors—a perfectly vicarious, voyeuristic experience for me that I keep to myself. Ben is my surrogate AIDS patient, a rehearsal for my own and surely imminent troubles, my fellow compatriot in a country that regards us both with suspicion since AIDS for the Japanese is a foreigner's disease, not a gay one. Unable to tell the difference between gay and straight American boys, this is a country that by default discriminates equally.

Once, early in our time together, Ben hyperventilates very dramatically in the middle of the night. Worried, I make him go to the hospital. I think back seven years, to when I had to take Hank in the middle of another night to the hospital, too. A lot has changed in that time, however, and now I am aware of nuances that Ben, sick with worries, is not. I see those minute but unmistakable signs of nervousness when I tell the emergency room doctors what his symptoms are. I see the doctors edge ever so slightly away from us. This has happened to me, too, when I was the one who needed the help of a stranger in the middle of the night. The difference is that then, because it was me, I thought in the back of my mind that they were probably right to do just that.

*   *   *

"The long closing of the country (about 250 years) to the outside during the feudal period indicates," writes one modern scholar of Japanese society, "how Westerners were seen to be a real threat. They were often thought to be the source of epidemics."[3] And an Englishman tells Aschenbach he would do well to leave today, instead of tomorrow. "The blockade," Thomas Mann writes, "cannot be more than a few days off."[4]

December.   Dan arrives for a much anticipated two-week visit. When he comes out of customs at the airport, he scans the crowd looking almost desperately for me: he is thinking, what if John's not there? What if he, three months back in Tokyo, has found someone else? Someone new, or someone old?

I am there, in fact, hours before the plane from Seattle is due. Those days when I dropped boyfriends casually are gone. Fear of infection is part of it, but the need for constancy, even boredom, in the face of an epidemic is a much bigger part. The past three-plus months I have clung to the very idea of Dan, thinking my timing in leaving for this sabbatical year could not have been worse.

So I am there in the lobby waiting for Dan. Narita, Tokyo's new international airport, has already at the end of 1986 the feel of an old airport, one better suited to a poor country. The once wide concourses are narrower now, crowded with concessions pushing tacky souvenirs and kiosks hawking soft pornography, a chaotic Asian bazaar enclosed in glass and concrete. Already too small when it opened, Narita and its single runway serve the world's biggest city. Hundreds are sitting on the floor upstairs waiting to depart. Down here on ground level, other hundreds are busily milling around. Welcome to teeming Asia. How can anyone hope to contain our modern pestilences?

There are two doors leading from customs into the reception area, and with typical disregard for the people who use this airport, there is no way to tell which of the doors any passenger might emerge from. I run back and forth between both, artfully dodging passengers who have already arrived with their baggage carts piled high with luggage and the souvenirs of a shopping spree in Singapore, Guam, Los Angeles, or even Seattle.

1971.   Haneda airport was a quiet affair, few flights in or out compared to later years. The chartered plane that brought me from Saigon landed in the middle of the night, and we had to wait outside of immigration until it opened early in the morning. Past the inspectors, I entered a small hall with a few signs in English, but what I noticed was the bright sunshine pouring through large planes of glass into a massive hall cooled by unseen, but surely equally massive, air conditioners. In this country, I think, they can make us comfortable.

I waited for the new friends I had made on the plane to get through customs themselves, and then we found the driver who, as promised, was holding a cardboard sign alerting us to the bus that would take us to the downtown hotel. There, after as much as two years in Vietnam for some of us, we would reenter the world. Here was Japan, a place that strikes so many Western visitors as wholly exotic, but which to us had every sign of American normality.

Pierre Loti writes at the start of his novel: "At dawn of day we sighted Japan. Precisely at the foretold moment Japan arose before us, afar off, like a clear and distinct dot in the vast sea, which for so many days had been but a blank space."[5]

When Dan does emerge, I am fortunately standing directly in front of him. I am the first person he sees, and he breaks out in his big boyish grin. Later I will ask him what he would have done if I hadn't been there. Dunno, he says. Gotten a hotel room, flown back the next day. I note, of course, that he answered swiftly enough to reveal he had, in fact, prepared such a contingency plan. Pathetic homosexuals, I think, who can do such things to each other. Evil bitches all. Like Dan, I am always ready for rejection and humiliation. But can I promise I'll always be there for him?

Our hosts put us, two to a room, in a small business hotel owned by the commercial arm of a Buddhist sect near Ueno Park in the older, eastern half of the city. On the bus into Tokyo, a nattily dressed young female guide chattered on endlessly in her heavily accented English about this sight and that. I paid no attention except to the interesting fact that we had landed in Japan on the anniversary of an earthquake that, nearly half a century ago, had leveled Tokyo. Sirens, she told us, would go off all over the city at noon to commemorate the disaster.

But my attention was focused elsewhere. Stephen, a large American about my age, had also been working for a humanitarian group in Vietnam, but in Danang. I was drawn to him immediately, not only because of our shared recent history, but because he was handsome and, I sensed, interested in other men. When we got off the bus and it became clear that we were being randomly paired off for assignment to the hotel rooms, I made sure I was standing right next to him when our turn came. "Room 417 for you two boys."

I decided that it would be risking my new domestic harmony with Ben to bring Dan to our little Mejiro house for two weeks of sexual revelry. So I rented from Iida-*san*, my former landlord in Nakano, a small studio at the end of the long covered arcade outside of Nakano station, not far from the Broadway where Tetsuji, years earlier, had worked and I had often visited. There, Dan and I would have privacy, a place for him to sleep off his jet lag at any hour he wished; a place where he would be assured access to a Western-style toilet (his biggest concern in planning this trip); and a place where we could make love without worrying about either Ben's sleep or his prejudices.

Narita airport is far from Tokyo in the first place, and Nakano is at the far end of the city after that. But despite Dan's exhaustion from the long flight, I cannot afford anything more commodious than public transportation, which means first a shuttle bus from the terminal to a train station; a train to a subway; and then a long walk through the shopping arcade to our little room. He has two little bags and he insists on carrying the heavier one.

It is now a Sunday night, but that is Tokyo's busiest shopping day of the week and the place is packed with evening strollers. The narrow walkway from the station to our rented room has a high glass roof over it, and shops and restaurants, most with brightly lit or even neon signs, are stacked three stories high. *This is the Broadway arcade*. Dan, though I worry about him, is dumbstruck by the scene: the human commotion, the cacophony of sounds, but most of all the carnival of lights and banners and billboards, each in-scribed with marks he cannot decipher but which dazzle him all the more, mesmerizing this American with only the initial mystery of the East. *Just what do all these Chinese characters mean?*, he thinks to himself. *How many times did I walk this way to visit Tetsuji?*, I am thinking to myself. Later in his stay, Dan will begin to complain of "English deprivation"—unable to read even the simplest street sign, he discovers a hunger for meaning he had never known before—but this, our first Tokyo night, is literally spectacular. *Why do I feel like my past is still my present?* Dan's First Day in the Orient. *My last chance*.

Lafcadio Hearn, traveling through Yokohama on his first day, was also stunned by the "magical characters" all about him. In 1889 none would have been electric, but just as wondrous. Hearn wrote:

I see Chinese texts—multitudinous, weird, mysterious—fleeing by me, all in one direction; ideographs white and ark, upon sign-boards, upon paper screens, upon the backs of sandaled men. They seem to live, these ideographs, with conscious life; they are moving their parts, moving with a movement as of insects, monstrously, like *phasmidae*. I am rolling always through low, narrow, luminous streets in a phantom jinrikisha, whose wheels make no sound.[6]

Room 417 was a small rectangle, with two narrow day beds lined up against opposite long walls.

After unpacking and washing up in the bathroom down the hall, Stephen and I went out to have Our First Day in the Orient. Vietnam cannot count, because that was, we and millions of other young American men will realize later, a journey into ourselves and nowhere else.

Stephen was the kind of man I wanted to be. Big, with a deep voice, square-jawed and with a big American-boy grin. Chuck, the older boy in my Cub Scout troop; Chris, who played right field when I was in left; a shirtless and buff James West battling the brainy Doctor Loveless (and surely, like us, his unrequited lover) with his gentlemanly brawn.

It was very hot that late afternoon and Ueno Park across the busy street from the Hokke Club hotel would have provided no relief, even if we had ventured out that way. We wanted the city, the hustle-bustle of an affluent Asian city without any fear of being blown up by little boys or girls. The only thing we talk about is what we'll do back in America, which is start college, him on Long Island and me in New England.

At some point that afternoon, we are standing on a street corner when a parade turns toward us. On a huge float on a flatbed truck towers over us pedestrians a naked woman stretching with her arms outstretched upwards, and her legs spread wide. Later, someone will tell us that it was street theater.

Suddenly, this monster-woman's vagina opens up and young Japanese men and women with long hair and dressed in loincloths come streaming out, running amok, shouting words at the top of their lungs that neither Stephen nor I can understand. We look at each other and laugh. I think to myself: this is a good start to the seduction.

That night, after a dinner at a cheap restaurant where we had to lead the waiter outdoors by the hand and point at the plastic model of the food we wanted to eat, we wandered an area near the Ueno train station that was clearly where the local action was. Years later, now fluent in Japanese and very knowledgeable about Tokyo's secret places, it is in this neighborhood that I will pick up a Japanese truck driver at a public bath frequented by men who like sex with other men but do not think themselves homosexual. But this, My First Night in the Orient, Stephen and I stumble into an upstairs nightclub, chosen purely on the basis of its charming misnomer: Rounge Zero. This is years before I would start drinking seriously, but I made sure that both Stephen and I got tanked up good.

The lights are low, the music is Coltrane. Lying back against the vinyl banquette, a cigarette held between his fingers, his mouth open to laugh at a joke I have just made, Stephen and I are in Asia.

In that little Nakano room Iida-*san* had rented me at a discount, we sleep on a double futon we keep out most of the day, since we make love whenever we are both awake and feel like it. A first night and then two weeks of always-safe sex. Months of celibacy and the newness of our relationship make us so eager for each other that I forget we are in Japan, and recall it only when I wake up after our post-coital naps and see the signs of foreignness all about me: the tatami mats on the floor, the glare of the cheap florescent light over head, and the muted sounds of Japanese being spoken in the next room.

I don't remember when, or even if, we ever spoke about the rules of our lovemaking. Dan is the first of my lovers with whom I have never, as they say, "shared bodily fluids." *I kiss his forehead from left to right.* There has always been a debate, of course, over just what constitutes both "sharing" and "bodily fluids." *I trace his lips slowly with my tongue.* Friends back East tell me they only give head with a condom, but folks in Seattle say no one gets infected through oral sex. *I draw a wet line from one nipple to the other, right to left.* Similarly, my Boston informants tell me butt-fucking under any conditions is out, that rubbers will eventually break, but Shawn in New York insists that tops don't have to worry. *I follow the line of hair from his navel down to his cock.* I suppose if Shawn is right, then it's our wonderful versatility that's gotten us into trouble. *My head disappears down there.* Everything has become a negotiation, a matter of diplomacy. *I work my way up the shaft in a slow spiral.* I am not good at talking, it has always destroyed the erotic for me, so I have to proceed by hints, by body language articulating limits I do not cross, will not permit to be crossed. *I get the thickest part of his head slippery with spit.* As a boy I had a neighbor who would not let us kids cross his yard to get to the elementary school. *My fingers play with the weight of his warm, limp testicles.* And a coach who would not let our team shower after practice without him in the locker room. *I would like to swallow him whole, but that is where I stop.* In Japan I am a foreigner, there are some shrines I cannot approach. *Can I push my fingers in this far?* A line drawn in the sand, of course, is always an invitation to cross it, and for years I wanted the Japanese to accept me. *His hips begin to gyrate, issuing an invitation.* But I never succeeded. *But I put my fist around his big dick, and jerk him off.* Rules are not easily broken, unlike rubbers. *He kisses the top of my head, affirming my prudent decision.* This is their country, after all, and not mine.

Stephen and I stumbled back to the Hokke Club hotel laughing and carrying on as if to deliberately upset both the staff and the others in our group, whom we have confidently decided over drinks at Rounge Zero were definitely not cool like us. Back in Room 417, we undress. He pushes me playfully back onto my narrow bed, where it is a foregone conclusion we'll spend the next half-hour, if not the night.

I kiss his forehead, his lips, play with his chest, excitedly fondle him everywhere. He does the same to me, only rougher and with all the insistence that the larger and more handsome male can command. He squirts into my mouth: later that night, when we wake up for another go at it, he'll shoot deep into me. It is 1970 and there are no rules. There were only two boys and the thought that all of the Asian continent lay behind us, and all of history before us.

My sabbatical year is divided into two unequal halves: Before Dan and After Dan. But I am really referring to something that happened three days before he arrived.

As autumn turned into winter, my "bronchitis" does not go away. Dr. Yamada has done all she can, but it is not enough. I reach that point that so many of us reach, just like I would years later during that especially hot summer that sends me to the "small and dreary" building in Seattle, when knowing was worse than not knowing.

I need, despite my professional pride, to see an American doctor. I want to speak in English, let all my fears fly out of my mouth in nuanced speech, make the kind of subtly communicative eye contact impossible, I worry, with a Japanese physician. So I travel early one cold Monday morning to Saint Luke's International Hospital, which later will open a plush new wing but then, in the winter of 1986, is unexpectedly grim and dark. I fill out the forms, am briefly interrogated in front of other patients by a brusque nurse, and take my seat on one of the long, uncomfortable wooden benches. I wait for my name to be called.

*   *   *

His first full day in the Orient means going together to the department stores in the Ginza. Dan had carefully chosen six dress shirts, ironed and hung them where he'd see them the next morning when he packed before leaving for the Seattle airport. But he forgot to bring them after all that, and so our first errand is buying him shirts.

We are Tokyo *flâneurs*, strolling the wide sidewalks outside elegant shops on a sunny winter afternoon. We soon found some suitable shirts (on sale, if still four times what Dan was used to paying) on a discount table in the Seibu. Then we spend the next couple of hours walking almost aimlessly. My thinking is that this is as good a way as any for Dan to soak up what Tokyo looks, smells, feels like. I stop in at a coin dealer I know about who will sell us cheap bullet train tickets to Kyoto under the table. Dan is impressed by how well I know my way around.

He is fascinated by everything he sees. Dan has come to Japan with absolutely no expectations of what he will find here, other than me, and of even that he had been none too sure. He has read no guidebooks, consulted no better-traveled friends. He is entirely in my hands. He does not even have a map. He will do anything I want.

Stephen never did go to his own bed that night. We stayed together in mine, tightly glued together by the semen and spit that had dried hard between us. When I woke the next morning, it was with his long soft penis pressed up against me. I move my legs enough to rouse him, and while I ride him one more time before we have to dress to join the group meeting downstairs I think: I will do anything he wants.

Although I am among the first outpatients to register that morning, it seems that hours pass. Finally, when I think I hear my name garbled over the ancient public address system, I make my way to the specified examining room. Opening the door, it is my turn and not the doctor's to be surprised: a Japanese man swivels around in his chair to welcome me. Isn't this an *international* hospital, I say to myself. Shouldn't I be seeing a *white* doctor? As I realize with shame how ridiculous my assumption is, the doctor politely asks me if I can speak Japanese. I reply, yes, and the interview begins.

This doctor takes no X rays, prescribes no medicines. He tells me that bronchial infections always need a long time to heal and that I should not be alarmed. He says all this with a calm confidence that I find hypnotic. "Go home, don't exert yourself, stop worrying." One day soon, he assures me, you'll be fine.

How different from my visit to the Yamada Clinic early this month. Today, there is no probing, no X rays, no extensive note-taking. This doctor is not incompetent, quite the contrary: he knows his business and is not concerned over my little troubles. Have I ever met a doctor in whom I have wanted more to trust? I think: I will do anything he wants.

When I walk out of Saint Luke's, it is a now beautiful sunny winter day, the kind Tokyo has many of. I feel a rock of untold weight gone. For some reason I believe this doctor, or at any rate choose to believe him. Mejiro is a long ways from Saint Luke's, but giddy with the idea that I have my sabbatical, my career, and my life back, I decide to walk home, look in the shops, buy flowers, spend too much money on lunch, read trashy magazines in coffee shops. Tokyo is mine again. There is no work done that day, no novels of people slowly being killed by bomb-related cancers eating away at their organs. I've had it with the body and its concerns for this one day. And most wonderful of all, that the next morning, a Tuesday in the middle of December, I wake up in Ben's house, take one very deep breath, and know instantly that my lungs are healed.

Tsukiji, the neighborhood where Saint Luke's is located, was once the sole place that foreigners with business in Tokyo were allowed to live. Long ago, it had been a neighborhood for the mansions of some of Japan's leading daimyō, but when foreigners were consigned there it had fallen on harder times, and was one of the licensed quarters for prostitution in the city. Now, the fish market and the Buddhist Honganji temple are there, but the walls around the temple remind one of the walls that must have once separated the foreigners from the Japanese.

While I am in Japan this year I hear of other ghettos being readied for us. Real estate developers envision a manmade island in the middle of Tokyo Bay, where foreigners and "Japanese who have lived abroad for a long time" can dwell in Western-style apartments, enjoy foreign-language schools and cinemas, eat non-Japanese food, and be spared the discomfort of normal Japanese life: where we can be happy among our own kind. My more cynical friends dub this plan "Dejima Gardens" in a reference to a similar island used centuries ago to confine Dutch traders in Nagasaki.

Now filled in and part of the city proper, Dejima was originally a fan-shaped island in the Nagasaki harbor where in the seventeenth century first the Portuguese, and then the Dutch, were allowed to live and trade once all other contact between the Japanese and foreigners was prohibited. No Dutch women were permitted there, and one can imagine that despite the threat of punishment, some Japanese women crossed over to the island to their lovers. *Rashamen*, a word that can also mean "sheep," was the term for the mistresses of foreign men, coined perhaps because they were known for wearing the woolen garments of their European lovers.

Back in America, where we have our own history of confining Japanese "for their own good" as well as "our" own, one hears Congressmen muse about the merits of placing HIV+ people in camps to let the "general population" sleep more easily at night. William F. Buckley, a radical libertarian, alternatively proposes tatooing. Cuba does quarantine its HIV+ population, and in 1994 I will read of young Cubans who deliberately infect themselves in order to be moved out of the "general population" and into the confinement of a place known as Las Cocas—"The Common Good." Enrique explains that "We gave ourselves AIDS to liberate ourselves from society and those laws about obligatory work, and live in our own world."[7] I understand Enrique perfectly; so would Jean-Paul Sartre. There are times when we are confined against our wills, and there are times when we choose, in accordance with our wills, to confine ourselves. But there are also times that are both: when the rules we are handed and cannot change become the stage where we resolve to embrace who we are, to be our being, to exist our lives. And that stage, I learn again this year of my sabbatical, is not Tokyo or Seattle or any real place at all.

Bainbridge Island is just across from downtown Seattle, separated by a bay that the ferryboats cross in less than half an hour. It is a popular place for the city's professionals to live. Its small towns now have streets lined with bistros and little shops. But it was not always that way.

The island was discovered by Captain George Vancouver in 1792, only at the time he did not realize he had set foot on an island. Chief Kitsap never told him otherwise. Later, it was Captain Charles Wilkes who gave the island its Anglo-Saxon name, in honor of one of the heroes of the War of 1812.

Bainbridge, despite its patrinomy, had a peaceful nineteenth century. Port Madison and Port Blakely were the lumber mill towns that brought the first immigrants, later waves of whom would find work in the shipyards and agriculture. Bainbridge was particularly suited for the cultivation of strawberries, and by 1903 one of the farms had a first-generation Japanese owner. The Japanese-American population of Bainbridge rose slowly, then steadily after 1910, and by 1942 there were forty-three of their farms there.

*   *   *

On his first post-jet lag weekend night in Tokyo, I take Dan to Ni-chōme. Never good at directions, and now in a country where no sign or billboard makes linguistic sense, he is totally in my hands. At this hour, he could not even return home without my help; but he trusts in me entirely, with a faith that even then puts his life at risk.

In 1921 the State of Washington passes its Alien Land Law.

My favorite places in this neighborhood are the minuscule little bars down alleyways and up staircases that only foreigners who know the scene well ever frequent; where a knowledge of Japanese language and the more subtle ways of cruising are required. But tonight, with Dan in tow, I go along one of the larger streets and then down rather than up a flight of stairs. I open the door to Fuji, a dark rectangular bar whose three bartenders loudly yell out welcome in the Japanese fashion.

Dan orders a beer, I a glass of white wine. For a while we stand idly, and then settle at a small table with several chairs around it near the bar. The bar's stereo is playing some old hit from the seventies, and Dan has a big grin on his face. The strangeness and the familiarity of Fuji almost make him laugh, and in fact the giggles he unsuccessfully suppresses briefly attract the attention of the few other customers there at this early hour.

One of the three bartenders, to Dan's surprise and obvious interest, is a tall, young blond. Dan makes eye contact, and the young man—"Hi, my name's Howie"—comes over to our table to join us.

Howie, we learn quickly, is from California and has worked at Fuji for four months.

Fuji is a bar that caters to foreigners, and no doubt Howie was recruited to make those customers feel at home, though all the bar's bartenders speak English, or at least enough to sell drinks.

Out of the corner of my eye I think see someone I think I know. *Dan: "What's it like working in a Japanese gay bar, anyway?"* God, it could be Stephen, if he had never aged. *Howie: "Oh, great." (Grin)* He is standing by the seats at the bar, talking to two Japanese. *Dan: "I mean, is it like Los Angeles?"* I can't help but stare at him and his raw beauty. *Howie: "Uh, well, like, yes and no."* He is the same as Stephen, just a generation later. *Dan: "Are you going to stay here long?"* Now he notices me noticing him, but his gaze doesn't linger. *Howie: "Hey guys, how about some more drinks? I'm pretty thirsty myself."* I jar no memory for him. *Dan: "What can I buy you?"* It is not Stephen.

Howie looks over our shoulders as the door swings open and a large, elderly foreigner walks in with a young Japanese in tow. Howie and this foreigner obviously know each other.

I look at Dan, but am thinking back to another young American, who worked in another Japanese gay bar years earlier. He was not as good looking as Howie, but somewhat more interesting.

There are a dozen bars like Fuji in Ni-chōme, where foreigners can come freely and meet Japanese as well as each other. Part of Howie's job is making sure everyone who comes in gets to meet somebody; he makes introductions as he pushes the booze. No American so inclined need leave Fuji, or its like, alone. Within a few month's time, all of us who live here are usually and securely ensconced in a temporary marriage, lasting just as long as, but no longer than, we remain in Japan.

"There are now four of us," Pierre Loti writes in *Madame Chrysanthème*, "four officers of my ship, married like myself, and inhabiting the slops of the same suburb. It is quite an ordinary occurrence, and is arranged without difficulties, mystery, or danger."[8]

Nineteen forty-two was also the year that those forty-three farms—and fifty-four families—would disappear from Bainbridge Island. On March 24 the federal government issued a "Civilian Exclusion Order," subdesignated "No. 1," that declared the island a "military area." The Japanese and Japanese-American residents of Bainbridge were given six days to prepare for "evacuation" to "relocation centers" that the authorities had considered calling "residence control programs."

The Bainbridge Japanese were first lodged, if that is the right word, in a refitted livestock exhibition hall at the Washington State Fairgrounds: appropriately enough, perhaps, because eventually they were herded onto trains for the trip down to Manzanar.

Bainbridge was the dress rehearsal for the 120,000 internal exiles to follow.

I remember another Fuji. In the summer of 1974, I climbed Japan's most sacred mountain.

Stephen came with me. He was back in Japan then, too. We had stopped being lovers shortly after our return to the United States and did not mention the sex we once had ever again. This would be, in fact, the last time I saw him. Years later, he promised to put in an appearance at a party in

New York where I'd be. He never came. Even more years later, I heard he was married with two sons.

Fuji is high enough that the rain is swept up from lower elevations to higher, so you have to wear rain gear that closes at the pants and sleeve cuffs. The climb is not arduous, but it takes more than a day; in any case, since the point is to arrive at the summit in time to see daybreak over the western Pacific, everyone spends the night in the shacks that are there to accommodate us climbers.

We picked one that was still calling out to climbers that it had space; others had stopped, and I began to worry we would run out of options if we waited any longer. The staff told us to join the other guests sitting cross-legged on mats outside of the shack. Stephen, who by this time spoke better Japanese than I, soon engaged other young climbers in some banter, but I sat there quietly. Despite the early hour, we were all served a simple stew in large bowls and then brusquely instructed to go and use the outhouse. I got in line, did my business, and strolled back to the shack wondering how we would pass the time before nightfall and bed.

I did not understand the routine, however. Already, the young men who ran this place were directing us to go inside. It turned out to be one large room. Each guest, fully clothed and clutching his or her pack, was being packed in like sardines one by one starting from the back of the room. One with his head toward the wall; the next with his feet, and so on. At some point Stephen and I joined the line and were securely glued into place by the presence of Japanese climbers on all four sides of us. More and more people came in to join us on the thin straw mats, so many that no blanket was going to be necessary to keep us warm. When we were asked to turn onto our sides from our backs or stomachs so that even more sleepers could be squeezed in, I momentarily panicked. Usually not prone to claustrophobia, I suddenly saw that no path was being left clear for any of us to get up during the night, either to piss or to flee.

Stephen and I lay down as instructed. Our bodies, fully clothed, were pressed tighter and tighter together as others joined us on the floor. I remember joking with him about the erotic possibilities of these accommodations, but he declined to continue the flirtation. In no time he was fast asleep and I was left again to my thoughts.

We were going to bed while the sun still had not set past the horizon because they would be rousing us in the middle of the night, to feed us a breakfast and send us on the way up the short distance that still remained between us and the top of the holy mountain. Armed with flashlights, we would in a few hours form an immense human snake illuminating a path that cut through the last of the night. But that was still six hours away. At this moment, I continued to feel slight shoves in all directions as climber after climber was squeezed into the tiny spaces others had hoped to preserve for their comfort. Surrendering, I began to let myself enjoy the warmth of unknown strangers all around me. In Vietnam Stephen and I were warned not to trust anyone. But in this room of young Asian people, nestled together like young cubs in a lair as the rising wind outside drowned out the few snorers among us, I let all my caution go. Exhausted by the day's climb on the shifting pumice soil, it was now my turn to fall into a deep sleep little different from that of an infant at a mother's breast. I could feel Stephen's breathing, as well as that of the fellow climber to my back. Like a newborn with its parent, I felt the contentedness that comes from the union of one person with another—all of us in this fragile hut connected one-by-one in a single, huge chain of being. On one side, my first lover; on the another, a member of the race that I had committed to love as well.

December 1986

VIRUS FOUND IN BLOOD SAMPLES

Three blood samples donated in Tokyo were found to contain Acquired Immune Deficiency Syndrome (AIDS) antibodies, increasing the total of such findings nationwide among the public to nine, reported the Health and Welfare Ministry on Friday.

The ministry, which has been analyzing donated blood for possible AIDS infections since February with the Japan Red Cross, said one sample was donated in September and the other two in October, all by Tokyo male citizens, though it withheld their identities.[9]

We were woken in what seemed to be the middle of the night, but was in fact shortly before the first light. After eating we resumed our march to the summit, part of a long, bright chain formed by scores of men and women carrying torches. We were soon there, on the edge of a huge crater that had erupted in the past and will one day erupt again. But we were facing outwards, in the direction leading toward the Pacific Ocean, which on this exceptionally clear morning we could see—first gray, then greenish, finally blue. Standing behind Stephen, I put my arms around his waist and nuzzled my head against his shoulder. No Japanese there with us stared our way or even looked askance. The sight of the sea from the heights of Mount Fuji demanded everyone's full attention and did not permit even the distraction of these two Americans embracing tightly against the breezy chill of the morning.

We walked the perimeter of the crater, looked far in all directions, and then sat down on two rocks to wait while the sun warmed the day. Other Japanese did the same. It became ever quieter as many of the climbers started their descent down the mountain. Eventually Stephen would offer those sitting by us a cigarette with a gesture of his hand. The Japanese acknowledged Stephen's favor with a slight nod of the head and a low grunt. The two of them leaned back and blew smoke into the clean, clear air of Mount Fuji as if they were such old friends that there was no need to speak.

The sun was rising quickly and the orangey light that had first illuminated the stone of the volcano and the faces of the climbers was turning whiter, shortening shadows and burning up the mist below us. Stephen ground the butt of his cigarette with the heel of his boot and nodded once more in the direction of his new, mute acquaintance. Turning his head forward but not the least bit toward me, he stared out beyond the clouds to where the sea began.

"Ready to go?" I offered after a few minutes of silence.

"No."

Eventually I would cease my pursuit of other Americans in Japan, most of whom (I was convinced) were better-looking than myself. I gave up on trying to seduce men both so familiar and so unattainable. I was in Japan, after all, and so why not join my love of this country with my love of its men? So unfamiliar and so attainable. My vanity as well as curiosity would be perfectly served; my need for love as well as my need to know so easily reconciled.

But sometimes, in a Japanese habit I have never been able to break free from, the sight of a huge Calvin Klein billboard towering over a Ginza street or a J. Crew poster in some subway station brings me to a sudden halt. There, drawn to a young chiseled Aryan in his briefs or a brawny rugby player with legs covered with curly golden hairs, I study white manhood and have my longing for it remind me of the other lessons of my itinerant erotics. *There is a man more like me.* All around me Japanese people are rushing past, but I stand still for a minute and stare. *I can imagine being him.* If close enough, I have even reached out and stroked the chest of a blue-eyed swimmer or the strong back of an Armani model. *But only because I am in Japan, where our common race makes the impossible distance between his beauty and my ordinariness, here if nowhere else, mean nothing.*

"Okay, I'm ready. Let's start down."

It took a fraction of the time, given the slippery pumice of the mountainside, to descend to the fifth station than it had to climb to the summit. At Mishima I boarded a train for Tokyo, and Stephen one for Kyoto. That night Japanese friends asked how my journey to Japan's most sacred mountain had gone, and I answered that it is indeed a trip that everyone should make at least once in a lifetime.

JANUARY

The Theory of the Japanese People

The Japanese government has estimated that one Japanese in every quarter million is infected with the AIDS virus. A ratio that can hardly be true. It would mean that less than five hundred of its citizens are positive. Enough to count, but perhaps not enough to matter. Japan carefully calibrates its crises.

Dan and I take the bullet train to Kyoto, where we spend the first three days of the new year with Babette. Babette, whom I have never called by her real name, has been my friend since the early 1970s, when we both lived in Kansai—western Japan, meaning the cities of Kyoto, Osaka, Nara, and Kobe—and attended the international division of a local university. Married to, if soon to be divorced from, a Japanese flamenco guitarist, La Babette reigns as grand doyenne over the sizeable *gaijin* society of Kyoto, the ancient capital. Our three days with her are filled with parties, a couple she gives herself, but mostly ones she is invited to or simply knows about and crashes. Babette, and we her entourage, are free to go wherever we please.

*   *   *

Kipling visited Kyoto, too. He wrote of his arrival there in 1889 after leaving India:

> So we came to the very great city of Kyoto in regal sunshine, tempered by a breeze that drove down the cherry blossoms in drifts about the street. One Japanese town, in the southern provinces at least, is very much like another to look at—a grey-black sea of house roofs, speckled with the white walls of the fire-proof godowns where merchants and rich men keep their chief treasures. The general level is broken by the temple roofs, which are turned up at the edges, and remotely resemble so many terai-hats.[1]

Babette is aggressively heterosexual and has several lovers as well as a husband. But because she lives in Japan and is fond of other Americans, she also knows a great many male homosexuals. Dan and I meet several dozen of them (in my case, not always for the first time) over the course of our excursion. Gay men in Kyoto are different from us in Tokyo, both those who are Japanese and those who are not. As a city that prospers nowadays largely on its rarified aesthetics, Kyoto is a perfect place for artistic types from around the world. Many are studying some ancient art, preferably a dying one that can be rescued by the lucky arrival of a Bruce or Ariel or Stafford. Tea was my particular devotion when I was going to school in Kyoto years ago. Others of us are doing avant-garde performance, or applying old dyeing techniques to our postmodern constructions. Wolfgang tells me he's here to paint. When he shows me the five tubes of paint he is carrying in his shoulder bag, I ask him if that's enough. He tells me he mixes them.

Tokyo types like to make fun of Kyoto esthetes, especially when we learn they are supported by well-paying English-teaching jobs in Osaka commuted to under the cover of twilight. But this is New Year's, and I enjoy showing Dan a corner of Japan both outrageously, familiarly, gay and at the same time still exotic in ways that Tokyo no longer is. Odd people in an odd place, we are very much at home here.

One of Babette's holiday events is a dinner party she hosts at her apartment. It is a smallish place, but in a good neighborhood in the northeast corner of the city. I helped her finance her lease when she first moved in half a dozen years ago, which is to say I lent her money that I had borrowed in turn from Tetsuji, the poorest of all of us. In any case, nowadays Babette is financially secure, with several of the best paying teaching jobs inherited from a succession of long-gone foreigners, though a deadbeat husband is something of a drain on the family finances. Shōji is not to be with us tonight, and Babette does not mention why.

The dinner party starts late. Dan and I have been sitting around the *kotatsu* since late afternoon, not only to stay warm but to take advantage of the fact that we can drink for free at her house. I have always felt very at ease with Babette, so comfortable in fact that I can treat her as I would a sister, and her home as if it were my own. Japan always make fellow expatriates intimate, but in Babette's and my case we also have a history of special intimacies.

Babette is in her kitchen when, shortly after nine, there is the sound of her doorbell. Ravi and his Japanese wife join Dan and me around the low table in the living room. Ravi is a tall, good-looking and affable young man originally from Bombay but now a long-time citizen of the United States. Ravi, like Babette herself in only a few years' time, will end up in San Francisco—both minus their spouses. Babette opens a cabinet near the table at which we are gathered and extracts a bottle of Stolichnaya that she places with two glasses in front of Ravi.

"What is this, Babette? Do these guests of yours have their own *bottle-keep*?"

The wife looks puzzled at the name I use to call Babette. But I note that Ravi grins, intuitively grasping the camp joke. He shares in our intimacies, too.

"And aren't you going to bring them some ice?"

Babette, though she can hear me perfectly clearly in the tiny apartment, has her back to me in the kitchen and ignores my teasing. The phone rings and Babette leaves her guests to fend for themselves.

Ravi starts to ask me questions—who Dan and I are, what we're doing in Kyoto, and so on. I let Dan answer most of them, because I am curious about Ravi's wife. Eventually I will learn she goes by the name of Bo. She seems some years older than her husband, or she certainly looks that way. She is thin to the point of appearing ill, and has uncharacteristically long and stringy hair for a Japanese. The lines in her face are already hard. She does not wear the heavy makeup many Japanese women her age favor. I am sure that she has a colorful, muddled past. At best, a nature photographer specializing in the Himalaya summits, and who met her husband in Kathmandu; at the probable worst, the ex-girlfriend of Red Army terrorists who married Ravi out of misplaced third-world sympathies. Bo hesitates in her answers to all my questions, and prefers to look in any direction but my own.

I wonder what particular vice it is that has made her this uncomfortable a person.

It is when she pours out generous amounts of the vodka for Ravi and herself, and has to reach across the table to hand Ravi his tumbler of luke-warm alcohol, that I notice the track marks etched into the crux of her stick-like white arm.

> Kyoto fills a plain almost entirely surrounded by wooded hills, very familiar in their aspect to those who have seen the Siwaliks. Once upon a time it was the capital of Japan, and to-day it numbers two hundred and fifty thousand people. It is laid out like an American town. All the streets run at right angles to each other. That, by the way, is exactly what the Professor and I are doing. We are elaborating the Theory of the Japanese People, and we can't agree.[2]

Kyoto is full of people at New Year's, and this year cold but exceptionally clear skies bring out even the locals. Dan and I are swept along each day by the crowds at each of the temples and shrines we try to visit, but he does not care because everything, even the jostle of the crowd, is new and interesting. Through Dan I find myself enjoying Japan more than I have at any time since arriving here last September.

During the day Babette has associates upon whom she has to pay the obligatory New Year's calls, so Dan and I are free to wander about as we wish. I have my favorite places from when Babette and I attended school here fifteen years ago; and unlike Tokyo, where my favorite places are bars and restaurants that disappear one by one, these old places in the ancient capital are here forever.

On our way up a hill toward Kiyomizu temple, we run into a lanky young blond walking his bicycle down in the opposite direction. I recognize him at once as a former student from one of my first-year Japanese classes several years ago.

"Hi, Professor Treat? Do you remember me? Darron. From Seattle. The UW."

Of course I remember, though I had been planning to pretend not to, in order to avoid just this conversation. Dan stands off to the side, his interest suddenly compelled by some cheap pottery for sale in a stall, in case the fact that I have a male lover with me in Japan is not an opportune circumstance at this moment.

A brief exchange confirms that he is living in Kyoto now but that I am only passing through.

As we watch him walk his bicycle down the hill, snaking his way through the stream of Japanese pilgrims headed our way, Dan remarks how attractive Darron is. I do not know why I bother to say that he is not my type, because there was once a time when he most certainly was.

His longish blond hair bobs up and down in the distance, still visible among the sea of black.

The conversation around the dinner table turns to Ravi's latest project once Babette comes in to join us, a big platter of appetizers in hand for us to pick at. He is photographing families still at work in one of Kyoto's oldest and most venerable industries, kimono-dyeing. The pictures, he tells us happily, will go on display first here in Kyoto at one of the trendier small galleries specializing in the work of local foreign artists, and later in Santa Cruz.

Dan and Babette begin to have an animated exchange about the special Japanese food prepared at New Year's, a topic neither of them knows anything about. I listen to Ravi explain his photographs.

"The point is not *ethnographic*, that's all been done before, of course, you see. Nor am I terribly interested in the *aesthetics* of the textiles themselves—I'm working in black and white anyway."

"Then you're especially interested in aesthetics," I offer, thinking back to Wolfgang.

Ravi's wife yawns, and looks over my shoulder at something on the wall behind me. While listening to Ravi talk, I refill both their glasses. Neither returns the favor, a serious breach of etiquette in Japan.

"No. Rather, what I'm after is the *narrative*, the one woven, you see, by the interaction of both the family at work on the silk, and the life-history of the silk itself as it is transformed into the commodity. The pictures have to be *read* as a sequence, but not necessarily linearly, you understand."

Will it be a book, I ask, thinking I have grasped the concept. Ravi frowns and lifts the tumbler to his lips.

"I'm not a commercial photographer. I wouldn't be here in Japan if I was."

Years later, when Babette takes me to Ravi's penthouse in downtown San Francisco, I will ask him if he is still photographing. He will dismiss my question with a wave of his hand and a small laugh.

*   *   *

One other night while visiting Kyoto, Dan and I venture out without our hostess and make our way to another of my old favorite spots.

The New Rug was down an especially narrow and dark alleyway in the bar district near the Kamo River. I could only guess the name referred to the toupees so many of its rather mature clients sported, but this night, years since I'd been there, we are the only customers. I should have been able to guess then that the New Rug would soon be out of business. We order two extremely pricey glasses of beer.

One of the staff, a very young man with the crew cut favored by high-school boys and lots of loose bracelets about his wrists, sits down to join us. He says his name is Yūji, and asks us where we come from. He speaks Japanese to us as if it were the most natural thing in the world. There are no more monolingual tourists in Japan—the country is too expensive for casual interlopers. We all live here now, and that is why Yūji doesn't register any surprise when I tell him we come, in point of fact, from Tokyo.

Yūji is good-looking and obviously bright. He knows all about several of the writers I am researching. He holds Dan's hand the whole time we talk, lightly stroking it with his fingers.

We finish our beers, settle the bill, and say good-bye to a pouting Yūji. He tells Dan to come again soon. He follows us to the door, and then out into the alley, never once releasing Dan's left hand from his own. He insists on giving my lover a kiss, and Dan, charmed by the boyishness of it all, returns it. I think to myself: if he lived here, Dan's penchant for younger men would do him well. He would soon find a Yūji (or Masa, or Fumiaki, or Kenji) for his very own. Experience teaches that rice queens are made, not born. I am made less jealous by this little scene than I am irritated to realize that, in America, I must be that very boy for him.

We move on to another nearby bar. Sebon, the Japanese approximation for French "C'est bon," is also a venerable institution, as is its owner. I have been there before, but it has been too many years for him to recall my name. But I remember his.

After ascertaining that I can speak Japanese, he places us not at the piano bar, but at one of the small tables alongside it. He takes our drink orders, and a waiter puts a minuscule bowl of rice crackers and sweet dried peas in front of us. Dan has already been in Japan long enough to know this will make our drinks dear. He asks discreetly if I've got enough cash on me to get us through the night.

We are the only foreigners in the bar tonight, though many do come here as a rule. International guides for gay tourists are nearly useless when it comes to the chapter on Japan, but Sebon has always been there under "Kyoto." Sensing an opportunity to entertain everyone on this rather slow night, the Master comes over with a flourish and sits with us for the sole purpose of asking us in a voice loud enough for everyone to hear where we are from, what kind of men we like ("Am I your type?"), how we like Japan, and so on. He goes on to tell us that of course Kyoto is better than Tokyo, he wouldn't dream to going to Osaka anymore, that he once had an American boyfriend who loved him very much and begged him to move to Chicago with him, that of course he could not leave his beloved Kyoto *ever*. He insists, in a voice loud enough for everyone to hear, that I *must* be that foreigner with the huge penis—uncircumcised!—he spotted earlier today at the public bath. Performance over, he takes his bow by making a few bitchy comments in high Kyoto *okama* patoís—just so that there is some nelly aside *they* understand that *I* cannot—and moves back behind the counter to resume his attentions to his regular customers seated at the bar.

Dan understands little of what is said, but he enjoys all of it, as always. He is precisely the kind of foreigner who does well in Japan, and who the Japanese themselves always like best. We leave Sebon and, at Dan's shy urging, go back to have a nightcap with Yūji.

After our trip to Kyoto, and now about to go through airport customs on his way home, Dan's suitcase begins to vibrate when a little switch inside is accidentally pushed on. Dan steps out of line, we repair to the men's room, open the suitcase, and throw away two C-size batteries. No one else could have any idea why these two American men in a single stall are laughing so loudly. Later, I will panic at the thought of what might have happened had a customs officer demanded an inspection of the Mysterious Vibrating Valise. Would my name be entered in the computer? Or, just maybe, would the inspectors have laughed along with us?

Babette has served the stew and side dishes. It is now past midnight when Ravi's wife Bo, suddenly enlivened, finally begins to talk excitedly. The vodka has been entirely consumed, as well as what was remaining in the rest of the liquor bottles. All of us are now helping ourselves without ceremony to Babette's small stash of old dope. Ravi seems perturbed by what Bo is talking about, which is in some sort of half-English, half-Japanese code that I cannot fathom. Increasingly annoyed at her husband's crossed looks, Bo gets up, goes to the entryway, puts on her shoes, and leaves. Ravi throws her purse as she motions to him wordlessly that she needs it.

She returns a few minutes later, quiet and for the first time that evening with a smile on her face: a stupid, happy smile that does not go away for the rest of the night.

January. It is now the middle of the month. My research proceeds nicely, and my good health means that I have regained my scholarly detachment. I have settled into a comfortable routine with Ben, varied only by his real illnesses and rather more frequent bouts of hypochondria. The house is drafty, but a small electric heater warms my cold room, where I work steadily through more stories and novels. In the middle of the day, I go out for a walk, a bowl of noodles, a cup of coffee, a look at the Japanese papers. Three times a week I spend a couple of hours at the gym to try and rebuild a body that has atrophied after months of involuntary sloth. Weekday evenings are usually spent with Ben in front of the television, but on weekends our different sexual orientations make a difference, and we agreeably go our separate ways.

Ben brings the English-language newspapers home from his office, and pours slowly over every article. So it is only days later that I get to read them myself. In the January 17 edition, I read that the Japan Red Cross reports a total of ten HIV+ people in Japan. That is about as many as were living in my old apartment building back in Seattle at the corner of Summit and John. In America, the Centers for Disease Control are estimating a million and a half infected individuals. Japan, as always, is different. Not ten who test positive; not ten "known at present"; not ten "approximately." But ten. Exactly. But I know better, because I am reading this article a week late. That same day, as yet unreported in the press, the number is being revised upwards to eleven.

Death in Venice

And all the while he kept doggedly on the traces of the disreputable secret the city kept hidden at its heart, just as he kept his own—and all that he learned fed his passion with vague lawless hopes. He turned over newspapers at cafés, bent on finding a report on the progress of the disease; and in the German sheets, which had ceased to appear on the hotel table, he found a series of contradictory statements. The deaths, it was variously asserted, ran to twenty, to forty, to a hundred or more; yet in the next day's issue the existence of the pestilence was, if not roundly denied, reported as a matter of a few sporadic cases such as might be brought into a seaport town. After that the warnings would break out again, and the protests against the unscrupulous game the authorities were playing. No definite information was to be had.[3]

January 17 is also the day that doctors in America can prescribe AZT for their patients. For the first time, we think we might live. At last, a drug they say works. A drug that will, however, eventually kill you all by itself. But ideally, no sooner than any of the other afflictions that ravage us; and which make us live more intensely and with more meaning than any drug will ever allow.

The gym, in keeping with my modest means, is the public one in Takada-nobaba, where the shogun's horses were once corralled but now where students and foreigners find cheap rooms to rent. It is just down the big hill and up a little one from Shimo-Ochiai: a twenty-minute walk along twisting side streets and across busy intersections. The Shinjuku Sports Center is a new building, and maybe the best public gym in the city. Ben used to go swimming there until the stares at his very un-Japanese body got the better of him. When I go, in the early afternoon, it is nearly always empty except for a few mothers accompanying their children to swimming lessons. And for the other white men who, like me, congregate in the weight room.

I do not work at all, so I could come here anytime. The other Americans are English teachers whose day at the office does not start until evening, when their students get off work and are free to attend class. So we are here together: some of us every day, some just two or three times a week. Soon I know them well enough to nod hello each time we meet crossing the large room from one muscle machine to the next. But in my entire sabbatical year, I will never speak a word to any of them. Not everyone is as taciturn. In fact, they all chatter away about a myriad things: girlfriends, cheap tickets back to "the States," plans to quit their shitty jobs and make a million bucks by going into business for themselves. I am too shy to join in. They sense my reticence and leave me be. But their company, alienated as it is, is a frequent (three times a week, to be precise) reminder of just where it is I come from and one day will soon return to.

In a report that will create hysteria for more than a week, the government's AIDS Surveillance Committee reported that, for "the first time," a Japanese woman has contracted AIDS. "A 29-year-old habitual prostitute living in Kobe," we read, "had sexual intercourse with a number of men including non-Japanese."

> Doctors said the woman told them she had lived until six years ago with a
> non-Japanese sailor who had had homosexual relationships. . . . From these

facts, the committee concluded that she was infected with the AIDS virus while living with the sailor.[4]

The *Yomiuri* reports that Miss A had "relations" with a hundred men. (Maybe she wasn't a prostitute. Maybe she just liked sex. How many men will they say I had sex with?) The paper also says that "seven years earlier" Miss A "had lived with a foreigner."

Seven years earlier Tetsuji was living with a foreigner, too. We met one night at a bar, went home together, and spent two years with each other. It came to an end only when I decided in favor of America and my career and, as a corollary, against Tetsuji's happiness.

Tetsuji is an artist, a sculptor and a painter. His work is colorful, and borders on a playful formlessness. He now lives outside of Tokyo with his new lover (an American who took Japanese citizenship—someone who will not abandon him as I did) and a great menagerie of animals. Birds in particular: exotic ones, the noiser the better it seems, all kept in large cages built right into the side of his house. I think when I am most fearful: maybe I was positive back then and Tetsuji will die too, like Miss A. The newspapers will say he "seven years earlier lived with a foreigner." He will be called "Mr. T." I will have no name at all. And though I know we are not supposed to blame ourselves, it doesn't get us anywhere, it only eats up the days left to us, it's part of our self-loathing. I ask myself when I am most prepared for the truth: Tetsuji, what do you really think of me?

Kobe is the center now of Japan's AIDS panic, due to Miss A's recent death. In 1995 I will again be in Japan when, *that* January, an unexpected earthquake will strike this city and destroy all Japanese assumptions about who is safe, and who is not, from sudden death. I will see the Japanese react with incredulity when, crowded in front of television sets, I watch them watch a beautiful city, a city renowned for its history of foreigners, go up in flames. Do they think: I could be there? I could be dying in Kobe? Only because I happened to be there? *Where were you then?*

Babette did not always live in her present apartment. At the beginning of the 1980s, she rented a small, traditional house attached to a minor temple in the southeast of Kyoto; it was there, on another New Year's holiday, that Tetsuji and I stayed during another of my visits.

A traditional house means one that is *wareme-darake*, "full of cracks." Tetsuji and I froze even underneath the heavy futons that Babette and Shōji, her then-new husband, lent us from their own bed. But Tetsuji, like Dan years later, was willing to put up with any number of discomforts in order to be in Kyoto at the start of the year because that is where I wanted to be.

Tetsuji had been to Kyoto before, as a middle-school student on a class trip, but this time he wanted to see the less famous but still important temples. He led me about as I would lead Dan half a dozen years later. Our sightseeing typically took place in the morning; we would use the afternoons, when Babette and her husband were out of the house, to make love, which we did daily on our little trips. The evenings were spent with Babette and Shōji at one of the local student dives, where she was well known and was always extended plenty of credit.

Report. The *Asahi* on the eighteenth quotes Shiokawa Yuichi, chair of a government commission charged with formulating AIDS policy, that the syndrome is now a danger for "people living ordinary lives." He proclaims 1987 Japan's "AIDS Year One."

New Year's in 1980 was exceptionally cold, or at least I remember it as such. Tetsuji did not have as warm a winter coat as I did, but he did not complain. He seldom complained about anything, even at my increasingly petulant, soon to be cruel, treatment of him. Was that New Year's the start of my using our lovemaking, under the guise of passion, to tell him things I did not have the words for, by hitting him with blows just on the line between passion and violence? Even as I made love to him, by using male sex as male aggression? I yelled the Japanese equivalents of "bitch" and "cunt" at him, screwing being the excuse to let him know not only how much I treasured his warm, receptive body, but how much my love for him contained some inexplicable measure of my distress at not being him. At *wanting* to be him?

At nine in the morning on the twentieth, Miss A dies. The paper reiterates that "she had about 100 customers, including foreigners . . . and had lived with a foreigner with bisexual tendencies." She continues to be referred to in the press as "Miss A"—the Hester Prynne of My Sabbatical Year. The press also persists in claiming her Japan's first AIDS casualty—whatever happened to all those Japanese homosexuals who last year "had returned to their residences in America?" Or who had died in America without ever coming home? The crisis, in other words, is recalibrated this month.

On the evening of the nineteenth, a talk on AIDS sponsored by the city of Yokosuka, the location of a large U.S. naval facility, draws an unexpectedly large crowd. *Miss A, how were you doing just then?* Within three days of Miss A's death, 2,487 people will have telephoned authorities in Kobe to ask about AIDS. *Were you dying peacefully like in the movies?* By mid-February, that number will have swelled to 100,000.[5] *Or with tumors in your eyes, fungi blocking your throat, water in your lungs suffocating you, shit and piss in your diapers, all your practiced composure gone in a second as you beg for help?* AIDS Year One, and counting.

After the three-day holiday, Tetsuji had to go back to Tokyo to work in the frame shop. I stayed on a few extra days at Babette's house. One day I went to Kobe, telling Babette I wanted to sightsee, but in fact I wanted to to visit Shōji. Not Babette's Shōji, but my Shōji, a Japanese man I had known in New York who returned to Japan when his father died to help with the family business.

This Shōji had also been married to a American. Michael was a high-end colorist on the Upper East side who preferred Japanese men. It was through Michael that I first met Shōji. When Shōji initially went back to Japan to visit his father at the start of his illness, Michael and I had had a brief affair that started at the Wildwood on Columbus Avenue and ended a short time thereafter at his Pines share on Fire Island. But we continued to be friends until we lost track of each other in the middle 1980s, by which time the incentive for tracking down old lovers was seldom there.

> Women, especially sex workers, immediately came to be viewed as the "vector" moving HIV from the sex and drug underworld to heterosexual men, who then passed it to their wives, the "vessels" of procreation.[6]

Shōji met me at the Nishinomiya station and we went back to his apartment. He made me lunch while we talked about New York and recalled funny stories about Michael. Soon he seduced me, no doubt thinking me a souvenir for the man he loved but had had to leave; and I seduced him, thinking him *not* the man who had just left for Tokyo, and whom I was perhaps not loving anymore. As we coupled on his futon warmed by bright winter sunlight, I squeezed him tight in my arms, told him he was beautiful and wonderful. Where were the violence and the insults with which I made love just a couple of days earlier with Tetsuji? With the man I thought I *loved?* Why is Shōji just Shōji, but Tetsuji always *Japan?*

*   *   *

I wonder who that sailor is, if that is what Miss A's own Kobe lover was. Some of the weekly magazines tell me he was a Greek; one of the papers says he was thirty-seven when they moved in together. Where is he now? On a ship? In the grave? Let's give him a name, even if the press will not. Pyramus, lover of Thisbe? How about: a Famous Greek.

Later in January, Tokyo city officials say that by the end of 1986 thirty-three Tokyo residents are HIV+. "However," the *Japan Times* adds, "the number is not necessarily high as the 1,614 people tested were mostly homosexuals."[7] So don't worry, they mean to say, unless you are a homosexual or you sleep with one. I am, and I do.

I am a professor of Japanese literature. I take stories, the stuff we live by, and handle them as gingerly I would anything so fragile. I read novels about people and a place of which I only have the most imperfect understanding; and then I profess them, hoping not to dull their insights with my banality. What have I in common with a Meiji intellectual, a frightened geisha, a reincarnated Buddha? Empathy, even when it is for a story, is akin to sexuality; and so it comes in orientations. Some novels are a desire for the other, others a search for the same, and some a witness to a brilliant, short-lived streak of light that defies the rote calculus of difference and identity.

The students, now half my age or less, have their own reasons for reading these novels. They are practical these late, twentieth-century days: they want to arm themselves with the knowledge that will serve them in business and industry. When I began my studies in the early 1970s, Japanese literature was esoteric, effete, aesthetic, and useless. It was perfect. Now, when a corporate Japan looms so large before us, its literature is geopolitical intelligence, the key to new forms of wealth and power that the state has retained me to decode for the next generation of American workers. My old escape is today these students' patriotic pursuit. Every trip to the classroom is a reminder of how different the novels are for them than they are for me. I want the novels I teach to be dazzlingly different, beyond our ordinary ken, quicker and cleverer than we can ever be. They want them to be instructions, like the little booklets that come with Sony stereos or Canon cameras.

In that classroom, however, there are always two or three students, sometimes more, who want what I want. They are twenty years younger, but little else is changed. That look, that way of posing a question or phrasing an opinion. A telling enthusiasm for one novel over all others; a curiosity no other classmates share. They are not here because it is Japanese literature, but because it is another ticket out. Still a perfect escape. They sit in the front row, come to my office hours, tell me how beautifully strange the stories are. We never, unless it is years later, talk plainly. There is no need to. They understand me and I understand them.

> Unlike the matter of physics, philosophy, or classical literature, the matter of Oriental studies is arcane; it is of import to people who already have an interest in the Orient but want to know the Orient better, in a more orderly way, and here the pedagogical discipline is more effective than it is attractive.[8]

I come from a long line of homosexual professors of Japanese literature. I perch on the upper branches of a special family tree whose roots go deep. Edward Said never told us just why so many of Europe's Orientalists went east, aside from a politely Victorian reference to a "different type of sexuality, perhaps more libertine and less guilt-ridden." There is, however, one—"Dirty Dick," as Said calls him with affection or disdain, I cannot tell which—who somehow shook "himself loose of his European origins" and veered closest to the truth.[9] How could this have happened? What could have been different about Sir Richard Francis Burton? A white man dispatched beyond the Bosphorus, hardly to conquer, or even to be conquered: but rather to be, amid the company of soft Persian boys or manly Bedouins, something that England and France would not bear to imagine within their borders, much less allow; though Europe's dreams, like mine and those of my two or three special students, have long been this very thing.

> The didactic speaker, therefore, *displays* his material to the disciples, whose role it is to receive what is given to them in the form of carefully selected and arranged topics. Since the Orient is old and distant, the teacher's display is a restoration, a re-vision of what has disappeared from the wider ken. And since also the vastly rich (in space, time, and cultures) Orient cannot be totally exposed, only its most representative parts need be.[10]

Nagasaki, like Hiroshima three days before it and like Kobe half a century later, is a city where death came unexpectedly. A bomb meant for Kokura will, because of overcast skies, be sent its way and dropped on a little neighborhood of Christians, whose forebears had been slowly boiled alive by authorities scandalized by their foreign faith. Atrocities in Japan, too, are carefully calibrated.

*   *   *

There is a movie about AIDS whose story line has Sir Richard fall in love with Patient Zero Gaetan Dugas. The film, entitled *Zero Patience*, is a musical comedy. (Yes, we are that far into this nightmare.) Dan and I see it in London one summer, where Burton's work and that of others on older branches of the tree fill the British Museum with booty that spills the secrets of their private desires as well as the Crown's imperial demands. I think: for Dan, Burton cannot be more than some nutty limey pedant who measured penises; and for the clueless heterosexual watching this movie, Dugas is just some queen with a funny accent. But for me, when I watch the film's two leading men screw on screen, I see the two parts of me at once, both the white man with a burden and the wide-grinned Huck Finn of a boy in a new place. No difference, yet nothing the same—the bizarre and beautiful spectacle of an indivisible embrace.

"I measured one man in Somali-land who, when quiescent, numbered nearly six inches. This is a characteristic of the negro race and of African animals."[11]

There is one guy who comes to the gym before I do, but who finishes up about the same time. The shower stalls at the Shinjuku Sports Center have curtains, but he like the other Americans never pulls them closed. His body is muscular and lean, but most impressive is his penis. It is very long and dark and uncircumcised: I imagine in my fantasies that he is Puerto Rican. He takes quite a long time showering, rubbing every part of his sinewy body repeatedly with the special soap he brings with him. I make sure, whenever I can, to be in the stall diagonally across from him.

His back is especially beautiful. It is wide at the shoulders and narrow at the waist. His deltoids are dense mounds of strength. But one day, he steps out of the stall to towel himself off, and thus stands closer to me than ever before. There, across the masculine stretch of his back, I notice skin covered with small pimples, as if some odd kind of acne had gone wild. But I know what it is, and I do not need to look for the track marks on his beautiful smooth arms that would be the proof.

Soon a kind of fairy tale is woven about this alphabet-woman, nameless no longer once one of the more brazen weekly magazines publishes both her photograph and real name. She lived in Kobe, a city founded for and by foreigners in the nineteenth century. Miss A's wake was held, appropriately enough, in a Christian chapel. A headline in the January 28 *Japan Times*: "Woman AIDS Victim Dreamed of International Marriage." She is disposed of as a *rashamen*, a pariah to society and a traitor to the race. At the very end, we are told, she refused to accept food and thus, it is implied, accepted the wages of her sins.

Enrique might like Ni-chōme; we "live in our own world there." There is Ikebukuro for something less conventional, Ueno for those fond of truck drivers; but Ni-chōme, with its cheap drinks and central location, is home. I met Tetsuji there, just as I have met other Japanese and visiting foreigners over the years: all our paths converge.

Japanese literature, if an unusual profession in America, is more common in Ni-chōme. Japanese gay men must think half the male homosexual population of America is employed to teach haiku. At home, we are scattered on campuses across the country; but here, during our summer breaks or yearlong sabbaticals, we are all neighbors in our virtual village. We trade gossip, talk of who's going where, and most of all we laugh at jokes inseparably gay and American. And of course we chat up new Japanese friends, let them practice their English on us (or they our Japanese on them), occasionally make those well-practiced arrangements. Those of us with money stay out late, grab cabs home; those of us with less rush to catch the last train back to our far suburban stops.

But however many or few, these hours together are necessary—a comfortable habit for some of us, a rite of passage for others. Sometimes I run into a former student now a Ni-chōme acolyte. I introduce him to friends, buy him a drink, continue his education. Here, we are one.

In Japan, it is a white man's disease; in America, if it isn't mine it belongs to a black man. As late as 1988, a white journalist married to a African woman could write with impunity: "How curious it would be if the source of the Nile and the source of AIDS prove to be one and the same, that huge teeming lake in the dangerous heart of darkest Africa." With as much hate and fear this same journalist calls his own country, the Homo Heaven, a "great land whose politically admirable but epidemiologically lamentable motto is E Pluribus Unum."[12]

Shimada Masahiko, one of Japan's younger novelists, writes in an essay:

> You can see a certain tendency in what contemporary Japanese literature has been introduced abroad. Just what do, for example, Mishima, Tanizaki and Kawabata have in common? There can't be many who would think these writers are at the center of our literary history. What's unfortunate is

that in foreign countries, homosexuals have introduced these writers claiming just that. This is worth taking a close look at. It was the gays abroad who first started reading and translating Japanese literature. In America there's a gay bar where American scholars of Japan can meet and have a good time reading English translations of Mishima Yukio.[13]

Death in Venice.   Japan, unlike Africa (or its ciphers Haiti and Harlem), can never be the "source" of AIDS; but it can surely be its final destination, if all the ramparts are mounted. *For the past several years Asiatic cholera had shown a strong tendency to spread.* And they will be, because I am here on sabbatical. *Its source was the hot, moist swamps of the delta of the Ganges, where it bred in the mephetic air of that primeval island-jungle, among whose bamboo thickets the tiger crouches, where life of every sort flourishes in rankent abundance, and only man avoids the spot.*[14] "In the 1970s, who summoned the uninvited guest from the far Dark Continent, via Haiti, to America itself," instructs a learned Japanese ethnologist, "were the gays."[15]

The War of the Worlds.   "Before the cylinder fell there was a general persuasion that through all the deep of space no life existed beyond the petty surface of our minute sphere. Now we see further."[16]

In Seattle, there is a small neighborhood near the gay part of the city, but not quite adjacent to it. At first it was only a good restaurant and a few restored old homes; later, all kinds of shops and apartment buildings go up to accommodate the gay men who like the cozy scale of the neighborhood and its relative quiet. Soon, the local newspapers have given this little place a new name, christening it part of the city's 1980s revival, but never crediting the gay men, and the few gay women, who make Madison Valley their home.

Eventually plans are announced to build an AIDS hospice here, and the money is raised. But the straight owners of the businesses who have followed the gay people into this neighborhood object and take their case against this building (it, too, our home) to court because it will "destroy the nature of the neighborhood," by which is meant discourage business.

One night, someone does what has to be done, and across the picture windows of the store owned by the leader of this heterosexual vendetta against our hospice is spray-painted: *WE BUILT THIS NEIGHBORHOOD.*

The 1970s were the decade in which gay men, released from the clutch of their rural hometowns by the economic collapse of America's heartland, migrated to the coastal cities, where perhaps access to the open seas held out the promise of yet another ticket out. In downtowns we often uneasily shared with other minorities, we of all colors were Africanized like shy native bees eager to mate with angrier strains. Those of us who are white stopped talking like white men, if we still talked like men at all. Now In The Life, we went to the Paradise Garage or places like it across the nation. We eagerly gave up the twangs and gawkiness we inherited from our pale fathers to mimic a culture that had long ago learned to turn the tables armed with little but style and wit. They called our music Urban Progressive to take note of the demographic change, but the rhythms were unmistakably black and the lyrics gay. Altogether and without regard to the color line that made us all our lives, until then, "white" or "black" or something in-between, the crowd was tribal, the slang impenetrably ours, the way we moved no longer without defiant meaning. We chose to dwell in a weekend third world even if we drove expensive cars and lived uptown. We cast our lot with Fanon's heroes, and Aretha's, too: with those who understood long before Hegel and with much more panache what is The Truth of the Master; with a nation parading the genius that being a captive people provides in queer compensation.

Now we know there was a price to pay. To share in the moral purity of the slave is to refuse the privilege of being his owner. Our wilful Africanization meant it was all that easier for America to make the darker peoples and their fellow travelers equally "high risk," so fuck your fine car. The test for white gay men after AIDS is whether we understand the poetry of the blues as well as the drive of the rhythm, to understand that to be free is to be condemned to freedom. And for white gay men in Japan, all our existential choices and their due are written out as large as the words on that billboard on the way to Ben's house.

> Casually ask your date if she's ever had sex with whites, blacks, Central Americans, East Africans, merchant marines, American military personnel, people with weak bodies, and homosexuals. Also inquire if she's had sex with men who have been abroad on business. Be wary of women who like reggae, Prince, Michael Jackson, African music, and black contemporary. Special caution is needed with women who like soul and frequent discos where blacks hang out.[17]

In the spring of 1982, the Paradise Garage held the world's first benefit for a mysterious disease some called "Saint's disease," after the name of the club so many of its early victims patronized.

*   *   *

Shimada Masahiko writes further:

> The Tokyo I live in today is really pathetic. These waspy Japanese guys have got a bit of money to spend, they feel very superior to Americans and other Asians, but for some reason they all want to act like foreign homosexuals and blacks. In places like Shibuya and Roppongi they tell television reporters to their faces that they want to become negroes.[18]

A joke. What's the hardest part of telling your parents you've got AIDS? Convincing them you're Haitian.

The party in Ravi's South of Market penthouse started very late. Babette took a nap before we left for it, while I sat on her fire escape and watched the lights of the traffic illuminate Divisadero while smoking a joint. By the time we arrived the place was packed, but Ravi spotted us immediately. I was impressed that he remembered my name despite the years since we had met in Babette's Kyoto apartment. He led us out to his rooftop pool and introduced to other former Japan expatriates, all of whom had, like us, moved back to lead lives that for any of many reasons Japan would never allow.

"That's Ravi's new friend, Samuel." Babette motioned with her cocktail towards a tall black man dressed in a dark Issey Miyake suit once Ravi had drifted off. "He's been living in the penthouse since the fall." Whenever Samuel laughed the deep resonance of his voice swept over the crowd.

"I think I recognize him. Didn't he live in Tokyo?"

"No, Kyoto. He modeled in Osaka. You might have met him when you and Dan came for New Year's. He was living for a long time with some sister-boy bartender named, uh, Yūji, I think. Then Ravi came along. End of story. Beginning of story."

Whatever happened to Ravi's Japanese wife, I will ask Babette as we are in the elevator going down from his San Francisco penthouse several hours later. "Bo, wasn't it?" Dead, Babette will say. From what?, I'll ask, not really all that curious but just as some kind of reflex. "Ravi never said. I guess we all just thought it was an overdose, maybe AIDS, who knows." And Ravi himself? Is he all right? Babette, lighting her cigarette, will shrug her shoulders as the doors open into the empty lobby.

FEBRUARY

Morals Business

Now that "people leading ordinary lives" are at risk, the Japanese government acts. Interagency discussions that started last year about barring entry to HIV+ foreigners go public to test the reaction.

The War of the Worlds

> Citizens of the nation: I shall not try to conceal the gravity of the situation that confronts the country, nor the concern of your government in protecting the lives and property of its people. However, I wish to impress upon you— private citizens and public officials, all of you—the urgent need of calm and resourceful action. Fortunately, this formidable enemy is still confined to a comparatively small area.[1]

The possibility that something like this would happen had already occurred to me. If they pass some law, I'd refuse to take the test—half out of principle, half out of fear. I'll never travel to Japan again. A professor of Japanese literature, like an English rock star with a drug conviction, permanently persona non grata in these islands. Would it destroy my career? Probably not. What could be better for it than than having to appreciate my chosen object of study, like the deeded object of my desire, from afar? And never possessing it? I would become (even more, since I am already) a voyeur reduced to stealing glances at a nation of fellow voyeurs. Now this libidinal scenario seems really possible. On the fourth of the month (the same day that we read "Liberace Reported Near Death"), the *Japan Times* warns me that "methods of legal control of the killer disease AIDS are now under consideration":

> The plan was revealed after a Cabinet meeting Tuesday when the justice minister urged [Health and Welfare Minister] Saito to take legal measures to counter AIDS since no law exists that would deny entry to Japan of foreigners believed to be AIDS carriers.
>
> Saito said that the Health and Welfare Ministry is now considering enacting a new law or resolving the issue under current preventive laws covering either infectious disease or venereal disease.[2]

How will they tell, I wonder? Quarantine all sensitive young men at Narita immigration? Have Hitachi develop a lightening-fast antibody test, to be administered at airline counters around the world when we try to check in? Or just ask around?

The Japanese have plenty of words to denote how we really know what we know these days, even in a country as dominated by electronic media as this one. *Uwasa, kuchikomi, kagekoto, goshippu, fūbun, sekenbanashi*: all can mean what we say with our "gossip" and "word of mouth" and "the talk around town" and, most of all, with "rumor." These things are everywhere of course, but especially among us, and never more than since AIDS. Both homosexuals and people with the virus appeared for those crucial first years on no network or journalistic or medical screen, so other drums were beat. "I heard," someone told us, "that they had to remove a dead gerbil from his butt"; or "Are you kidding? He lived with Jim Nabors for years!" We trade in rumor because they give us the news, but also to make ourselves kin, among whom even if we cannot exchange bodily fluids, there are still a few comfortable secrets to trade.

> What I find most difficult is distinguishing between reality and fabrication when crises stir up their inevitable confusion. Rumor has become a form of communication well suited to this present period of official mendacity. In fact, we are long-winded producers and greedy consumers of reports that spread all the faster for their patent absurdity. When it first appeared on the scene, AIDS was as mysterious as a punishment from heaven, so rumors flew thick and fast. One of them involved germ warfare, and its persistence

reflects the spirit of general paranoia this epidemic inspires in groups at risk.[3]

At risk. A young and pregnant Japanese housewife, who had sexual intercourse with a hemophiliac before marriage, is discovered to be HIV+. No foreigners in her life, no trips abroad: only the sad luck of the draw. What law will they concoct to protect "people leading ordinary lives" from her? For her fetus, the Diet ponders mandatory abortion; for the mother herself, social ostracism will suffice. In the February 20 *Asahi*, I read of another hapless housewife. Her neighbors have plastered their *danchi*, or apartment complex, with flyers that say "Mrs. A in Apartment XXX once worked in the 'morals business.' This kind of person threatens our way of life. We must demand she take the AIDS test."

Fifteen years ago in Osaka, I worked in the "morals business" too. That summer I had a job as a bartender in a small Osaka piano bar, the kind of place with nearly as many bartenders as customers. I was employed, of course, illegally. My race and gender protected me from the police. Would I now be liable for the same deportation that the Matsumoto "hostesses" are subject to?

> *"Peccatum illud horribile, inter Christianos non nominadum."* The subject is so horribly repulsive and distasteful that the writer would have preferred to close his eyes to the existence of this awful phase of human depravity and pass it by in silence, but friends, in whose judgement he places entire confidence, have pointed out that the very nature of this work demands at least a passing allusion to one terrible form of venery which prevailed in Japan in the latter Middle Ages.[4]

I worked at Men's Club from five in the afternoon to five in the morning, with one fifteen-minute break at midnight. All of us bartenders would arrive at the same time and greet each other with the Japanese equivalent of "Good morning" despite the late afternoon hour, as is the custom among those of us working in the "morals business." My first job was always to help clean the bar, which, because I was the newest employee, meant scrubbing the small and generally foul toilet that was at the back. Men's Club had that slightly metallic, slightly rancid smell that was the compounded effect of the sewers, the fitful air-conditioner, and last night's stale booze. Then I would run errands such as buying groceries that would be fashioned into the little snacks we would offer the customers later that evening.

Some would show up early. I recall a couple of women who would stop in each week for sloe gin fizzes after shopping at the nearby department stores. At five in afternoon this gay bar was not yet a gay bar. Men's Club was located in the Kasayamachi section of Dotombori, the once-theater but now restaurant-and-club district that took its name from the river that once flowed through Osaka. Osaka nightlife, like Osaka people themselves, is different from that of Tokyo. More lively perhaps, but certainly more earthy and never far removed from the mercantilism that long defined their city. But was it only for money that I began to work in Osaka?

> In the early part of the Yedo period (commenced 1587) traces of the sur-
> viving customs of the preceding civil wars lingered on, and as unnatural
> practices (which had grown up in armed camps) had been introduced into
> the metropolis, and were rife in the city, there were, of course, depraved
> persons who provided accommodation to gratify the infamous tastes of the
> times. Among the play-actors were a number of vicious and wholly aban-
> doned characters who did not hesitate to pander to their patrons and submit
> to outrageous physical indignities for hire.[5]

My own salary was three thousand yen for each night's work, less than a dollar an hour. Women friends of mine working in upscale clubs in other Osaka entertainment districts like Kita-Shinchi or Umeda could easily earn a hundred bucks a night, plus cab fare back to Kobe or Kyoto or wherever it was they lived.

But sometimes I got little bonuses. A steady customer might, at certain times of the year, give his favorite bartender a tip that could be as much as hundreds of thousands of yen. I did not work at Men's Club long enough to collect those kinds of perks. But there were other benefits to my employment there. *Among working boys there are vast differences in attitude.* At least once a week some customer would ask the head bartender, whom everybody called Kewpie, if he (once, she) could "borrow" me for a while. The answer was always yes. *Some entertain their patrons in a daze, concentrating only on paying off their proprietors.* I was never consulted and I never minded. I was twenty years old. I could always be counted on to perform. *Then there are those, full of feeling, who think, "Even these brief pangs of love for me must be deeply felt."*[6] Even if it was not always the adventure I looked forward to, there was that envelope subsequently passed to Kewpie and then, just a little thinner, to me.

My young American body, skinny and smooth, long and white, held a certain appeal for some. The drink, the bath, the embrace, the murmured requests, and at last the low long sounds in no language other than the one we were all born speaking. I liked most of the men, perhaps only because they liked me. Naked, atop a futon on a floor of straw mats, or sprawled across a bed in a high-rise hotel, there was if only for the moment him (not *them*) and there was me (never *us*). If history was there too, I do not recall it: as with so many invisible things, if we do not see them they might as well not exist at all.

February 25

FEAR OF AIDS SPARKS STRINGENT GOVERNMENT REACTION

A government pamphlet on the disease—illustrated with a drawing of a perspiring Statue of Liberty clasping a book on AIDS, towering over a trembling Mt. Fuji—advises readers to avoid contact with prostitutes, drug addicts, homosexuals, and "people from countries where there are many AIDS cases."[7]

Has anyone ever seen the human immunodeficiency virus? Watched it find our cells' receptors, hold on tight, use its enzymes and proteins and whatever to pollute its close embrace with fatal poisons: in miniature, an act of love-making that mimics our human own? Is the mating of one virus with one cell the same thrill we find between ourselves and those of other races and nations? These little things may be more innocent than we suppose, tiny organisms in search of a union in order, like us, to forget, to forget.

Men's Club closed only one day a month, on each second Sunday. But it really was not a day off. We bartenders would do something together, like go to the beach or visit one of the religious shrines that Osaka "morals business" people patronized. We socialized after work as well. Men's Club closed late, but there was always some Korean restaurant or yet another bar for all of us to go to and be waited on ourselves. The bartenders were my constant friends that summer, though at its end I would desert them, as I would later Tetsuji and as is always the prerogative of the insolent person who has crossed a border.

> Beautifully dressed, handsome, and effeminate looking young men wandered through the city carrying about with them various kinds of incense in *kiri*-wood boxes wrapped in light-blue silk cloths, and, under the guise of selling incense, wormed their way into the mansions of the nobility and gentry, but in the course of time the custom was abolished.[8]

Kewpie, like many homosexuals in Japan, was married. One night after we closed up, Kewpie invited me to go back to his apartment to meet his wife and join them for dinner. We drove to a far suburban *danchi*, where Kewpie and his wife lived a dozen floors high in the sky. Since it was only six in the morning, his two children were still asleep in their own bedroom. But Kewpie's wife kept the same nighttime schedule as did Kewpie himself and had a complete dinner ready for him, and me, when we arrived. I do not remember what we talked about, but do I remember what happened. After dinner, Kewpie told his wife I'd be staying over, so she should sleep on the living room sofa. Kewpie took me into their bedroom and, shades drawn against the morning light, we took our clothes off and got into bed. I remember that as we made love he stifled his moans with a pillow so as not, I suppose, to disturb his wife only one small room away: like me, prone on her bed in internal exile. Like us, I am sure, wide awake and trying to forget, to forget, to forget.

A Dutchman in seventeenth-century Japan wrote:

> I cannot forbear taking notice, before proceeding any further, that on the chief street of this town, through which we passed, were built nine or ten neat houses, or booths, before of which sat one, two, or three young boys, of ten or twelve years of age, well dressed, with their faces painted, and feminine gestures, kept by their lewd and cruel masters for the secret pleasure and entertainment of rich travelers, the Japanese being very much addicted to this vice.[9]

On the little Dutch island of Dejima in Nagasaki a century ago there was a place also known as "Men's Club." It was where foreigners and Japanese met to discuss the issues of the day and problems of mutual concern. A small but noteworthy footnote in the modern history of Japan and the West.

Today, the former Men's Club is now a historical museum.

The average Tokyo household is said to consist of a husband, a wife, and 1.5 children. We read these statistics about Japan, and even more than we assume of such data about ourselves, believe that they really tell us something about Japan and the Japanese. We picture that small apartment, a white-collar worker meek outside the home but a bit of a tyrant within it; a wife devoted to her children to the point of excess; and that 1.5 child, ever moody and encased in her stereo headphones in a futile effort to win some degree of privacy. We do not imagine a man who dreams of being a poet; a wife who has taken her neighbor as a lover; the child who needs more attention, not less. The Japanese are not individuals to us, only ciphers of a still strange and exotic race, incapable of our own many differences unless they are those odd fetishes we associate with their country's ever stranger and more exotic mores. We do not imagine Kewpie and his wife, and certainly do not imagine a Kewpie and his wife who, eagerly or begrudgingly, have made room in that same small apartment for a gangly young American who spoke bad Japanese and left his foreign smell on their bedding. Or maybe, that is precisely what we imagine of a people whose rules are our own rumination.

I climbed another holy mountain that summer.

The drive to the mountain shrine was in the early morning hours, in a darkness so complete I could not tell where we were headed. Somewhere in Nara prefecture, I want to recall; in fact, it was a pilgrimage as ethereal and otherworldly as any ghost story gathered by Lafcadio Hearn a hundred years ago.

We parked the car in a large lot nearly full. All of us bartenders who had squeezed into the tiny Corolla got out and started our ascent. Unlike other pilgrims at other shrines—or perhaps, unlike this same one during daylight hours, with more respectable worshipers—we were a noisy crowd, with madeup faces and high heels, or tuxedos and cummerbunds, or kimonos far too gaudy for paying humble respect to the gods. My fellow Men's Club employees seemed to know everybody, and greetings were shouted across the evermore crowded path as we neared the shrine. I knew no one other than the Men's Club bartenders I went with that night, and I clung close to them.

The shrine was lit poorly with strings of bare light bulbs, but some of the crowd were carrying candles. Before the shrine, we purified ourselves with water from the stone cistern, approached as close as we could, clapped our hands in supplication and threw coins in the offering box. On the way back down the hill, I was introduced to men and women from other bars, not only in Osaka, but Kyoto, Kobe, and Nara itself. Cleansed and blessed, the comraderie was intoxicating.

The drive back to the city took us into early daylight. As prearranged, the five of us went on a long detour in order to stop at a beach. We changed into the bathing suits we had stored in the trunk. That early in the day, we were of course alone and could strip naked in the parking lot without concern. No one was shy about taking a good look at me and joking about my genitals, which I would later learn had already been reported on by some of the Men's Club patrons. I enjoyed the attention, especially the teasing. Naked once again, in the warm morning sun and in the company of friends who liked me, the months of anger and frustration and embarrassment of being an American in Japan, a white man in Asia, dropped away and cleansed and purified me, if only for a moment, more than any little prayer I had murmured in a mountaintop shrine.

February. *"Is it all right to go into a hot springs bath that a foreigner has been in?"* This is the month that the government was figuring out how to keep us out. *"Should I be worried about having shaken hands with a foreigner?"* But this is the month we started coming to Japan in suddenly larger numbers. *"I used a glass in a bar that a Philipina hostess might have used. Can I get the virus that way?"* We notice, if no one else does. *"Is it safe to go to America?"*[10] Is it all right to stay in Japan?

It is widely reported in both the gay and mainstream American press that dextran sulfate, originally developed as an anticoagulant, prevents or slows the replication of HIV. Japan is the one country that manufactures and sells this drug for medical purposes, and HIV+ people are coming to Tokyo to buy it. Those of us living in Japan are asked to get it for friends back in America.

We purchase it at the American Pharmacy, located near the Ginza. The American Pharmacy is well known to expatriates. It is where you can get Vick's Formula Cough Suppressant, Summer's Eve, Dr. Scholl's Original Foot Insoles. It is now the place, with its prominent location and English-speaking staff, that is selling dextran sulfate to people who, only the day before, have gotten off jumbo jets from San Francisco, New York, Paris. Some of these men are the healthy representatives of underground buyers' clubs, but others, visibly ill, have come on their own. Their symptoms aggravated by jet lag, they find they have to stay in Tokyo longer than they planned, for the American Pharmacy has a large sign near the register, handwritten and in unidiomatic but perfectly plain English, and English only: "Only One Box of Dextran Sulfate Per Customer Every Day." The rationing system that is speeding gay men to their deaths across America has made it to Japan.

Some years ago Tetsuji and I went to a midnight showing of *The Rocky Horror Picture Show*, which, as in America but on a minuscule scale, had developed a cult following in Japan. We walked from my apartment to the huge Koraku-en amusement park between Kanda and Suidōbashi and found the small theater already full of young Japanese who, like their counterparts in Greenwich Village, had come dressed as their favorite characters. Frank was the most common, with Riff Raff and Columbia a close second and third.

Again as in America, drag was very popular. In a room where I was probably the only American, Japanese boys were Magenta and Janet, and a few Japanese girls were Rocky or Eddie. I remember how, at the most deliberately maudlin moment in the film, candles were taken out of pockets and purses, lit, and raised high above the heads of the audience. They were doing what audiences had long done in the United States, and that was of course the why of it. But what I recalled in Suidōbashi that night was not the Village. It was the candles my fellow night travelers had carried with them to the top of a Japanese mountain shrine almost a decade earlier in the company of Japanese who did not do drag just for the fun of it, but because it was their profession. And a few years later, holding a candle myself at a midnight AIDS vigil in Seattle, in the company once more of cross-dressers, I would finally figure it out: hold the damned thing high enough and no one notices how unreal you really look.

Shimada Masahiko has written his own novel about homosexuals. In Japanese it is called *Mikakunin bikō buttai*, which Shimada translates as *Unidentified Shadowing Object*.

> Takamado Luchiano. Real name: Takamado Osamu. Thirty years of age. Presently unemployed. Until last year worked at a gay bar in Roppongi. Three years ago at the age of twenty-seven, underwent gender reassignment in Singapore. No criminal record. Certified to teach traditional singing. Coworkers at the gay bar say he is quiet but intelligent. His youth, luminous makeup looks and long limbs made him the bar's most popular host. But he suddenly quit in October of last year.[11]

It was fun dressing up as outlandish characters and going to see the *Rocky Horror Picture Show* in Korakuen. *Give yourself over to absolute pleasure.* I was good as masquerading, not just as a homosexual who needed to be otherwise much of the time, but as a white man in Asia, where there was a long tradition of pretending to be someone else other than we were. *Swim the warm waters of sins of the flesh.* "A little dyestuff and three yards of cloth," wrote Rudyard Kipling of his white Indian, Kim, "to help out with a jest." "Is it," Kim wonders, "too much to ask?"[12] *Erotic nightmares beyond any measure.* Sir Richard did it, and Lawrence did it even more. *And sensual daydreams to treasure forever.* What made them so good at disguises? Why did they enjoy it so much? Was there anyone underneath all that makeup and drag? *Can't you just see it?* "I am Kim," he tells himself. "I am Kim. And what is Kim?"[13] *Don't dream it—be it.*[14]

DRUG TO PROFIT AJINOMOTO

A recent World Health Organization report warns of spiraling world-wide growth in the number of people with AIDS. . . .

Ajinomoto Co., Bristol-Meyers' sole DDI supplier, is expected to reap profits of several billion yen starting next fiscal year from its part in the $2 billion market.

Considering this development and Ajinomoto's rock-bottom price, now is a good time to pick up Ajinomoto shares.[15]

AIDS is one of the periodic great levelers in history. Like Pompeii, bubonic plague, or the earthquakes of northeast China. At times, death makes no distinctions and fells everyone in its path.

Treatment for AIDS, however, is something different. If you can afford the prices, Welcome Burroughs—or Ajinomoto, or any of a host of trans-national pharmaceuticals—you might live a bit longer, or at least die with fewer diseases racking your body, and, if luckier still, then in a bit more comfort. So we read the Internet, go to information meetings, compare notes with friends who have different doctors, devour everything we can get our hands on. No group of patients dies better educated than we do. No one is ever sick, he just has "health issues" that require further study. But we all do die, which makes us and our scourge different, and worse, than the wrath of an Italian volcano, the pestilence of rats, or the subterranean rumbles of an unsettled planet.

> Luchiano was suffering from a temperature of thirty-nine degrees centigrade, and wandered the day in nothing but fog and the ground. Although until just the other day there had been someone with her, now he was nowhere to be seen. Or maybe he never existed, and her imagination had concocted an illusion in order to avoid loneliness. But even so, a high fever and fatigue was debilitating her imagination, obliterating her companion and instead tripping her up.
> "I will not die," she kept on praying to herself. "Before I die, I'll find someone to cling to, and make myself his constant presence."
> Before she knew it, she had taken off her clothes and was naked. She was losing a couple of pounds every month now, and could count her ribs just by looking in the mirror. The skirt she had bought three months ago is too big for her now. Only her breasts did not shrink or wither away. In fact they seemed even bigger and heavier to her, since the muscle tissue supporting them had atrophied. These breasts, unlike a camel's hump, did not serve the function of storing nutrients.
> Her range of vision had narrowed. Little particles, something like sand or pollen, was now part of the fog. Perhaps the particles were grains of just-refined sugar. When they collided with her skin, she felt their heat; when they touched her lips, they tasted sweet. No, the sweetness had to be coming from the drugs. The tiny particles that had sunk in from her sink had led her exhaustion to drowsiness and lethargy.
> She was seized by a baseless idea. Could these particles be a colony of the virus? Melting quickly like snow when they reach the skin, invading the body proper, eating away here and there at its structures? Surely this fog with its particles will become a viral storm like a snowstorm and destroy me.
> The ground became resilient. Each time she stepped on it, like a damp urethane mat her foot left a depression, and was encrusted with a gray mucus.[16]

My friend Jerry, who lives in Tokyo with his lover Jaime, tells me that he has been sending his old college roommate Michael dextran sulfate for months. Michael is doing pretty good. He's got Kaposi's sarcoma but not much else. A year later, when dextran sulfate like everything else will have been demonstrated to be useless, or worse, Michael's doctor tells him that it hadn't been the dextran sulfate that helped, it was those horse-sized capsules of

Valium he took. *Valley of the Dolls*, we conclude, has been a good influence on us after all.

For years Jean Pearce has been using her *Japan Times* column "Getting Things Done" to inform foreigners living in Japan how to find replacement bags for their Hoover vacuum cleaners, or locate an English-speaking podiatrist, or buy Kosher cold cuts, or send the kids to an international summer camp in the mountains. Now she also dispenses advice on AIDS testing, access to AIDS treatment, AIDS support groups, AIDS hot lines. In one column she tells us that large-sized condoms are available from (where else?) the American Pharmacy.[17]

> When the fog and the density of the particles became denser, and it was hard to breathe, Luchiano discovered a hot springs before her. She caught her breath out of the joy of finally encountering something with form. Running towards it while inhaling the particles, choking on them, she takes a dip in the water after checking its temperature and depth. But her body had already reached a point just short of efflorescence, and it began to sizzle like sulphuric acid poured on metal, and then to dissolve in the water. A dazed Luchiano sat up and tried to leap out of the springs, but both of her corroded legs snapped off just below the knees, and she fell back into the water up to her head. She was now unable to get out. Her hair and eyeballs and ribs and the callous on her foot's little toe all melted away, leaving no traces behind. Two gelatinous lumps about as big as fists, with uncountable numbers of tiny air bubbles in them like fish eggs, were floating lightly on the surface of the hot water. They looked liked the silicon that Luchiano had had injected into her breasts. Silicon says nothing, feels nothing, and those two lumps of it were all that remained of her former self.[18]

Roland Barthes writes:

> The Oriental transvestite does not copy Woman but signifies her: not bogged down in the model but detached from its signified. Femininity is presented to read, not to see: translation, not transgression; the sign shifts from the great female role to the fifty-year-old paterfamilias: he is the same man, but where does the metaphor begin?[19]

February.   Japan's most widely read literary theorist, Karatani Kōjin, is quoted on the subject of AIDS in a respected weekly:

When I got interested in AIDS some four or five years ago, no one knew what it was. We suspected it was some sort of autoimmune disease, and that's why I was interested. But later, as soon as I learned it was entirely something "exterior," I wasn't interested anymore. (*Laughter*) In other words, all the mystery disappeared once we knew it was a sexual disease not confined to homosexuals.[20]

Hey, I've got a mystery for you. Several, in fact. Which of us is going to go next? If you're in a relationship, is it better to be the first or the second to go? Which would you choose: to keep your sight or trade it for maybe a few months' more life? Who gave it to whom, anyway? Why is this happening? AIDS may not be "confined to homosexuals," but it is dazed gay men who line up in a country halfway across the world for their one daily box of some funky hocus-pocus drug we hope will work but god knows how.

In central Africa traditional healers work their magic with faith as well, and I'm sure that some of us are flying there now, too. The insolent among us cross over the border into Tijuana, or gather herbs in Tibetan valleys, or enroll at ashrams in India. There are many mysteries; they grow more numerous and stupefying every day, and I will thank you to leave them alone: without mysteries, there will be no miracles either.

Unidentified Shadowing Object. Luchiano stalks Doctor Sasakawa everywhere he goes. "The doctor laughed so hard he bent over. Just think, both the AIDS organism and Luchiano have the exact same personality. Luchiano had crept into his perfectly ordered perfect life, and while mutating just like a retrovirus had destroyed everything."[21]

"Transvestites," Barthes ruled, "are in hot pursuit of the truth: what most horrifies them is to be *disguised*: there is a moral sensitivity to the truth of clothes, and when one possesses it, this sensitivity is very touchy: Colonel Lawrence endured many an ordeal for the right to wear the *San*."[22]

Poststructuralism is, my sabbatical year in Japan, more fashionable than back in America. Japanese theorists, some of them gay, see structures under duress everywhere, binaries that slip away and explode into pieces like nuclear particles.

But that is not all. Among retroviruses, that associated with AIDS has the singular ability to attack and seize the T-4 cells that coordinate the immune system. It goes without saying that the immune system is what distinguishes between the self and the non-self, and wards off whatever non-self (whether a pathogen, or a transplanted heart) invades, thus preserving the self's identity. When this mechanism is attacked by the virus, its defenses against the non-self collapse; all sorts of opportunistic infections and anti-immune conditions occur that can lead to death. That is how AIDS—Acquired Immune Deficiency Syndrome—earned its name.[23]

Unidentified Shadowing Object.   "AIDS is a tough character to deal with. As you probably know, the cells in a human being whose immune system no longer functions cannot distinguish between themselves and anything else. That is to say, it is a case of 'I am the Other'."[24]

Roland Barthes was born in Cherbourg in 1915 during a great war, and his grandfather had been a great explorer of Africa. Barthes's own battles and adventures would take place at a sanitorium at Saint-Hilaire, where as a young man he was treated for years for tuberculosis. Hemoptysis. Pleural effusion. There were many relapses. A hole in his right lung. Eventually these things, revived in 1980 by the trauma of a stupid traffic accident, killed him. In between, he was a Marxist, then a structuralist, and lastly a theorist of desire. Now we claim him as a gay man, and his ideas as queer, though Barthes himself loathed such words as dangerous betrayals of perhaps his desire as well as his class.

Yet at Saint-Hilaire he first admitted to others that he was attracted to young men. Odd, we might think, that a sterile hospital could encourage such fertile confessions. But he was there, after all, to be cured; and homosexuality, like a retrovirus, is chronic.

AIDS—acquired immunity deficiency syndrome. Since the first case was announced in 1981, this lethal scourge continues to elude a cure, and is spreading with a fearful vigor: an evil star illuminating the late-century evening sky with ominous light. Infection is via blood or sperm, and thus it has hit hardest hemophiliacs, who rely on blood products; addicts who use needles; and most of all homosexuals who engage in anal intercourse. Consequently AIDS has the apocalyptic air of an accursed plague. That image, now in place, shows no sign of dissipating today, when infection by heterosexual sex is no longer unusual.

Of course danger attends this image. It has become a new means for eliminating those at the margins—first and foremost homosexuals—by labeling them. What is odd, however, is that homosexuals themselves have

accepted this, and cite it as a stigmata for recognizing their own prerogative.[25]

In his autobiography Barthes wrote: "A life: studies, diseases, appoint-
ments."[26]

Luchiano also recognizes his prerogative. "And everything will combine with
the prohibited blood in my blood, cause a chemical reaction, and then blow
up." *Luchiano sees things very clearly.* "The explosion will smash me into
little pieces and scatter me all over Japan." *Luchiano has a plan.* "Actually,
I'll get into the jet stream and go to America and the Soviet Union, too."
Luchiano, the Oriental Transvestite, means to act up. "Everyone who breathes
the particles of me will get sick." *Luchiano loves everybody.* "Men and women,
children and the middle-aged, members of parliament and secretaries, alco-
holics and pious Christians, each and every one will die intoxicated with me."
Luchiano is our leader. "My particles will make everyone in the world equals.
I'll have as much power as a hydrogen bomb." *Luchiano, the destroyer of
worlds.* "Me, the useless queen. A *queen* with no family and with AIDS."[27]
Luchiano.

Barthes' first lover, Michel Delacroix, died of tuberculosis in 1942, and at
least one more of his boyfriends had been a patient at the sanitorium. What
kinds of knowledge did Barthes have when he died, on the eve of the disease
that would claim others of his beloved? And what things would he have had
to learn, to face, to confess?

> I became ill at a time when tuberculosis was a disease which made the
> patient the object of a taboo: the taboo of contagion. Besides this, it was a
> very long, very slow illness. You did not know yourself how it was progress-
> ing since you felt no pain. Except in the most serious cases, you felt perfectly
> fine and it was only the doctors who decreed you were ill. So you had to
> live with this kind of superior medical decision hanging over you for years.[28]

February. The university where I am a visiting scholar this year invites me
to give a talk to the Japanese literature faculty. I chose as my subject a long
novel about a Hiroshima survivor named Motoko who is a painter by profession. I tell my colleagues about how she tried to use words to describe what
had happened to her in August, 1945. But words did not work. The first
person failed her; so did the third. Painting allowed her, I go on to say, the

exercise of pure form. But there too she despairs. Everything she attempts to put on canvas is already dead, nothing but *things*. Surely, one of my colleagues asks, that is a problem for all modern painters. The incommensurability of experience and representation. But do all painters, I ask in response, kill themselves over that problem?

The Japanese poststructuralist explains further:

> What is unique about AIDS is, in fact, that the virus is a "retrovirus"—a reverse transcriptase containing oncogenic virus. A normal living creature carries DNA as a blueprint of itself, but a retrovirus uses its RNA, once it has invaded the cells of a host, to manufacture DNA that is then made part of the host's own. What happens consequently is that the host himself becomes unable to tell if he is Self or Other. Unless we imagine some science-fiction means whereby genetic surgery could extricate the virus' DNA, the host has no chance but to live out his whole life carrying it within him.[29]

Unidentified Shadowing Object. "I don't know the difference between myself and AIDS. It's not that I've caught AIDS; AIDS has *become* me. Maybe I'm dreaming. Everything I see looks like me."[30]

Barthes' doctors at first reassured both the patient himself and the public that the injuries sustained in the traffic accident were, while serious, not mortal. He will recover, the press reports said. But the doctors in 1980 were not the doctors who had treated Barthes in Saint-Hilaire, and they either did not know, or underestimated, the power of those bacilli lulled into remission decades earlier to reassert themselves and kill the French poststructuralist.

American poststructuralists have written about hosts, too:

> One of the most frightening versions of the parasite as invading host is the virus. In this case, the parasite is an alien who has not simply the ability to invade a domestic enclosure, consume the food of the family, and kill the host, but the strange capacity, in doing all that, to turn the host into multitudinous proliferating replications of itself. The virus is at the uneasy border between life and death. It challenges that opposition since, for example, it does not "eat," but only reproduces. It is as much a crystal or a component in a crystal as it is an organism. The genetic pattern of the virus is

so coded that it can enter a host cell, turning the cell into a little factory for manufacturing copies of itself, so destroying it."[31]

I learned all this as a graduate student at Yale, when in the 1970s I learned to deconstruct: to look for the repressed, the absence, the marginal, and use it to reverse and then resurrect, smugly and ironically, the grand structures of our even prouder faculty for reason. And to make incommensurable experience with representation. Somehow, my sexuality had already proposed this intellectual project. Has anyone explained why so many of our theorists, and we fans of them, are homosexual? Perhaps because it is the perfect revenge. With our secrets safe inside, we dream if only in our little essays and classrooms of having the last word, the final repartee, and with camp flair and queer wit (little different from the drag queen's repartee) delivering the supremely devastating blow to our enemies. Hold those candles high.

> Could it be that metaphysics, the obvious or univocal meaning, is the parasitical virus which has for millennia been passed from generation to generation in Western culture in its languages and in the privileged texts of those languages? Does metaphysics enter the language-learning apparatus of each new baby born into that culture and shape the apparatus after its own patterns?[32]

The Yale deconstructionist ends his own little essay on hosts and parasites by calling the latter "the uncanniest of guests."[33] I prefer to think of one parasite in particular, the Human Immunodeficiency Virus, as a tourist instead. Guests are presumably invited, whereas tourists can descend on you unwanted. They never know their way around, but instead stumble about and always ask us residents of the neighborhood stupid questions. Sometimes they don't even know the language.

> In fact various Others have taken up residence within DNA which otherwise provides the basis for the pure identity of species and their individuals. Stated another way, various heretical pages are inserted into a bible. The original exists in point of fact in the cross-sectional intertextuality.
>
> Regarded in this fashion, one cannot help be surprised at the perfect correspondence of the process of DNA mythology being deconstructed by reverse transcriptase theory represented by a retrovirus, with the process of logocentrism being deconstructed by so-called poststructuralism.[34]

In bed with Kewpie that early morning, he told me I was his first foreigner. He wanted to examine every part of my body, compare the unfamiliar with the well known, feel the differences and the similarities. I enjoyed the worship. He took his time, and indeed did it twice, both before sex and afterwards. Had I changed somehow in the interim? Was I lighter, he heavier? He the wiser for this lesson? (And what had I learned?) Or was I no longer a foreigner, and instead the sated lover, someone to be *seen* rather than observed and measured? The sun was painfully bright now, and we could see each other clearly in the light that poured in even through the tightly drawn curtains. My skin was so pale next to his, my body so much bigger. I heard the singing of two little children being given their breakfast. A mother tells them to hush, papa's sleeping. The deconstruction of love.

MARCH

The Social Situation

I am back in Seattle for most of this month. Tokyo has nice springs, but it is not spring yet; Seattle's spring, though cold, gray and damp, is here, however, and I look forward to cheating Japan of the last of its winter. But my reasons for returning to the United States just now are more necessary than that. I will attend an academic conference in Los Angeles, see my Seattle doctor, and most of all spend time with Dan, whom I have not seen for two months. I get a cheap ticket on Thai Airlines with my departure and return timed so that the Japan Foundation, my patron, will be no wiser.

The plane arrives in Seattle on schedule, and Dan is there waiting for me excitedly. He has never disappointed me. He is older than me, but ever so much more boyish in his enthusiasm for our lives together. In the years to come I will do things to make him doubt that I share that ardor. But on this early and raw March day, my plane in at an ungodly hour, he waits for me outside customs thinking about how good it is to have me back.

My timing on this trip, as it will turn out, is not good. On March 31 AIDS legislation that would deny HIV+ foreigners from entering Japan is formally introduced in the Diet. One parliamentarian publicly announces his support, citing evidence that AIDS can be transmitted by mosquito bites or by exchanging toasts of sake.

111

LAW WOULD BAR ALIENS WITH AIDS

The law proposed by the LDP's Social Affairs Division also reportedly requires "suspected" aliens entering Japan to document that they are not infected with the virus.

They did not elaborate on what was meant by "suspected" aliens, nor did they indicate what sort of certification would be required.[1]

Sir Richard Burton, who traveled widely, identified those countries in which, for reasons of climate, pederasty is both endemic and largely tolerated. *Terminal Essay*. He described homosexuality as if it were a disease, an influenza or such, that was restricted to those environments just warm enough for the contagion to thrive. *1. There exists what I shall call a "Sotadic Zone," bounded westwards by the northern shores of the Mediterranean (N. Lat. 43°) and by the southern (N. Lat. 30°).* This theory is not as crazy as it sounds. *Thus the depth would be 780 to 800 miles including meridional France, the Iberian Peninsula, Italy and Greece, with the coastal regions of Africa from Morocco to Egypt.* There are good reasons why, in places where the sun shines long and hot, that Sir Richard found what he had sought: dry and hard and in perfectly plain, bright view.

Seattle lies near the forty-seventh north latitude, nowhere near the Sotadic Zone. In all the Hollywood nuclear disaster movies, we're always the first city to get blown to smithereens by the incoming Soviet missiles. No one ever places a World War III survival movie here. Seattle always goes first. We know that everyone is dead there because no one in southern California can raise us on the shortwave radio.

The city proper is an irregular isthmus of land pockmocked by water in the form of lakes, rivers, canals, and the brine of the Puget Sound. It is neatly sliced off at the top and bottom from suburbs that stretch down to the state capital in Olympia, and up past the Boeing factories in Everett. Half a million-plus people live in this hourglass shaped-city, a green-gray expanse of hills and valleys, and most of the gay people are found in the central neighborhoods collected at its narrowest point.

In the most central of those central neighborhoods, amid so many high and mid-rise hospitals and clinics that it has earned the sobriquet Pill Hill, is located the "small and dreary" King County Public Health building. It is surrounded by clinics and apartment buildings favored by the aged and infirm

who need them regularly. It is close enough for most of us gay men to walk
to, though it is on one of Seattle's many hills that we must climb in order to
do so.

All winter Barbara has been phoning me to say that her constant lethargy and
headaches must mean AIDS. Who knows, Barbara might very well have it, I
think to myself, but her notorious hypochondria makes me doubt it. Braver
than me, she goes to take the test one day. She tests negative, promptly takes
the test again, and then a third time. Each visit, a different doctor reassures
her she does not have HIV.

But Barbara does not believe them, and why should she? *Every time I
went to the hospital, my suspicions increased, says Tacite Eiji.* In Japan the
doctors lie. *Each time 30 cc of blood was taken for liver tests—but to my
laymen's eyes, it seemed the amount was too much.* They do not tell terminally
ill patients of their illness: cancer is always "a breathing problem," a "stomach
ailment," or a "liver condition." *Another time, I was sick in bed, with my
swollen lymph glands being examined.* They think that this makes the dying
person's last days easier; perhaps it does. *So I indirectly asked whether it was
AIDS and the doctor persisted in saying there was nothing to worry about.* But
imagine a Japanese woman, her husband often away on business trips to
America or Southeast Asia, whose constant slight fevers and dizziness tell her
she has been infected on account of his infidelities. *Every day I ran in circles
with worry.* Who then goes to the doctor, is told there is no sign of the virus,
yet remains convinced that she is only being humored, as she will indeed
humor her own parents when their time to die comes. *I thought, "I am
probably infected, and if I am, it will turn into AIDS and I will certainly die."*
That woman goes crazy, of course, in the tiny rooms she inhabits with
her children. *Wait a minute. I'm not aware of any telltale symptoms and the
doctors have said nothing, so I'm probably just fine.* The panic and the dread
take over as each new ache, every stray itch, is more proof of what she knows.
But lately the doctor's attitude has been strange. She becomes convinced not
only that she has AIDS and will die, but that she has already passed the virus
on to her children. *Should I really trust him?*[2]

When I moved to Seattle in the early summer of 1983, it was with very little
idea of what the Pacific Northwest was. I had imagined Seattle to be an arc
of pristine, emerald green islands along a bay, whose inhabitants all commuted by kayaks from their houseboats to work in big office buildings made
of logs. I was not entirely wrong.

It hardly mattered where my fantasy ended and the real began. Seattle was the West Coast, a far edge along the big sea where I yearned to be. At the same time it was not California, where I already sensed I would not belong. Only some of us like it here in the far and stormy upper left-corner of the country. Like Japan, the rain here makes for an aesthetic, as do the close mountains and warm mother-of-pearl gray skies. Many of us who did like it in the early 1980s were homosexual. We still are. But the city's reputation today for being a pleasantly mellow and tolerant place is not its true history.

March 23. "According to one Ministry health official," reports the *Japan Times*, "doctors fear that some patients, if told they are AIDS carriers, might commit suicide or become socially irresponsible and intentionally infect others."[3]

> I experience the uprooting of the AIDS community, its sudden social ostracism, in much the same way as Americans of Japanese descent in California lived through their internment in camps from 1941 to 1943. There only crime was to be suspected of hampering the war effort, a suspicion based solely on the fact that they belonged to a group "at risk."[4]

Ruth Benedict was born in 1877 in upstate New York, where she had a very proper Victorian upbringing. Her Puritan stock, however, gave way to passion in the early 1920s when, driven together by the suicide of a mutual female friend, she and Margaret Mead became lovers. They consummated their relationship while traveling in the West to the Grand Canyon.

> It was not until 1989 that Tacite learned he had been infected, after peeking at his chart in the hands of his doctor. The doctor had been staring at the chart, saying nothing, so Tacite leaned over and saw for himself the character "+".[5]

Terminal Essay
   2. Running eastward the Sotadic Zone narrows, embracing Asia Minor, Mesopotamia and Chaldæa, Afghanistan, Sind, the Punjab and Kashmir.

One hundred years before I was born, Seattle was founded when the steamer *Exact* out of Portland disembarked ten adults and twelve children on a beach. They were met by two young men who had already arrived from the south on foot and had begun the construction of a cabin. It was raining that day, and reportedly some of the women cried in dismay at the sight of their new home. But as long as San Francisco would have need of their timber, these settlers were assured a future. Western civilization had its foothold in the far northwest, and the local Indian chief who would lend his name to the new city was, in the eyes of his descendants, foolishly inclined to help.

One desolate December, a few years from now, a Japanese college professor will commit suicide after convincing himself he had AIDS, although tests had twice proved he was not infected.[6]

"Western civilization," Benedict wrote,

> tends to regard even a mild homosexual as an abnormal. The clinical pic-
> ture of homosexuality stresses the neuroses and psychoses to which it gives
> rise, and emphasizes almost equally the inadequate functioning of the invert
> and his behavior. We have only to turn to other cultures, however, to realize
> that homosexuals have by no means been uniformly inadequate to the social
> situation. They have not always failed to function. In some societies they
> have been especially acclaimed.[7]

Dan takes me from the airport back to his house on the hill overlooking our neighborhood. Fremont is just west of the University District, a place once not much but light industrial plants and dreary little bungalows. Then it had its hippie phase, and now it is home to a lot of women, feminist or counter-cultural, and more and more gay men like us. We go, because my nostalgia insists upon it, to the Still Life Cafe, where we are among the company of casually dressed women with weathered faces and practical hair, and bearded men with earrings and ponytails. We order black bean soup, carrot cake, and double-short lattes for our breakfast.

"God, it's good to be back. I miss this."

Dan beams, but as if an afterthought he asks just what it is I have missed.

"I dunno. This place. The air, the smells. Seattle. This funky cafe with chairs that don't match and tables that rock. Not Tokyo at all."

Dan tells me what is new. It has been a mild winter, and a lot of flowers and shrubs have already bloomed. He's been busy at work and has hardly taken a day off. The point is that he should work as hard as he can while I'm in Japan, so that we can take time off together when I get back for good at the end of the summer.

"How's Brock?" I ask. "What's he up to?"

Brock has gone back to Ohio, I am told over the last of my carrot cake. After he lost his sight he could not manage the house he and Henry had lived in on Dan's same street.

"So who's living there now?"

"Dunno. I see cars in the driveway sometimes, but never any people."

After we finish at the Still Life, Dan drives past Brock's old house on the way to his own. The rhododendrons in Brock's yard are blooming crazily, given all the recent rain and warm temperatures. I am about to tell Dan we should take a picture and send it to him in Ohio, but then I remember that he is blind.

"She was unaccountably gay," reminisced Margaret of Ruth, "and mischievously refused to tell us anything."[8]

Terminal Essay

3. In Indo-China the belt begins to broaden, enfolding China, Japan and Turkistan.

The Japanese have their own stories of how homosexuality spread to their islands. The most popular is that it was brought back to Japan by Kūkai, the Empty Sea, a monk who brought True Word esoteric Buddhism back with him from China over a thousand years ago. Centuries later, a less than disinterested Christian missionary named Padre Gaspar Vilela claimed that it was Empty Sea who had invented *peccado nefando*, the "accursed sin."[9] He also invented the Japanese syllabary, compiled the first Japanese dictionary, and, according to his followers, was spared physical death and still dwells immortal in eternity.

Terminal Essay

4. It then embraces the South Sea Islands and the New World where, at the time of its discovery, Sotadic love was, with some exceptions, an established racial institution.

"The etiology of sex perversions, in instance after instance," Ruth Benedict tells us, is "intelligible from the social side, from a consideration of the whole culture."[10]

*   *   *

Homosexuality, it is presumed, was a habit Empty Sea had acquired while living in Chinese monasteries, where he believed it best restricted. Otherwise, what would become of the species? Buddhism teaches that the last stage of the world will be that of *mappō*, the End of the Law, when people will no longer live by Buddhist truth or attain enlightenment. Homosexuality then, like AIDS now, is said to be a portend of destiny.

March.   I am busy meeting with colleagues and students at the university. Dan and I drive in to campus together, and then home again at night, but in between our paths do not cross. Only a few people know we are lovers, though our mutual homosexuality is well known. No one would expect a professor of Japanese literature to be otherwise, but a fag scientist is something altogether different. People talk. Dan takes care not to be too obvious about things, out of consideration for his untenured, assistant-professor boyfriend as well as himself.

At night I use my free time back in Seattle to read a single novel, a very long one. *The Shade of Trees* is the story of two lovers in postwar Nagasaki, one a married artist unsure of his talent and the other a woman of Chinese descent burdened with supporting her family. When I began my study of Japanese atomic bomb literature, it was as an American, a citizen of the nation that used a weapon that contaminated hundreds of thousands with a slow killer. But by the spring of 1987 I feel as much a victim as a victimizer. I cannot read a page of what happened in those years before I was born without my own heart pounding, my own palms sweating. I stand in a different place now in history, and if it is not the same as those two lovers' place, it is nonetheless at a crossroads where for one moment our paths converge.

Eventually Margaret would leave Ruth for a man, and Ruth would fall in love with the next woman in her life, Natalie Raymond. Later would come Val.

> Many of our culturally discarded traits are selected for elaboration in different societies. Homosexuality is an excellent example, for in this case our attention is not constantly diverted, as in the consideration of trance, to the interruption of routine activity which it implies. Homosexuality poses the problem very simply. A tendency toward this trait in our culture exposes an individual to all the conflicts to which all aberrants are always exposed, and we tend to identify the consequences of this conflict with homosexuality. But these consequences are obviously local and cultural.[11]

Dan continues to be glad I'm back, even if it's only for a few weeks. Our relationship is still a new one, and my sabbatical has come too early in it. We make love with a special passion both compensatory and anticipatory: passion we've missed over the past months since his Tokyo visit, and passion we've yet to miss in those to come.

One day we go to visit a friend who, since my move to Tokyo last fall, has received his diagnosis and is in the hospital with a brain fever that in the summer of 1987 will be one of the things that finally kill him. I do most of the talking, because I can distract all three of us with stories about Japan. Josh will never travel anywhere anymore, but he closes his eyes as I take him to my house in Mejiro, introduce him to Ben, bring him along to dinner at Jerry's and Jaime's, tell him about my research. I neglect to talk about the AIDS hysteria in Japan, out of concern for him; I neglect to talk about my own fears out of concern for Dan and for myself.

As war began, Ruth Benedict met Ruth Valentine. Her appointment book reads:

Sept. 17, 1939—To Bradleys with Val
Sept. 19, 1939—Val to dinner
Sept. 21, 1939—Val's invitation to stay with her
Sept. 22, 1939—*Canceled NY trip*[12]

Terminal Essay
5. Within the Sotadic Zone the Vice is popular and endemic, held at the worst to be a mere peccadillo, whilst the races to the North and South of the limits here defined practise it only sporadically amid the opprobium of their fellows who, as a rule, are physically incapable of performing the operation and look upon it with the liveliest disgust.[13]

It was in June 1944 that Ruth Benedict, then a social science analyst in the Foreign Morale Division of the Office of War Information, was assigned to study Japan. She began writing *The Chrysanthemum and the Sword* a month after the end of the war.

I believe I first read it in high school. I was excited to read about a country where the people were so different, so attuned to each other rather than to solely themselves. In my little New England town I saw the possibility of going someplace where, oddly enough, I might belong precisely because it is so dissimilar.

*   *   *

The Shade of Trees is one of the novels I knew I would have to read, but had too long put off. I was not prepared for how difficult reading this book would, in fact, be. I had tried to start it last November, when I was living alone in Nakano. Sitting in my little studio, feeling my bronchitis' dull throb on some days and sharp stabs on others work their way up my throat and across my lungs, I read a novel about two lovers who, because they had gone into Nagasaki not on August ninth but a day or two later, thought themselves free of radiation disease. I read about two lovers whose health slowly deteriorated over the years but only prompted, in the man, ever more shrill and pathetic protestations that no, he could not be a victim, it had to be something else. It won't happen to us. The doctors make Asada's denial easier. Even if Keiko knew the truth, that did not make facing her own suddenly abbreviated mortality any easier. The terror of being left alone is what finally overwhelmed her.

"Therefore I shall speak only of sex perversions," writes Ruth. *"It was that young mixed-race man whom I loved that infected me," says Luchiano, "the one whose photo hung in my room."* "On the Plains of North America, the transvestite, a man who has assumed women's clothes, occupations, and lived as wife with a husband, is an accepted institution." *He wasn't homo, he just had a big dick, and it must have been that sex drive of his that got him into trouble.* "Among the Dakota he was exclusively a passive homosexual, active homosexuality being on the other hand a sexual offense; as was also the woman who tried to live as a man." *It looks like he got the virus from the female photographer who took that nude picture of him.* "The regular transvestite, the so-called berdache, was allowed, but was regarded with a certain ambivalence." *He only learned he's got AIDS when she died.* "Behind his back he was called 'he' and jokes were made." *He panicked and went wild, had sex with everyone.* "Fathers whipped little boys for dressing up in girls' costume— the only occasion on which informants remember ever having been whipped—because the danger of transvestism was so real to them." *I don't know for sure, but I bet he passed it on to a hundred others.* "Nevertheless, once the rôle was chosen, the berdache was honored for his industry and strength." *I don't particularly hate him. It's not like he infected people deliberately.* "He was the 'best wife' for he outshone women at their own occupations and could also provide game for the larder, which women did not do." *He was a frightened, lonely boy, and probably just wanted others to share his fate with him.* "The point of interest in connection with this discussion is that the berdaches were seldom to be distinguished physiologically from other men." *He hated fags, so he looked for girls he could die with, and brandished his stiff cock.* "Nor were their characteristics evident from early childhood."[14] *He's dead already.*[15]

I do not really know what got me interested in this topic of the atomic bombings. Was I born with a predilection for dark things? Do I actually enjoy hopelessness? No stories I heard as a boy growing up in rural New England ever could have led my imagination to Hiroshima or Nagasaki— unless what brings now to these records of the end is the adult reaction to an adolescent fear. I am part of that generation that had to rehearse its dives beneath the classroom desks at the wail of the siren. I am part of that generation that sensed how fragile the balance of terror was. I was taken out of school one October by a mother who was frightened to be left alone while her husband, our father, was on his annual hunting trip in northern Maine. We went with him that year, where we might have survived had Kennedy wagered wrong. I am part of that generation that walked down streets and saw buildings here and there marked as having bomb shelters. I am part of that generation that "stockpiled" dusty canned goods in our basements, there to allow us to outlive enemy isotopes.

Japanese atomic-bomb literature is full of stories of families who thought they might survive but do not. I got used to them over time. Narrative and aesthetic closure in the genre grew to demand death, not life: the only arrangement that is both realist and symmetrical.

Ruth Benedict died a peaceful death on September 17, 1948. An unexpected heart attack fell her several days earlier, but she was resolved to stay alive until Val could return to California. They spoke at length the afternoon she got back, after which she soon expired.

Benedict was sixty-one at the time. Her death was mourned as premature, but that would be a pretty good run for a male homosexual nowadays. I suppose the only thing better would be, like the Virgin Mary or Empty Sea, to be taken up into heaven as is and not have to die at all.

Every day now, thirteen years after the end of the war, was spent by both Asada and Keiko catering to their states of poor health. The development of what was pronounced a "chest ailment" doubtlessly meant that the life they had once eagerly anticipated would now never come. Yet the suffering that ensued was an inducement to keep on living. One could say that the suppression of their fears, as well as the strain of their infirmities were now part and parcel of their lives. Each of them had their own health worries, and those worries were the reason behind their psychological deterioration. Nagasaki's ordeal of thirteen years ago was something from which the city was recovering, but that was the consequence of how normal people get on with their lives. It had nothing to do with how those who were sick might think. Neither of them, until now, had imagined what illness might actually mean. Even now, as it was sinking into their consciousness, they denied its import. But such evasion itself was the work of their weakened state. The anxiety brought about by the spots that appeared on Asada's wrist made a mockery of their charade.[16]

My own coughs seemed worse when I tried, unsuccessfully, to read this novel last November. Now, in spring, I can look back on my autumn and think: yes, sure you were sick, but you are also a hypochondriac.

Freud suggested a correspondence between hypochondria and homo-sexuality via the narcissism that underlies both. To imagine some part of one's body inflamed, tender, or hot is tantamount to imagining it aroused and eroticized, or so we are told. But I have another theory. The body that is threatened by illness, either real or illusionary, houses a mind for which only the internal exists, and nothing external. It makes all reference purely to itself and objectifies nothing. Nor does it eroticize anything; the hypochon-driac can think only of his pain, never his pleasure. But out of that pain comes the realization what true pleasure once was, and can be once again.

Abruptly the fear of another sexually transmitted disease, AIDS, has leapt into the ranks of the hypochondriac's fear. Even more than syphilis in the eighteenth and nineteenth centuries, AIDS is a real and extremely grave problem, but in addition its freight of shame, terror, uncontrollability, and blame make it a perfect focus for hypochondriacs. AIDS centers increasingly receive calls from individuals who had one sexual adventure eight or nine years ago and are now terrified that they have AIDS and have given it to their faithful and probably ambivalently loved and resented spouse.[17]

Am I a hypochondriac because I both love and resent? Or because I am a homosexual? Or a narcissist? Or is it because I live in Japan, a nation that obsesses over its ailments? The Japanese language has a dozen words for hemorrhoids. Or is it because this particular disease (though not the only one, as Asada and Keiko know) is so mysterious, stealthy, and cunning? Every new bruise is a reminder, an omen, a riddle. But I still have to wonder: just why do I inflict wounds on myself deliberately? Stigmata of what private passion are these?

One day I am seized by an odd combination of panic and remorse. Back in Dan's house, our intimacy briefly restored, I suspect for a second that maybe he is lying (not speaking all the truth) to me just as I do to him, and just as Asada and Keiko do. (He looks well enough, but we haven't spoken plainly yet.) *The Shade of Trees*, now that I am close to finishing it, does not seem a novel at all to me. I marvel at "the accidents of my history" that took me this year to Tokyo. To my house with Ben, and to be alone with my illness, to read books and write my own.

In both this novel and my own life, men turn to liquor for companionship. Asada and I drink because we are frequently depressed and frightened. Dan does the same, but while I am back in Seattle this month, we find a way to use our reunion as a good reason to drink more than ever. We drink at home and we drink when we go out. We drink all the time. It might look to the world as if we are living it up because, together again, we mean to have a good time. But in fact, we are merely inviting along our very best mutual friend to join us in what, after a cocktail or two, becomes two men retreating once more into their frightened, shy seclusions.

Of the many things Ruth Benedict learned, some were these, as she writes in *The Chrysanthemum and the Sword*:

> Homosexual indulgences are also part of "human feelings." In Old Japan these were the sanctioned pleasures of men of high status such as the samurai and the priests. . . . It still falls, however, among those "human feelings" about which moralistic attitudes are inappropriate. It must be kept in its proper place and must not interfere with carrying on the family. Therefore the danger of a man or a woman's "becoming" a homosexual, as the Western phrase has it, is hardly conceived. . . .
>
> Intoxication is another of the permissible "human feelings." . . . Drinking *sake* is a pleasure no man in his right mind would deny himself. But alcohol belongs among the minor relaxations and no man in his right mind, either, would become obsessed by it. According to their way of thinking one does not fear to "become" a drunkard any more than one fears to "become" a homosexual. . . . At urban *sake* parties men like to sit in each other's laps.[18]

The things that Dan and I do not want to talk about are neatly repressed by booze, our major form of recreation. We go out one Sunday to a brunch and have several drinks. Then we take a ferry to a party on Bainbridge Island, given by two men who are famous for their lavish entertaining. We are already drunk when we arrive, which means the entire day will be spent in the haze we enjoy so much on these very gay occasions.

I know almost everyone at the party, mostly gay men my age, race, and socioeconomic class with whom I have socialized regularly since I first moved to the Northwest in 1983. I moved here in the midst of the great gay migration, which brought men like me not only to San Francisco and Los Angeles, but to all the coastal cities, Seattle included. Art, my lawyer, is there, as is my dentist Christian. Art grew up in Chicago, and came here after graduating from law school in Michigan; Christian is from Connecticut, not far from where I grew up. Everyone fits in so well here, it's the perfect place to come to. I like to think that I've come home.

It was a job that brought me to Seattle, but most of the gay men who moved here chose it for more personal reasons. For some it was the mountains, for others the rain they find soothing. But for some the reasons are harder to explain. Seattle, like the Alaska it psychically borders, lies at the distal edge of the American continent. Geographically, it means we do not leave it easily, or conversely are visited often. Psychologically, it means the world we inhabit here is very much one of our making, the news we read in the papers heralded as if from a foreign country. One can prefer, after all, to be in internal exile.

Dan quickly goes off with another colleague from the university to repair together to the bar. It is staffed by two young and toothy blond twins wearing suspenders but no shirts underneath. They smile and chat affably with Dan and his friend as they prepare their drinks.

I mingle. My half-year absence means I am greeted warmly by acquaintances I would ordinarily have little to say to. Japan? Oh, it's great. Glad to be back for a visit? Sure, yeah, of course.

Almost everyone here is white. I am not quite reaccustomed to this. Everyone is so big, too. Their voices are loud and they stand too close together. They wear too much cologne and don't excuse themsleves when they brush by. Are American buttocks really this wide?

Bainbridge Island is now a Euroamerican preserve for Seattle yuppies fond of taking ferries. But Bainbridge Island was not always that way.

*　　*　　*

Dr. Ruth Benedict, Professor of Anthropology at Columbia University, wrote the *New York Times* on March 6, 1942, on the subject of the coming internment:

> America has reason to be proud in considering the loyalty of these American-Japanese and their dedication in our war effort, even at great personal cost. We must use this offered cooperation to the full, for our own sake as well as theirs. We must echo Governor Olsen's statement to leading West Coast Japanese about evacuation: "We need Japanese leadership, because it is a program of and for Japanese-Americans."

The house of our friends on Bainbridge is a big L-shaped affair built before World War II. They added a guesthouse and stables for Bruce's houses. Bruce takes me out to see his animals, big martinis in our hands. On the path to the corral, we pass someone who looks familiar, but who says hello only to Bruce and not to me. Once he is out of earshot, Bruce tells me he's an old friend who's moved out here from Seattle to spend his last months in their guesthouse.

This Old Friend has his own place for the duration. He must be glad. What an impossibly elegant exile. What a piss-perfect quarantine. A win-win situation for everyone. A voluntary evacuation.

It was March 31, 1942, when Bainbridge's Japanese-American families were loaded onto the trains that conveyed them from Puyallup to Manzanar. It was March 31, 1987, that the Japanese Diet began to deliberate what might have been my own expulsion.

Back in the main house, Bruce has to run off and greet newly arrived guests. I wander by myself to admire the home and its furnishings. Everything has been restored to look, I imagine, the way it was more than half a century ago. I am admiring the restored paneling in the hallway when Old Friend walks up to me.

"You like it? I was one of the zillion friends who gave up weekends for an entire summer to get that right."

He tells me that his name is John and that we've met before. I do not recall that, but I see no point in correcting him. John leans against the wall, his bony left shoulder and hip pressed against the newly stained paneling.

"Bruce says you're staying in the guesthouse."

"That's right. I've got my own house on Lake Sammamish up for sale. Know anyone looking?"

I wonder how he manages to get to his doctors in Seattle from Bainbridge. His face is gaunt, drawn, lined with deep wrinkles. The eyes are jaundiced, and I notice makeup trying to disguise a lesion on his neck. The ferry ride from here is short, but then it is a steep walk uphill from downtown to the hospitals.

"Do you see much of Russ?"

I do not know who he is talking about. Is he mistaking me entirely for another person? There used to be someone in Seattle, or so I have been told, who looks just like me.

"Russ. Used to work at the Deluxe Bar and Grill. Sandy's lover. Russ Tamanoki. I thought you two were good friends. After Russ got his diagnosis, he went back to Idaho for a bit, to stay with his grandparents, but then came back here. Or so I hear. Have you seen him? Sandy's dead you know."

No, sorry, I don't know Russ and I didn't know that Sandy, whoever that is, is dead. I begin to mumble something about getting another drink, but John beats me to the punch and turns around to talk to someone else. Someone who really does know him.

Dan rejoins me when, new drink in hand, I enter the library.

"Bruce says it was built in the thirties by one of the big farming families who lived around here. Pretty neat, huh? Doesn't look like farmers lived here." The house is open, spacious, spare. It appeals to Dan's sense of style.

"I wouldn't have thought anyone back then on Bainbridge would have wanted a house this modern. It's great."

Looking out one of the picture windows on the back side of the house, I notice a clump of bamboo growing lushly along the edge of the patio. The tall stiff bracts undulate in the soft, late afternoon breeze. They cast fuzzy shadows on the patio concrete, quick calligraphy spelling out a familiar story. This house, I suddenly realize, had to have belonged to a Japanese-American family. I can sense it in its spaces, its use of plants, in the way it is oriented to the outdoors, from the spare lines that make it as perfect for tasteful gay men today as it once was for a immigrant family remembering a country they had left behind.

"Bruce has researched the whole history of the place. An old farming family named Tamanoki built it."

John is being helped into a chair out on the patio. I watch as two men of my generation help a third, looking decades older, get comfortable in this rare March day of warm sun. They share a joke, laugh, and look my way: through the window, into the room, and right at me.

What could Sir Richard have had in mind when he coined the word "Sotadic" to describe where we live? Sotades, the Obscene of Maronea, lived in Egypt during the third century B.C.E. Perhaps it was for his lewd and scurrilous Greek poems, poems that eventually so irritated King Ptolemy II that he had him wrapped in lead and thrown into the sea. Then again, maybe Burton saw in Sotades' invention of the palindrome the beauty of opposites that are also identical. Here on Bainbridge Island I sit in a chair in Bruce's living room to watch John, outdoors in the light, sit in his. His gaze turns away from me and moves slowly toward the lush Pacific Northwest landscape that will survive us both, but I know that he is thinking about me and whatever past he shares with the person he mistakenly thinks I am, just as I am needlessly thinking about whatever common future we both may face. In a week's time I will be back in Japan and back at working hard to forget all this. But at just this moment and here in this farmhouse long haunted by memories, John and I are indeed old friends as perfectly same and different as any palindrome.

APRIL

Special Friends

I notice him even before the plane takes off. He is on the other side of the aisle, two rows ahead of me. Big, American, he might have played football in school. He is reading a Japanese magazine, not a comic book, something more serious. I stare as his strong left arm, triceps outlined by his polo shirt, turns the pages slowly. I see more of his head whenever he glances at other boarding passengers making their way past us toward the rear of the aircraft. A square jaw, a full head of hair, and beautiful baby skin—he has the look of both a man and a boy. On my way back to Tokyo today, I am reminded of what America is still very good at manufacturing.

Dan brought me to the airport only two hours ago. He stayed with me until I had to give my boarding pass to the gate employee and walk down the jetway. He is probably back in his house now, surveying its emptiness and trying to adjust to being by himself again. And I am already thinking about men other than him.

The newspapers report that a Japanese housewife, afraid that she has AIDS, kills herself and her own child.

* * *

He gets up to put the magazine into his backpack stashed in the overhead compartment, giving me the opportunity to study his entire young body stretched to its full length. His ass is perfectly round, the proverbial melons stuffed into gray jeans. His biceps are full, and his shoulders powerful. His hands are large, I can tell, as he grapples with his luggage. His sinewy back muscles arch as he helps a fellow passenger with her own belongings. She is a Japanese woman, young and beautiful herself, and I see him smile as he speaks a few words to her in a voice whose deep masculine resonances make their way back to me.

Dr. Matsuda, Japan's sole authority in the treatment of HIV disease, says:

> What most surprised me when I began my work in AIDS was the fact that male homosexuals existed in this world. . . . There are an extraordinary large number of men who have sex with other men. That was really a shock. . . . I told my male homosexual patients, you may catch AIDS, stop your risky behavior, find a nice girl fast and marry her.[1]

The flight back to Tokyo is always a hour or so longer than the other way around and, given the earlier time of departure, harder to sleep on. Having this young man to study (probably an English teacher on his way back to Japan after a brief vacation back home in Iowa) gives me one more way of passing the time.

I put down my book and look ahead once again. One of the stewards, a Thai probably around the same age as the English teacher, is serving drinks at the head of the aisle. I notice that he notices me noticing the oblivious English teacher. I detect a small smile on his face, as if to say, yes, I see him too. Later in the flight, when I have to pass the steward on my way to the restroom, he says hello and flashes me his own wide grin. Somewhere over the Pacific we share our little secret. Over international waters, no nations here except for the ones we invent for ourselves.

April.   Looking back at my calendar for this month, I notice that every third day I had penciled in "pill." My Seattle doctor must have prescribed something for me, but I no longer remember for what. But I see "pill" written in for all the rest of the months in 1987.

The steward is good-looking too, with classic Thai looks complemented with eyes that sparkle with obvious intelligence. Like stewards everywhere, this one is clearly gay. All through the long flight I am the grateful recipient of special treatment because I am too. Where did this guy come from? A village near the northern border, or a good family in Bangkok? What does it take for a Thai to imagine a life dispersed among continents? During one of the inflight movies I am able to have a short chat with him in the galley and learn that he has a lover in Seattle. Do you know him? Sorry, I don't. I live in Tokyo. Oh, really? What part? Where does the airline put you up when you're in town? Why don't I mention Dan?

When the plane gets in at Narita, I scramble to be directly behind the English teacher as we queue up to exit. Somewhere after passport control I lose track of him. But as my airport bus starts to pull away, I catch a final glimpse of the Thai steward. He is standing with his colleagues at the curb, waiting for his airline's minivan but once again smiling broadly at me through the smoked glass of my window.

> AIDS is no game—except in Japan. Medic, an Osaka-based software company, is selling a popular video game in which players simulate the experience of AIDS from HIV infection to death. . . . The plot of the game centers on a 25-year-old who strays into a red-light district and later suspects he's become infected with HIV. Players then have several choices, including promiscuity, suicide or a life with a girlfriend who also has AIDS. The game, developed by an ex-medical student, is meant to be educational and entertaining.[2]

As a boy I always wanted to grow up to be an astronaut or comic-book superhero. They were my 1960s American version of the adventurers and explorers who made the modern world, except that they were making the future. Maybe my future, I would hope, as I looked at their strong bodies fight against the unknown in the first instance and evil in the second. I also wanted to be John Glenn, or at least his son. I could be, depending on my mood, either the fatherly Batman or adoring Boy Robin. Captain Kirk, I already knew back then, could have me as his lover since it was his job to go where no man has gone before.

Dr. Matsuda, Japan's sole authority on the treatment of a minority that does not exist there, says, "I now believe that it's probably a good thing that there's one doctor in Japan who understands male homosexuality."[3]

*   *   *

April.   The prominent monthly journal *Chūō kōron* publishes a lengthy essay by scientist Yonemoto Shōhei grandly entitled "The Basic Theory of AIDS." It is apparently meant to serve as a kind of primer for the literate public in all the aspects—medical, social, political—of AIDS. A man of science, Yonemoto begins by specifying his terms: "I will henceforth refer to American homosexuals as 'gay,' and to Japanese homosexuals as 'homos.' "[4]

I had toy models of the Mercury, Gemini, and Apollo spacecraft. One Christmas I got a cape and a play ray gun. I wanted to go to the stars, or at least fly like Superman to far continents and save the world. My best friend Jackie and I would go to our treehouse in my backyard and plan our intergalactic attacks. Was I already looking for an escape in these fantasies? Was I already preparing to be Sir Richard Francis Burton?

For the Japanese, "homo" or otherwise, Yonemoto writes, "sex is psychologically forbidden and repressed; that is why there is such a big demand for such visual adjuncts as pornographic photographs and comics." But "there are any number of psychological and cultural reasons," he explains,

> why gays in America have established a compulsive sexual lifestyle that appears to be inordinately promiscuous. Fundamentally speaking, in both Europe and North America there is the tendency to seek a more substantial sexual lifestyle; and since normal sex is impossible for gays, the exchange of bodily fluids takes on a particularly vital meaning. Moreover, given the high degree of societal discrimination in those countries, when one gay recognizes another there is a comparatively strong urge for the two of them to have sex with each other.[5]

I know what I am doing this night, my first one back in Tokyo after my month in Seattle with Dan, when I go out to Ni-chōme and head straight for the bars. I go to the one that is frequented by foreign airline stewards. I am restless after being away a month. Seattle was home, and great fun, but now I want a little adventure. No cape or toy ray gun in hand, perhaps, but I've got adult things in mind to play with nonetheless. I want to find that Thai steward. I have a "comparatively strong urge," as the scientist Yonemoto would put it.

There are Japanese who think that every obvious homosexual they see is actually a Korean; and there are Koreans in Japan who are convinced that homosexuality is a Japanese problem. So many races always darker than our own, so many beastly sexual drives: black people in America fornicating constantly, *burakumin* in Japan doing it with the sudare blinds rolled up, and homosexuals everywhere given to indiscriminate coupling. But, after all, we are different. Let's not pretend otherwise. It is only the "we" that changes. Once I believed that as a gay foreigner in Japan, I was spared xenophobia and chauvinism (both our own and theirs) because they were some Japanese people just like me, people whom I knew as well as myself and, in one case, loved. But now in 1987 there is a new invisible fraternity, a new international conspiracy. *Mabuhay*, Jesusa. *Shibaraku*, A-chan. *Sawadee*, Mr. Thai Airlines.

Sir Richard was a great British soldier, explorer, ethnologist, archaeologist, poet, translator, linguist, amateur physician, botanist, zoologist, geologist, swordsman, and raconteur. And homosexual, according to many. Unfortunately his widow, Lady Burton, burned almost all of his private journals and diaries after his death, including his extensive notes on farting.

> When in early 1987 a Japanese prostitute from the city of Kobe was diagnosed as having died from AIDS, the assumption that she had been infected during sexual contact with a foreigner was reached overnight. "Her death," one Japanese newspaper concluded, "was the result of an infatuation with Europe."[6]

Sir Richard was born at Torquay, in England, on March 19, 1821. His youth and then most of his adult life was spent abroad, first in France and Italy and then, later, the East. He never felt fully English, or fully anything. A handsome man, he was always convinced of his ugliness. He was in restless exile, a stranger who crossed borders to track the devils that drove him. He contemplated, we are told, writing a biography of Satan. What he did do, was explore Asia and Africa in the course of a life: the result of an infatuation with the East.

Rumor. I run into Chan in Ni-chōme while looking for the steward. He says he's got news for me. Movie star Takakura Ken, Japan's answer to Rock Hudson, has checked into the American Hospital in Paris. Diagnosis? *Shit-te'ru wa ne.* You know.

I do not see my new Thai friend. Foolish of me to try, I think. If he flies in regularly, he's probably got a special friend. "A lover in Tokyo," as he might put it. Disappointed, but not quite ready to go home yet, I offer to buy Chan a drink which, ever eager to please, he interprets as an order to go off and get them for us. While I am standing alone, looking around the crowded room with no particular thought in mind, I see the English teacher from Iowa walk in.

When Burton was a child, he was caught in a measles epidemic that was, according to his biography, "probably the most critical single accident in Burton's life."[7] But rather than become the hypochondriac he might have been, Burton struck out in the opposite direction: he became a fearless adventurer who challenged the jungle and the desert with his body as well as his nerve. A pale Englishman who, whether in Africa or Arabia, was drawn toward precisely what was the most dangerous; and whose body was made heroic by the challenges of the exotic.

His name, it turns out, is Daniel. When he tells me that he is an English teacher, I check my impulse to say something about my prescience. The litany commences. So, where do you teach? In Takayama, he tells me, mentioning the name of a small city in the mountains quite some distance from Tokyo. He's spending a couple of days here before he takes the train back. He likes Tokyo, and spent his first six months in Japan here. As he talks I stare at his hands: bigger than I had thought earlier and connected to large wrists covered with short blond hairs that sometimes catch the light from the bright illumination over the bar's dance floor. I would guess he is in his mid-twenties. His voice still has a youthful timbre to it. And you? he asks. Oh, Tokyo, I say. Almost walking distance from here.

Chan returns with our two drinks, and I use his added presence as an excuse to move my own body closer to Daniel's.

It was reputedly Italian medical students who, early in life, taught little Master Richard about sex. As an adult, Sir Richard had a special fondness for boots, and in his last years owned over one hundred pairs.

AIDING THE STOCK MARKET WITH A
RUMOR OF AIDS

Notoriously volatile, the Tokyo stock market is prone to bounce like a yo-yo at the drop of a rumor. And there are flocks of sharpies who take advantage of this propensity to try and make a quick yen.

This is what happened on the afternoon of April 15 when Kabuto-cho . . . began buzzing like a beehive . . . Out of nowhere had come whispers that screen actor Ken Takakura had "died in Paris, a victim of AIDS."

His office promptly contacted him and was told that he was feeling fine. The canard was thus quickly put to rest.

But that did not deter plungers from trying to revive the waning fortunes of so-called "AIDS stocks" . . . shares in bio-chemical, pharmaceutical and rubber companies.[8]

By the late 1980s, unlike both the early 1980s and what the 1990s would be, Tokyo is overflowing with young Americans and Europeans working for the international stock brokerages and investment banks. Tokyo, before the bubble burst, was one of the best places in the world to make money, and nearly everyone there did. Living in high-rises and driving Jaguars, this was an alien nobility unlike any Tokyo had seen since the postwar American Occupation. And this time, many Japanese were getting rich, too.

Jerry lives in one of the main concentrations of these foreigners, but not the biggest. Most cluster together in Roppongi, Hiroo, and Yoyogihara, but Jerry is down a side street in Aoyama. It is a nice place, very fashionable in the eyes of his Japanese colleagues and friends and, to me, not like Japan at all. Jerry is not an interloper, or new to Japan. He has lived here for years, first as a student while working on his doctorate in marketing and now as one of the grand, queer masters of the scene. Because of his long experience here, Jerry is both more and less comfortable than are his fellow Americans, for whom Tokyo is both exotic and intimidating at the same time. For Jerry, it is no longer either. He thinks of leaving, and sometimes does, only to be back again after a year or two.

Babette introduced me to Jerry once when she was visiting Tokyo, and we quickly became friends. Jerry is tall, dark, and good-looking. I would have liked him no matter what. But our common link to Glen, and the fact we had attended the same graduate schools, made us especially good friends. Our shared sexual orientation really becomes the tie that binds. That we are attracted to very different kinds of men only helps.

Jerry had me over for dinner soon after we met. He prepared a perfect meal, many courses, lots to drink, and reefer both before and after. We talk about a lot of things: our pasts, our current work, people we know in common. Ordinarily, this would be part of a seduction. Not this time, however—it is as if we're old friends already, years beyond the point where this kind of easy intimacy can breed sexual excitement. I am too much like him for any further investment. A Great Gay Friendship commences.

This time, I do talk about Dan.

In 1846 Burton, traveling in the Orient, was struck down by cholera. He returned to England in 1849, all the while thinking he would never make it back alive. He made the journey with his dear Moslem servant, Allahbad, at his side.

The Perfumed Garden

> Others there retain boys as servants to see to their needs when they are traveling or journeying away from home. These boys are constantly in their company, and when they are alone and in close contact with them, they are impelled by their sexual urge to have intercourse with them, especially when they are relaxing or are alone with them in bath-houses or when they are drinking in company or are in a state of intoxication which induces an awareness of the charms, grace, suppleness and fine deportment of a stripling.[9]

Daniel is not one of my former students, but he is one of those younger men who, when we meet in Ni-chōme, I take it upon myself to tutor. No doubt there was a professor like me in his past anyway, someone who took a special interest in him, and vice versa, for reasons that later would become clear. He asks me a lot of questions about Japan and of course I act as if I know all the answers. That, plus the *mizuwari* drink Chan earlier provided, means I speak rapidly, with confidence and the knowledge that I am impressing this young man. This is a new way for me to score, I think: I'm the older brother who's been there first and is willing to share with baby brother the secrets of life. Daniel does not stop smiling. Was it like this when John Hanning Speke first met Sir Richard?

April.   On the twenty-sixth the *Asahi* reports that teachers at a Tokyo-area public school are debating whether a child, recently returned from New York where he lived with his parents, should be forced to take an HIV test.

America is where the Japanese fear AIDS originated. Sir Richard knew better. "Diseases," he wrote, "do not begin except with the dawn of humanity; and their history, as far as we know, is simple enough."[10] He never blamed India or Africa for the occasional illnesses that almost killed him, and which made him realize certain important truths.

Spring really has come to Tokyo now. I had opened the windows wide when I got home from the airport earlier this evening, and left them open when I went to Ni-chōme so that the newly warm air could permeate a house that had kept its staid odors captive all winter long. Tomorrow I will put away my thermal undershirts and get ready for the two or three months of fine weather we will enjoy before the monsoon rains, and then the humid heat, come to Japan. The change in temperature has me feeling great, and thinking about men.

Daniel excuses himself to go to the bathroom at the back of the bar. Chan catches my eye from across the room. Is he accusing me of what I know I am guilty of?

The Perfumed Garden. "The way to lay a catamite is first to get him on his side. You then lift the lad's thigh as you would with a pregnant women and crouch down in a squatting position with your penis poised towards his anus. If you like, you can kneel over him with your forearms resting on the floor. Alternatively, you can get him to lie on his belly and then go belly to back."[11]

Sir Richard's body was, in fact, the essence of his fame. Without it, there would have been no adventures, no great discoveries. He first donned a disguise when, at the request of his superiors, he visited the boy brothels of Karachi, which were rumored at the time to be corrupting British troops. His report, later widely circulated, compromised his career for years—no one could write of homosexuality without himself being accused of it. Then later, working for British intelligence, Burton stained his face with henna and, calling himself Mirza Abdullah and pretending to be half-Arab and half-Irani, went into the bazaars of the Sind. He would use this name again, most famously when he penetrated the holy city of Mecca. He had completed his disguise by undergoing a Moslem circumcision, a procedure he insisted on observing.

Sir Richard could pass as an Oriental not only because he knew them so well, but because he felt so little English himself.

One hundred years ago, Lafcadio Hearn lived through an epidemic too, and also saw how Japan responded to it.

From the upper balcony of my house, the whole length of a Japanese street, with its rows of little shops, is visible down to the bay. Out of the various houses in that street I have seen cholera-patients conveyed to the hospital— the last one (only this morning) my neighbor across the way, who kept a porcelain shop. He was removed by force, in spite of the tears and cries of his family. The sanitary law forbids the treatment of cholera in private houses; yet people try to hide their sick, in spite of the fines and other penalties, because the public cholera-hospitals are overcrowded and roughly managed, and the patients are entirely separated from all who love them. But the police are not often deceived: they soon discover unreported cases, and come with litters and coolies. It seems cruel; but sanitary law must be cruel.[12]

Sir Richard's body, the survivor of deadly diseases, transformed into the Other with the removal of his foreskin and used to make his way into the most forbidden places, was the instrument of his Orientalism. He skillfully deployed it to go where white men were not supposed to go, and he used it to do things white men are supposed to frown on, or worse. Perhaps he did not *feel* like a white man himself, either because he was attracted to men who were not or because he wondered if he were a man at all. Castration, we learn from his books, was one of his favorite scholarly interests.

Jerry tells me about his lover, too. He met Jaime in Harajuku one Sunday afternoon, when the latter was passing through on his way back to San Francisco after a business trip to Seoul. Jerry had had a Japanese lover, but was recently thrown over for a wealthy Brit. Consequently Jerry is, for the time being, not much interested in what we call (when we do not want others to understand us) "HCNs"—Host Country Nationals, an old diplomatic corps term we both picked up from Glen years ago.

Jaime is Mexican-American, a successful banker, a real romantic. His relationship with Jerry has been transoceanic but intense. Their mutual affluence allows for extravagant rendezvous around the world. And now, Jerry tells me over cognac, Jaime is quitting his job in San Francisco to move here into the Aoyama apartment by spring. For a moment I am jealous. Wouldn't it be nice to have Dan here with me. Then again, I realize, there would be so much less opportunity for adventure. Lady Burton stayed home in England; adventure, as Sir Francis knew, is what the East is all about.

*   *   *

Sir Rutherford Alcock, a witness to the birth of modern Japan, describes what happened in 1863 in the city that would soon become its capital:

> All failed, however, to give them immunity from the devastating cholera, which the United States frigate Mississippi is said, I believe correctly, to have brought over—a first fatal fruit of the treaty and their extended relations with foreigners! It swept many thousands from their cities; they say 200,000 from Yeddo alone. And one cannot be surprised that in the minds of the people it was looked upon as associated with the strangers, and a visitation wholly due to their established relations.[13]

Sir Richard's masquerade was unsettling to his fellow officers in India, who called him "the white nigger" behind his back. The line that crossed, so often and with such apparent relish, made his colleagues' Englishness as much of a drag as his own long, flowing robes and makeup. Years later, back in London, he would embarrass friends and colleagues by showing up at social functions dressed in those same native costumes. What was it about the Empire that both preserved it in the Orient and made it so fragile at home?

Luchiano was able to fool nearly everyone. He had the look, the voice, the walk, everything down just right. Japanese men are good at this, they don't have the prominent Adam's apples to give them away. Years ago in Osaka I invited a group of bad drag queens to a party I gave and even they ended up fooling a lot of the other guests. Luchiano was the perfect woman, and it was his perfect man who infected him.

Jerry is very excited that Jaime is coming. He's cleared out one of the closets in the master bedroom for all his clothes, and told all his friends there will be an immense party to celebrate his arrival. When will that be? I ask. No later than next April. And how long is he planning on staying? Jerry did not say anything, but only shrugged.

A week later we had dinner together again, but this time at a *kushiage* place on Aoyama Avenue. Jerry was still talking about Jaime all the time, oblivious to the food. Somehow we got onto the topic of AIDS, and I asked Jerry if Jaime knew his status. Why did I ask such a question? When I don't ask it even of the men I go to bed with? Jerry did not say anything, but only shrugged.

*   *   *

When Sir Richard traveled to distant continents, it was still quite an ordeal. Ships and their crews might have been reliable, but negotiating one's way through the pagan world was still fraught with danger. There was the problem, of course, of visiting other peoples who did not especially want to be visited, but just as menacing were the microbes, viruses, parasites, and infections that lay in wait for the intrepid European.

When Jaime came to Japan, it was via United Airlines, Business Class; Jerry had rented a chauffeured car to drive them the hour and a half back to Aoyama from Narita. The Japanese, by 1987, were quite accustomed to being visited by foreigners. And on our part, we no longer feared the suspect hygiene of the Orient. The most frightening diseases were now, after all, thought be aboard those jumbo jets headed east (or chauffeured cars driving west), coursing through the blood of healthy young men.

"Thus even before the historical accident of the outbreak of AIDS in the gay communities of the West," writes one American academic, "homosexuality was conceived of as a contagion, and the homosexual as parasitic upon the heterosexual community."[14] If this is true, it is doubly true of the expatriate homosexual in Japan, where our national and, if white or black, racial being is as plainly extraordinary as our sexual one.

"Unrestricted international intercourse," writes Sir Chamberlain of Commodore Perry, the first of America's Japanese interlopers, "was at the time regarded by all Christian nations as an indisputable right, a sacred duty."[15] American ships in Uraga Bay penetrate the Mikado's realm. Missionaries assume their familiar positions. U.S. Marine Corps jeeps don't stop at the traffic lights. Any of a hundred Hiroshis say to our many Davids: go ahead and fuck me if you want. *I want it too*.

In the last years of his life, Sir Richard translated and secretly published six books of Oriental erotica, which in England's nineteenth century was an illegal act. The Sanskrit *Kama Sutra* and the *Ananga Ranga* are well known. But one other was the Arabic *Al Raud al atir wa nuzhat al Khatir*, or *The Perfumed Garden for the Soul's Delectation* by Shaykh Nefzawi.

Jerry throws a big party to welcome Jaime to Tokyo and to show him off to his friends. When I arrive there around nine, the apartment is already packed with gay men, about two-thirds foreign and one-third Japanese. The air is full of cigarette smoke and loud, alcohol-enhanced voices that resound with the low notes of male larynxes.

I do not find Jerry right away. I know some of the other guests already, thanks to Jerry's introductions over the past half-year. William is the first to say hello to me.

"John, have you met Ichi?"

"*Ichirō desu. Yoroshiku onegai shimasu.*"

"Hello. Are you two special friends?"

Both Ichi and William laugh. Either I have embarrassed them, or this was a question whose answer I am supposed to know.

"We're going to Thailand next week. Ichi's never been, and I want to show him Changmai."

We're also going to Ko Samui, Ichi lets me know. I tell them about a great place to shop for Burmese antiques brought in across the border, and a good, cheap place in Bangkok near the bars to eat. (They've heard it all before; this is a trip we all take.) All the while I am thinking: that same steward will be on the plane with you, more international homosexuals on the move, this time north-south more than east-west, but still on the move. He will be serving drinks from his cart in the aisle ahead of you, and he will catch your eyes. He will give you that knowing look that says, I'm one too. *Unrestricted.* He'll be sure you get the Royal Thai Treatment. *International.* And that night, after you've checked into your five-star hotel and dined on seafood curries, you will take a cab to the gay bars in the center of the city, and one of you, if not both, will be on the lookout for that steward. *Intercourse.*

Sir Richard was always attracted to younger, good-looking men who were themselves looking for a fellow adventurer-slash-older brother. John Speke, whom the world considers his arch-rival in the race to discover the source of the Nile, was perhaps his favorite. Six years his junior, Speke was tall and lean, with hair, "as the natives put it, 'the colour of a lion's mane.' "[16] After spending six months with him in Africa on a trip whose "great object," according to their sponsors the Royal Geographical Society, was "to penetrate inland," Speke would write home that he was "practically wedded with" Sir Richard.[17]

Daniel and I will slide into a similar relationship. Like me, Sir Richard was always uncomfortable with his body and thought himself ugly, despite the fact that others found him pleasing. Early in life, he experimented with opium, and later drank heavily. And Speke, like Daniel, was a man whom Sir Richard wanted to shape in his own image and was not entirely pleased with the result when he succeeded. How does one stop a lover from becoming too much oneself? How does one identify, and not dominate?

The sixteenth-century *Perfumed Garden* was originally published in a European language when an abridged edition appeared in Paris in 1850. When Sir Richard used it for his 1886 translation, he pretended to be French himself, a subterfuge that is now regarded as having been necessary to protect his already battered fragile reputation.

But only one of his planned three volumes of the *Perfumed Garden* was published, and no version contained the famous final chapter on homosexuality. It was a complete translation of Shaykh Nefzawi's sex manual, under the new title of *The Scented Garden*, that Sir Richard was hard at work on at the time of his death. "I have put my whole life and all my life-blood into that *Scented Garden*," Sir Richard told a friend. "It is my great hope that I shall live by it. It is the crown of my life."[18] These are the sorts of things we usually reserve for saying about our wives, husbands, lovers, or children. But for Richard Francis Burton, work was apparently everything.

When I wander into the kitchen I find Jerry filling a pipe bowl with dope. He hands it to another of the guests and greets me with a bear hug.

"Have you met Jaime yet? What do you think?"

In fact I have not met him yet, so Jerry grabs me by the arm and drags me through several rooms until we are standing next to a small group of men laughing over a joke that we interrupt.

"Jaime, meet John." We shake hands and I welcome him to Japan. Jaime is short and dark and very well groomed. He has a handsome smile, and I like him instantly. His features are distinct and strong, Aztec in both form and color. He looks especially exotic here in Tokyo, where the New World is generally represented only by races originally from the Old. Jerry has done quite well for himself, I say to myself, and once more I remember my bottomless capacity for envy.

While we talk, Jerry disappears, only to return soon with the pipe. We pass it around, when Tom, a friend of Jerry's from work, resumes his long funny story, telling us about his recent adventure at a place in Ikebukuro where Japanese businessman can go and get pissed on by boy prostitutes dressed up like young schoolgirls.

Soon after he died, Sir Richard's widow was offered a sizeable sum of money for the unfinished *Scented Garden*. Not only did she refuse, but she burned the manuscript at once, along with forty unpublished others. A good Christian woman who tried in vain to make a believer out of her husband, she was doubtlessly scandalized by the decadent manners and customs of sixteenth-century Tunis.

I spring for the cab that takes Daniel and me to Mejiro. After a perfunctory tour of Ben's house, whose two floors and several rooms impress him mightily, I put some music on and offer him a beer. He sits in one chair, I in another. Eventually I let my right foot play with his left. *The plot of the game centers on a 25-year-old who strays into a red-light district and later suspects he's become infected with HIV.* By beer number three, Daniel has reverted to the boy he, not so many years ago, was. He giggles and bats his eyelashes and flashes me his sheepish grin. When I come back from the kitchen with another beer for myself, I approach his chair from behind and put my hand on his shoulder while telling him a story about teaching gay undergraduates in America. *Players then have several choices, including promiscuity, suicide, or a life with a girlfriend who also has AIDS.* As he is telling me about his college days in California, I bend over to put my arms around him. He turns his head to kiss me. I've got my arm down his shirt front when he asks where it is I sleep. *The game, developed by an ex-medical student, is meant to be educational and entertaining.*

Jerry's party goes very late. The dope and the liquor mean that I pass out on one of the sofas even while it is still going on. Eventually the stereo is turned off, and I hear the front door close a final time. Someone, Jerry probably, throws a blanket over me and I fall asleep.

My first dream is about Dan. He and I are in a car racing up a mountain road. I am driving, fast, as if we need to get somewhere right away. It is springtime, but halfway up we start to run into ice and snow on the asphalt, and Dan becomes quiet. I can tell he is nervous. Winter weather has always frightened him, and he thinks we may crash. My reaction, as always, is to drive faster. I do not like the way he is fearful at times. One of the ways I have always wanted us to get closer has been to do risky things together, but he always says no. I enjoy scaring him a bit, if only to show that sometimes I am younger than he is; and that I need to do what young men do.

When I am drunk I never sleep deeply, so I am quickly awake when, in the darkness of Jerry's living room, I feel someone pulling the blanket off of me and fumbling with my underwear. A hand extracts my soft penis, and a warm mouth soon goes to work on it. In no time I am hard, but along with my desire to lie here in the dark and get blown is the sudden realization who my invisible lover must be. I think: is this fair to my friend? The warm mouth works its way down my shaft. This could be the end of our friendship. A tongue starts to lick my testicles. Lie back and enjoy, I think. How often does this happen to you anymore?

I push him away in a moment of guilt, but he persists in making love to my genitals. When I come in his mouth I stifle my moan, worried it will reach the bedroom down the hall. I feel warm semen dripping against my thigh, and I rub it into that smooth Indian chest.

I can see he has a hard-on, so I let my own press up against him. He stands up, I kneel, unbuckle his belt, lower his pants, put his cock in my mouth. He runs his fingers through my hair. *What was I telling you about? Teaching gay guys Japanese literature? Yeah, sure, I've thought about it. Never did anything about it though.* I lay the bedding out, take my own clothes off, and let him put his entire weight on top of me. His trunk-like legs push my own apart. *So, what do you want to do? Yeah sure, I've got some. Over there by the lamp.* He tells me that he's got a thing or two that he can teach me. Go ahead, big boy. *Sir Richard loved John Speke.* Yeah, okay, that's it, take it easy, great.

Sir Richard never did discover the Nile. But what he did discover, according to the Introduction to his translation of the *Kama Sutra*, was "Indian sex."[19]

The next day Daniel had to get back to his friend's apartment early to pick up his luggage and make his train to Takayama. I let him screw me one more time after he got out of the shower, his damp body clean and fresh against me. All the while he had that boyish grin, the joy of discovering something new and wonderful. Indian sex.

"Damn," he says as he pulled his penis out of me. The fuckin' rubber broke, he says. "Shit." That's my line, I joke in the brief interim before the news sinks in. Damn indeed. Later that day I'll think, well, he's younger, and taking risks is what it's all about. Why should I now be spared what I have done to my other Daniels all these years?

In 1857 Sir Richard Francis Burton and John Hanning Speke, while on their search for the source of the Nile, became afflicted with eye infections. Speke was nearly blinded and had to depend on Dick for everything. (Later those roles would be reversed.) Looking for the origins of a river in a place that, more than a century later, would be where others imagine our present scourge began, John Speke would resemble that Famous Greek who also was blinded; who also wondered why he turned on a man who had, with all the love and arrogance of a father, sought to fashion him in his own image.

John Hanning Speke was killed in 1864 when, while hunting partridges at a country estate, he died of a self-inflicted wound perhaps accidental, perhaps suicidal. When Sir Richard, who had for years been unsuccessfully attempting to discredit Speke's claim to have beat him to the origins of the Nile, heard the news he collapsed into a chair and wept, according to Isabel, "long and bitterly."[20]

Unrestricted international intercourse has its risks. Some of those intrepid Americans who followed Commodore Perry onto Japanese soil got their heads loped off. Daniel will, if he hasn't already, have condoms break inside of him, too. I bet that every day a Japanese man, sometimes even named Tetsuji, has his heart broken by a foreigner with a plane ticket in hand. And as Sir Richard learned early on, little germs like to hitchhike rides. But free trade has always been our official queer foreign policy, despite its occasional glitches. Promiscuity for the insolent persons on the far side of borders is more than wanton fun or mere hormonal imperative. It is our way of saying these little kingdoms of yours do not matter all that much to us. I politely answer all the questions the immigration officer asks me, but he never asks the questions he should. *Are you bringing any fruit into the country?* No. *Have you traveled in any areas under a public heath alert?* No. *Have you ever committed a felony?* Not me. *Welcome to our country.*

MAY

A Play of Muscles

My new friend Jane and I go to see a Japanese production of William Hoffman's *As Is*, one of the earliest AIDS dramas written in America. In New York it was staged in the middle of an epidemic. Here in Tokyo it is produced in a place called the Sunshine Theater.

We meet early in order to have something to eat first. I met Jane at a party last Christmas and instantly liked her. As I see her wave at me from a distance in Ikebukuro station, across a crowd of commuters headed home after work, I am reminded again of how much I like her. Jane is in her mid-twenties, clever, and lively. My affection for her feels sexual, and I like that too. She is originally from North Carolina, the daughter of a prominent family from which she fled early in life. Jane lives in Chicago now with her new husband, except for this year when, like me, she is in Tokyo to do research. There are other things we have in common as well.

We pick a restaurant that serves cold noodles. It was my idea to go to this play, so I treat her to the meal. It is already warm this May, and we are glad the place has air-conditioning. Between the time when the waitress brings us the cool *shibori* towels to wipe our hands and faces clean and when she returns to take our order, we have already broached several intimate topics.

* * *

Komagome, famous for its eggplants, was old Edo's favorite "kitchen garden." Not far from it was Kōgaiji, another of the city's popular healing temples. Komagome today is still a place you can go for help. And to die, unless you kill yourself first. Hospitals were once places where one went never to leave, and for some of us they are that again.

In the play's last act a dying man, Rich, has sex with his lover Saul in a hospital bed. A sympathetic nurse draws the curtain around them. (The play, according to its author, was meant to be funny.) The actors are Japanese, and so is the language: I am unnerved by the implausibility of such a scene ever actually taking place in Japan. Watching this play requires the wilful suspension of disbelief I associate with kabuki, not the modern stage. I have seen Japanese productions of *Boys in the Band* and *Bent* and both times, like today, my Brechtian estrangement was more the effect of the audience, made up almost entirely of adolescent women, than of the plays themselves. But this one makes me especially ill at ease at the absurd voyeurism in which I participate. I alone am on stage and in the front row all at the same time, looking at an audience looking at me in both places.

When the play is over Jane and I have coffee. She admits to some anxieties of her own. She is married now, and monogamous, but with a past. There has always been in our short friendship a conversation we've been moving ever closer toward, but I am not sure whether mutual confessions would be quite the best way to have done with it. That would be too staged, just like the Japanese attempt at a gay American play we have just seen in the Sunshine Theater.

We avoid the awkward (or rather carefully circumnavigate it) by talking about other contemporary American plays we have seen performed in Tokyo. I share with her how odd I had felt sometimes, seeing my story—"my" meaning any number of things—translated not only into the Japanese language, but into a Japanese sense of the world. Sometimes that sense is our own, Jane and I agree, but often not. This is one of lessons of being an expatriate, she offers; and one of its conundrums too, I add. We are talking in English and occasionally, when we laugh, which is often, we attract the startled but curious attention of other customers in the café. You would almost think our lines are scripted, if poorly rehearsed; and the crowd around us a paying audience.

Komagome.   You could translate it loosely as "The cavalry has arrived!" The name supposedly dates back to a famous battle, but another theory holds it got its name because of its plentiful wild horses. Alternatively "Komagome" could be the Japanese corruption of a Korean name originally given the area by early immigrants from the peninsula. We should feel at home in Komagome.

Tetsuji was honest from the start: he was exclusively attracted to foreign men, which made him a *gaisen*, though the use of the word embarrassed him. He was different, though, from the others like him in Ni-chōme. He did not desire a big house in San Francisco with an older lover to pay the bills, or someone who could provide the white masculinity he might have felt deprived of. But I was no different from the other foreigners who also roamed these bars. I left Tetsuji crying the day I departed Japan to return to America, and I guess I was glad to be rid of him. He was only one of a million. Had I ever said such things to his face? Warned him of what had been bound to happen? Of course not. Even Pinkerton was braver. Why was it that I respected Tetsuji so little?

> Rich: You know, if we took precautions . . .
> Saul: If what? What? You always do that.
> Rich: I don't know.
> Saul: Would you like to?[1]

Later that night I think about a real-life hospital, the one in Komagome. There is a room there, I have heard, with six beds. Komagome is the only hospital, and those beds the only beds, reserved for AIDS patients anywhere in Japan. It is my imaginative home away from home, the place I think I might end up. I have already been admitted in my exploratory fantasies. I speculate about who my "roommates" might be, what we would say to each other when the nurses and doctors leave the room; what they would think of a foreigner in their midst.

Jane lives not far from Komagome, and I take advantage of a visit to her apartment one day to walk around it. It is a very big hospital. But somewhere, on one of the floors, there is a small room.

May 1981.   The flight got in to Hong Kong on time, and the hotel van took us to our room high over Kowloon. Tokyo is hot, but Hong Kong is a blast furnace even at night. Our suite, as big as my entire apartment and several times that of Tetsuji's little place, was ice cold with air-conditioning. I pulled back the curtains and we stood there looking at the bay and then Victoria beyond it: at an Asia that was also English and therefore a place where we might think the two of us, men who were in love despite the abyss of everything, might belong.

I stripped him of clothes, still damp from sweat, and started kissing the back of his neck. He became embarrassed that someone might see him naked despite the fact we were dozens of stories high in the air. I interrupted his mumbling to lead him to the bathroom, again an immense expanse of space unlike anything we were used to back in Japan. I leaned him up against the edge of the double-sink counter, put my arms around his chest, and admired his body in the huge mirror we faced. It was lean, muscular, and totally smooth except for his thick bushy pubic hairs. I was amazed how good-looking he is. There is no needless body fat, no blemish or sign of age. His eyes are perfect dark pools surrounded with light, and his mouth is beautiful, like a woman's. Next to him my pale skin and oddly arranged muscles look ludicrous. Why doesn't he revolt, throw me off of him, tell me this is no good, go find himself another beautiful man whose beauty would be his own, and so form a perfect symmetry?

I reached down and stroked his penis, played with his testicles, teased his navel with an index finger moistened with spit. When he was ready he let me know by arching his back and pushing his buttocks hard up against me. I worked my dick into him from behind. As we fucked in front of the mirror I watched his face relax as he started to enjoy being penetrated. His own cock got hard and flapped with a soft thud against the sink every time I pushed in deep. I enjoyed watching him, nearly full-length in the glass, being taken by a nearly invisible lover who stood exactly behind him, and thus out of view. For the first time in many months we ejaculated simultaneously, me inside him, and he, groaning his pleasure in two languages, onto the marble countertop of this five-star hotel's bathroom vanity. Asian and American sperm, spilt shamelessly all over real estate that empires both English and Japanese have ruled or (for a few more years) do still.

Years later I will be in Tokyo one November for a conference. I am in my minuscule business hotel room, the cheapest I could find, and I am sick. This little room, oppressive suddenly in its claustrophobic limits, concentrates my symptoms. I have the flu or something like it: a fever, aches all over my body, swollen glands. Except for the day when I have to give my talk, I lie in my little bed, popping hundred-yen coins into the TV at its foot. The NHK news tells me that a male patient being treated for AIDS-related disorders at Komagome Hospital has hanged himself to death in his room. He used the sash from his bathrobe. Gee, I think, he must have had a private room. That's odd. Or just maybe, it occurs to me, his five roommates looked the other way. Or helped.

"Such tragedies end as quickly as they begin," wrote Lafcadio Hearn of his year of cholera. "The bereaved, so soon as the law allows, remove their pathetic belongings, and disappear; and the ordinary life of the street goes on, by day and by night, exactly as if nothing particular had happened."[2]

That night Jane and I part back at the train station, now deserted except for the few drunken salary men catching the last trains home. I toy with the idea of inviting her back to Mejiro with me. It's late, and my place is almost walking distance, while hers is quite a trip from here. But the mood does not seem right. The play we had just seen was no romantic comedy. It was about two men, one dying, who make love not out of desire but out of a memory that might be rehearsed one final time, a eulogy more than a passion.

May. Kuwahara Eimatsu, a member of the Diet who is also a medical doctor, gives a speech on the topic of AIDS, which he attributes to *furii sekkusu*, "free sex." Because of social and familial prejudice, he says, AIDS victims want to be isolated; perhaps it's time to build them "special facilities." Then again, Dr. Kuwahara muses, now may be the time to rethink euthanasia— AIDS victims have lost the will to live, he tells me.

Kuwahara belongs to the Clean Government Party, zealously dedicated to sanitation.

AIDS CARRIERS SIMILAR TO COCKROACHES, EXPERT SAYS

In an apparent slip of the tongue [Shiokawa Yuichi], the head of the Health and Welfare Ministry's AIDS surveillance committee, compared people suffering from the disease to cockroaches.[3]

Just a few days after going to *As Is* with Jane, Ben and I are back in the same part of town to see the David Cronenberg remake of *The Fly*. Jeff Goldblum, the brilliant scientist, is "infected" with genetic material from an insect and slowly turns into a monster. Unlike the original, this eighties version has steamy, close-up sex. Goldblum's lover Geena Davis is horrified when she becomes pregnant with his mutant child.

Walking out of the movie house with Ben, my hands are trembling. I feel light-headed and my stomach is churning. This movie would never have been remade without AIDS. It is a Hollywood classic retrofitted for the age of retroviruses. It never would terrify audiences unless they worried that each of their sexual contacts is an infectious gamble, a toss of the epidemiological dice. Ben goes yeah, yeah. Just enjoy the fuckin' movie, he says. I like Ben, but this is where we part company.

> Rich: If we're careful. Do you want to?
> Saul: I'd love to. What do you think?
> Rich: I think it'd be okay.
> Saul: What'll we do?
> Rich: I don't know. Something safe.[4]

Vermin everywhere. Insects from cockroaches to flies. Feasting on carcasses. I'd always liked horror films until now, when Hollywood fantasies have begun to overlap with memories of dying friends, and my own privately financed fantasies. Flesh-eating parasites may be the very next opportunistic problem we are told to worry about.

I choose to walk home, to enjoy the quiet balmy late night and think about Hoffman's play. When I get home, the time difference is perfect for calling Dan. I do, but he is not home. Perhaps he has already gone to work, and is busy translating the laws of the universe into formulae that only he and his kind can understand.

For centuries we have been eating each other in orgies of narcissistic pleasure. In 1776 Ueda Akinari told the story well. *Robbed of his bright jewel, shorn of this garland in his hair by a sudden storm, the abbot wept till the tears ran dry and cried aloud till his voice failed him.* Sex with Dan is sex that consumes us whole. *In his extreme grief he could not bring himself to burn the body and bury the ashes.* Our bodies beside each other, what difference marks where I end and he begins? *He spent whole days with his face pressed against the boy's, clutching at his dead hand, and in the end went stark mad.* Tetsuji's body, while smaller and darker, is still my body in its lines and angles and warmth. *He began to disport himself as he had when his beloved was alive and well, and since he could not bear to watch the flesh decay, he fell to eating what was left, even licking the bones, until at last he had devoured everything.*[5] In its desire, its need to be someone else's, my lovers' flesh devours my own.

Unidentified Shadowing Object. Luchiano has but one wish. "There's no place to die, wherever I go. I need something I can depend on. It doesn't have to be a person. A camel or a rock or a cactus would do." She thought to herself that she wanted to know she was still alive by conveying her own body heat, her breath, her pulse, her sweat, and her saliva. Luchiano wants to give her own body up to another, or conversely, devour that of another.

Hong Kong is so far from Tokyo. Suddenly Tetsuji and I were in a place where neither belonged, where none of our languages worked well, where neither of us looked like a native. We are both former colonial masters of this bit of rocky coast and at the same time two lovers whose love is both the rationale of empire and its challenge.

May. *Rizu rainichi!* Elizabeth Taylor in Japan! A weekly magazine puts Liz's story first. She's here to talk rich Japan into coughing up some capital to help with AIDS research. And to sell her perfume.

While in town, a television journalist Tamaru Misusu asks her: "Weren't you worried that you had AIDS yourself when your friend Rock Hudson died?"[6] Liz replies: I know how the infection spreads. I have no reason to think I have it. Liz might have added: And how about you, Misusu?

May 1981. Tetsuji and I did not speak much on the flight back to Tokyo. We were tired after three days of sightseeing and screwing. Nearly all the passengers were other Japanese also returning after this brief break away from work. Tetsuji was asked by the Japanese people sitting next to us to take their photo with an impossibly complicated camera, but fortunately my white skin spared me from similar requests. What Japanese would ask a foreigner a favor, or even think he could understand the request? Tetsuji did not mind helping his countrymen celebrate their little sojourn away. He was in fact glad to oblige. I think: yes, he is Japanese, isn't he. In so many ways he will always be closer to these strangers than he will ever be to me. An American stewardess who looks like Candice Bergen asks me if I'd like a copy of the *South China Post*, and I say yes, sure.

"We have done scant justice to the reasonableness of cannibalism," Ruth Benedict told us near the start of her career, and shortly after meeting Margaret. "There are in fact so many and such excellent motives possible to it that mankind has never been able to fit all of them into one universal scheme, and has accordingly contrived various diverse and contradictory systems the better to display its virtues."[7]

Unidentified Shadowing Object.   Luchiano thought she could depend on Doctor Sasakawa, but he spurns her. For months she tailed him, tried to get him to fall in love, demanded he treat her with the same tenderness she felt for him. The doctor feels nothing but pity and disgust for this mangled, infected transsexual. And so Luchiano, out of love or out of revenge, does something to guarantee they will be always together anyway. She puts her teeth into his arm, draws his blood, and leaves a tiny bit of her own.

> After he was bitten on his arm, the carefully ordered world he had maintained until then was reduced to tatters. The AIDS virus destroyed not only his immune system of his physical body, but that of his reasoning and character. How, for example, would have Sasakawa answered this question before he was bitten?
> "Which terrifies you more, nuclear war or AIDS?"
> No doubt he would have said "nuclear war," since he thought AIDS had nothing to do with him. But now he would answer this way:
> "I look forward to both of them."[8]

"A comparison of the degree of fright and the location of the persons interviewed," writes a study of the panic incited by Orson Welles' 1939 *War of the Worlds* broadcast, "suggests that the listening situation of those who were within possible range of immediate danger was different from that of persons somewhat farther removed."[9] Social psychology, a very insightful science. Who could have guessed? That those of us at risk, who are "within possible range of immediate danger," might be different from those of us who are not?

Halloween 1962.   It was cold and very wet. The rain drenched my brother and I under the single bed sheet we jointly wore as a two-headed ghost. I remember my mother driving us from one of our aunts' houses to the next for candy and apples that dark night, as she tried to give us the Halloween we were used to back in Connecticut. But it was not the same. We were chilled to our bones, and we did not know our aunts or cousins very well. But we did know that the President had said something that had my mother frightened, and so we were frightened, too.

Halloween 1984.   It was also cold and wet, as most Halloweens in the Pacific Northwest are. The big party that year was at the Seattle Aquarium, where thousands of gay men in great ghoulish attire or horrible drag would converge, ostensibly for an AIDS benefit, but in truth for the sheer fun of pretending on the one night pretending is required. My date went as a 747 jumbo jet plane crash. Very Seattle. I forget what I was. Maybe the Space Needle with a gorilla climbing up it. It was a costume so good that I did use it again for several years. The look was timeless, for a time. I don't remember being frightened of anything back then, but by 1984 I must have been. Seattle is very far from Cuba, but not so far from Haiti.

But when the hush of the night was at its deepest, there noiselessly entered a Shape, vague and vast; and in the same moment Muso found himself without power to move or speak. I don't think that Halloween should be a night for everyone to dress up like our divas or starlets or celebrity fag hags. *He saw that Shape lift the corpse, as with hands, and devour it, more quickly than a cat devours a rat—beginning at the head, and eating everything: the hair and the bones and even the shroud.* We are meant to be Dracula, a witch, skeletons, or vampires. *And the monstrous Thing, having thus consumed the body, turned to the offerings, and ate them also.* We are meant to be frightened and frightening that one night of the year. *Then it went away, as mysteriously as it had come.*[10] The rest of the year it's all a big mistake. We don't really want your blood.

"But I must tell you one thing still concerning that island," wrote Marco Polo of Japan, "that, if the natives take prisoner an enemy who cannot pay a ransom, he who hath the prisoner summons all his friends and relations, and they put the prisoner to death, and then they cook him and eat him, and they say there is no meat in the world so good."[11]

Lafcadio Hearn was born on the Greek island of Lefkas, one of the Ionians, in 1850. He was the son of an Anglo-Irish surgeon major and a local woman named Rosa. He would be haunted by Greece all his life, though he left it at age two never to return. He always felt, as he put it, of a "meridional race": part of that Sotadic Zone so named by Sir Richard Francis Burton, whom Lafcadio would come to admire. "An Oriental," he would call himself, "by birth and half by blood."[12]

Sir Charles Napier, colonial master of Karachi and one of the great personal influences on Sir Richard, also had children by a Greek woman.

The desire to miscegenate was apparently rife in the Empire. Could it have been that the English masters had two natures to procreate? Sperm not spilt, but profitably invested: not to be wasted on cold marble countertops.

> Our generation thought, in all its innocence, that all diseases were curable, just as we thought until recently that there would be no more conventional wars, only nuclear conflicts, technological wars launched by push button and waged for a mere few hours between experts.[13]

In one of his writings Hearn tells the "queer tale" of a young girl who had a test for her prospective suitors. "With goblin gestures," he writes, "she wrung an arm from the body, wrenched it in twain, and squatting down, began to devour the upper half. Then, flinging to her lover the other half, she cried to him, '*Eat, if thou lovest me! This is what I eat!*'"[14]

The way to Ben's house leads down a long alley, and so I see it at least twice a day: a large bulletin board maintained by the local neighborhood office. Its notices are normally restricted to letting residents know what days the garbage is collected. But in the spring of 1987 a large poster covers almost the entire board. It shows the four main Japanese islands outlined in black. The spot where Tokyo should be projects out, as if a spotlight, and forms the map of another country: my own, a most ungainly shape. But within the crudely drawn contours of the United States loom the large, solid black roman letters **A I D S**. And the simple caption for me and my neighbors? *Eizu kara mamorō*, or "Let's Protect Ourselves from AIDS." Too late, folks.

Hearn, who because of his Greek mother would claim to be an Oriental by both birth and blood, wondered whether the Celts and the Mongolians were in fact racial relatives, with the Greeks in the middle. His birthplace was a land where he was meant to come from, if never to return. To his brother he wrote: "Whatever there is good in me . . . came from that dark-race soul of which we knew so little."[15] He ended his days in Japan, living as fully a Japanese as he could (and as they would allow) in perhaps the last nation in the world to believe it is pure and free of the baneful contagion of foreign blood.

A childhood accident left Lafcadio blind in his left eye, a disability that he riled against his entire life. He had had troubles with his own father, and so he can be numbered among our Greeks Famous and Infamous alike.

*   *   *

May.   Jerry's friend Michael is visiting, not just for his box of dextran sulphate but to be a tourist. He travels everywhere now, keeping his credit cards charged to the limit; he lives, as we kid him, "like a rich white woman." Michael moved back to Boston, having given up on San Francisco—"the worst weather," he says—but in fact he blames the city for his diagnosis. This month—"the best weather," we tell him—he has come to Japan.

Hearn came to Tokyo in 1890, and would eventually die there. The boy born "Paddy" and who took the Greek name Lafcadio as a young man died as Koizumi Yakumo, a Japanese subject. His obituary in the New York *Sun* would report that he had "formed some sort of domestic relations with a native." In the 1980s the papers would probably have referred instead to his "longtime companion." Some of us not born in Greece of Irish fathers, or who even do not travel to Japan, have also refashioned ourselves, taken new names, changed who we are. And not just on the last night of our Octobers.

Strolling in Harajuku, I point out to Michael the young religious proselytizers who stop passersby with promises of happier love lives and, of course, longevity. Michael's interest is piqued, and only half-jokingly shoots back, "I'll give anything a try."

I have my own visitor. Randy, a lover of mine many years ago, is here for a two-week stay. Randy's last boyfriend tested positive shortly after they broke up and now Randy is scared both for him and himself. He has a daughter from an early marriage to worry about. But he does not talk about any of this after the first brief report. I am not good at these talks, either, so I am relieved. Years later, he and I will have the full exchange we avoid now.

"Now the sky is blue down to the horizon," wrote Lafcadio Hearn on his arrival in Japan, "the air is a caress of spring. I go forth to wander through the queer old city."[16]

One Sunday Randy, Michael, Jerry, Jaime, and I go out for brunch. It is a beautiful spring day, and we are still wandering through Harajuku, the queer new city. I run into an acquaintance named Scott, a Cornell graduate student in Tokyo to work on his dissertation, but who has also decided to dress as a woman for the entire year he is here. Today, and it being Harajuku, he is in a simple Comme des Garçon black shift with open-toed sandals by Plantation. It's a political statement, he explains to Michael.

We sit outside at a café popular with gay men. Randy is a playwright, and Michael has theater connections. The two, though meeting for the first time, instantly fall into an animated conversation. Michael will be dead soon, but I later discover that he and Randy kept in touch until the end by both phone and letter. I imagine that I know what they said to each other, but of course I do not.

Hearn, dark of complexion and adorned with gold earrings, was believed to be descended, according to one biographer, from a "wayward, passionate sexuality."[17] He never believed he fit in anywhere, though Japan at times came close. I once thought I belonged here, too, though our own twentieth-century plague would make me wonder just how honest I had ever been with myself; or just how much my urge to identify with was in fact an imperative to dominate over.

> Saul: We'll think of something.
> Rich: Close the curtain.
> Saul: Do you think we should?
> Rich: Well, we can't do it like this.
> Saul: Right.
> Rich: Right.
> Saul: What if someone comes in?
> Rich: So what?
> Saul: Right.[18]

"He is fortunate indeed, " Auschenbach learned in Venice, "if, as sometimes happens, the disease, after a slight *malaise*, takes the form of a profound unconsciousness, from which the sufferer seldom or never rouses."[19] At the very beginning, I had such a friend, someone who took to his bed after years of this and that, and in two weeks was dead. He did not have AIDS because as yet we had no such thing.

> We thought we had finished with those medieval epidemics that once wiped whole cities off the map (like San Francisco, which has lost more inhabitants to AIDS than to all the wars waged during the city's history). Just when we had counted on being able to leave everything to the professionals and their technological arsenals, we're stunned to discover that we must fight as in the old days, with not only our own courage and personal resources to fall back on in the end. It's a duel with the Angel of Death, out on the narrow gangplank of the human immune system, not an exchange of long-range missiles.[20]

The house I live in is in fact not only a house, nor are Ben and I the sole occupants. The back half of it functions as a dormitory, and it is inhabited entirely by, we guess, Filipinas. Maybe they are students, although I am sure my Japanese neighbors think otherwise. We pass and greet each other with the universal "Hi," but we never really speak, much less socialize: gender, race, class, national origin, everything separates us. Or does it? *Eizu kara mamorō.* We are alike now, in the year of Japan's AIDS panic. Carriers of contagion, you below and us above but equally infused with a plague that our own cultures blame, in turn, other foreigners for. (Subic Bay boys out for a good time, Haitian refugees clinging to rafts.) Maybe we should stop in that alley one day and talk. Maybe we should take that sign down, or at least deface it with words from our own languages that we will understand and they will not. Here, we are one.

Hearn believed the Japanese, like himself, to be an amalgam of races, and therefore of characteristics. Underneath their "charming multiple coverings," he theorized, "there remains the primitive clay, hard as iron; kneaded perhaps with all the mettle of the Mongol, all the dangerous suppleness of the Malay."[21]

Did Arthur Waley, born Arthur David Schloss in Tunbridge Wells to Jewish parents in 1889, fit in anywhere either? He once would have been called an Oriental, too. A privileged education and those Bloomsbury friends could not have made up for a family tree with roots far from the English soil he seldom left. What was it like, to stay so still and prosper where his people were newcomers? And to dedicate himself to Oriental literatures, on whose pages were marked a myriad differences he transformed so well into the familiar? Waley told us little about his life, so we can only guess about that; and so other things, too.

I took my pill on the following days this month: the first, the fifth, the ninth, the thirtieth, the seventeenth, the twenty-first, and the twenty-fifth and the twenty-ninth.

Hearn might have felt at home in Japan because he was short. *"His appearance was forbidding,"* would say the obituary, *"if not actually repulsive."* He may have been an Irishman, but he never cared for Ireland. *"Only about five feet tall, with one eye totally blind and the other so disabled that he had to hold papers within an inch in order to decipher them."* Neighbors were frightened of him as a child, and dubbed him a "Devil's boy." ". . . *always ill-dressed, unkempt, slovenly; with the face of a weasel and the manners of an oaf.*" But the stories of the Irish fairies with which he grew up would become the Japanese ghosts he taught us all about. *"He was nonetheless one of the most brilliant and picturesque writers of his day."*22

Waley is the greatest translator of Asian literatures ever to have lived. Ruled unfit for service in the First World War, he tackled classical Chinese poetry while working in the Oriental Sub-Department of Prints and Drawings in the British Museum. Soon thereafter, in the 1920s, he added Japanese literature, not just poetry but drama and prose too, to his repertoire. His last work, "Colloquial in the Yu-hsien k'u," was published in 1966, the year of his death. The obituaries, unlike Hearn's, made reference to his great contributions to learning.

Unidentified Shadowing Object.   Dr. Sasakawa thinks again about AIDS and nuclear war.

> He existed in neither the past nor the present. That's just what he had to believe. But whenever he was alone, he inevitably found himself facing the past. He shouldn't do that. The Ken'ichi Sasakawa of the good ol' days and the Ken'ichi Sasakawa whose health was now hovering between life and death were both shadows of himself. What cast the shadow was nowhere to be found. Hiroshima, August 6, 1945. A man sitting in a stairway was enveloped in a gigantic ball of fire and was vaporized in an instant, leaving only his shadow behind. Ken'ichi Sasakawa was very much like that shadow.23

Auschenbach knows the secret. There *is* a plague in Venice, even if the authorities are in denial about it. Auschenbach has his own secret: his desire for the boy. That, however, everyone *knows*.

Both Burton and Waley married, but neither fathered any children. Both led what biographers called "separate domestic lives" from their wives. Their work, we are told, was their true love.

Burton was widely admired as a man's man, a role model for aspiring explorers throughout the Empire, while Waley was the bookish accessory at Bloomsbury dinner parties, where his wit as well as erudition served him well. But both men were explorers of mysteries not necessarily found in African jungles. They were masters of impossible languages, translators of impossible stories, and they poured their own selves into great books they brought home as imperial booty. Is there something about being a translator that especially appeals to us homosexuals? Especially if they translate languages whose very scripts make us wonder: what do those odd marks and strokes hide from us? And yet: what is it about *Arabian Nights* and *A Hundred and Seventy Chinese Poems* that also strikes us as so similar? In what they yearn for as texts in English, if not in what they once said in Arabic or Chinese? Foreign languages, clandestine codes, magic writing. Words, like some lives themselves, that never give up their secrets.

May 1981. Our first night in Hong Kong Tetsuji and I decided to take the funicular up to Victoria's Peak. Surrounded by Chinese, talking it seemed, as loudly as they could, we held hands surreptitiously. The heat had abated somewhat, and I was really enjoying where we were, with the lights of the city and of the boats in the harbor strung out like pearls below us. Tetsuji and I spoke English to each other while we were on vacation, something we had never done in Tokyo. Suddenly I realized that Tetsuji seemed like a different person to me, here on the South China Sea and speaking the fluent English he had mastered through a succession of foreign lovers. I had not realized how important language was to the way we had always related. Now it was clearer, as we translated our affection for each other into a language so much a part of me, and so finally remote a thing for him.

Burton and Hearn traveled the world. Waley seldom left England, and never went East. Holed up first in his office at the British Library, and later in his study, he concentrated on his Oriental poets. But his first wife, the older and worldly Beryl de Zoete, often went abroad without him. She would send interesting people she had met back to stay with him, including once a deserter from the French Foreign Legion.

"Fearing to become a laughing stock to the world," wrote Po Chü-I in the last lines of a poem translated by Waley, "I choose a place that is unfrequented by men."[24]

Eventually Jane and I would go to bed together, but only to sleep and only because Ben and I lacked an extra futon for guests. She was leaving Japan a few months earlier than I, and after moving out of her Komagome apartment needed a place to stay on her last night in Tokyo before boarding her flight to Hong Kong, where her husband would join her for a few days' vacation.

I made dinner that night for her and for Ben and his Japanese girlfriend of the moment. We were comfortably drunk by the time we went to my room. The thought crossed my mind to inch closer to her, let my arm fall across her back, see if she was as interested as I guessed I might be. But something held me back, even as it refused to let me surrender the idea quickly. I think: she's sure to reject me. I'm gay, she'd worry about AIDS, why complicate things. Or worse: perhaps she would laugh at me.

"And my whole life, every white man's life in the East," wrote George Orwell, "was one long struggle not to be laughed at."[25] This is also what men feel before women: or at least how I felt with Jane that night. The other sex, the other world: does everything conspire to turn us back into what we fear and what we always suspected we are?

Hearn would travel to, and live in, many places before discovering his final home in Japan. *Young boys—yellow and brown little fellows—run in naked, and swim out to pointed rocks that jut up black above the bright water.* Time spent in New Orleans inspired him to go to the French West Indies, where the charms of Martinique's island life entranced him. *They climb up one at a time to dive down.* He might, one guesses, have settled there and never gone further west to Asia. *Poised for the leap upon the black lava crag, and against the blue light of the sky, each lithe figure, gilded by the morning sun, has a statuesqueness and a luminosity impossible to paint in words.*[26] But there was still something not found that he was seeking.

"Impossible to translate," Hearn might just as well have said. To take something that makes sense in one place and force it to mean the same elsewhere. There is at base an idea there akin to the erotic, or perhaps I should say the homoerotic, at least in places where our desires are left in foreign languages: ancient scribbling on cave walls that others once understood but are forbidden to know now. I am sure that Burton and Waley loved their wives, and Hearn his entire family: but we will never know just how much of that love was our modern gloss of now lost, inscrutable languages.

> Without fear of exaggerating facts, I can venture to say that the muscular development of the workingmen here is something which must be seen in order to be believed;—to study fine displays of it, one should watch the blacks and half-breeds working naked to the waist. . . . At a tanning-yard, while I was watching a dozen blacks at work, a young mulatto with the

mischievous face of a fawn walked by, wearing nothing but a clout (*lantcho*) about his loins; and never, not even in bronze, did I ever see so beautiful a play of muscles.[27]

Waley married his second wife, Alison Grant Robinson, a month before he died. She was dedicated to his well-being and he to hers. On the day he leaves Tokyo, Randy makes me promise that, should I ever leave Dan, I will think about going back to him. Randy had had a chance to take me with him years ago, one winter morning in New Haven before he drove off to Dallas to make a new life for himself. He chose not to, but since then he has come to imagine that I am the one meant to see him into his middle, and then old, age. Maybe we'll marry a month before his death, or mine, years in the future. No children left behind to tend our memories, perhaps, but then, our work, like that of explorers and translators, has its own stubborn permanency.

Rich: So what are you waiting for? This is a little scenario Jane and I have rehearsed many times, but of course we will not stage it tonight. *Saul: I'm scared. Rich: So am I.* Sharing my narrow futon, I stroke her side and tell her funny stories. *Do you think we should?* In time we fall silent for a minute, after which I hear the sigh that signals sleep is near. *Saul: God, I want to.*[28] I think: this must not be unlike nights that Sir Richard had with his wife, or Arthur with his. Desires are there, but they seep out of us and rise, slowly like smoke, into the hot night air that stirs little above us, and that by morning will be gone.

JUNE

Syntax, Et Cetera

On the sixteenth the government announces the following statistics: 285 Japanese known to be infected; 246 men, eight women, one unknown; nineteen male homosexuals, 217 hemophiliacs, fourteen "men who have had sexual contact with other men," five other or unknown.

These categories are peculiar. They remind me of Borges' fabulous Chinese encyclopedia, of the "laughter that shattered" as one reader, a gay man now dead of AIDS, wrote. An encounter "breaking up all the ordered surfaces and all the planes with which we are accustomed," the Dead Gay Man said (and where we pause to ask: who is "we"?), "to tame the wild profusion of existing things, and continuing long afterwards to disturb and threaten with collapse our age old distinction between the Same and the Other."[1] *And you were thinking all the while: these are only numbers. Why are you so upset?*

The encyclopedia that tells us animals are divided into the categories of "(a) belonging to the Emperor, (b) embalmed, (c) tame, (d) sucking pigs, (e) sirens, (f) fabulous," and "*et cetera* (category 'l')." What might this same Chinese encyclopedia's entry be for "HIV-positive people" be? Perhaps the Japanese government could tell us. What is the difference between "male homosexuals" and the "men who have had sexual contact with other men"? And in a country as scrupulous with details as Japan, just how does one manage to become "unknown"? Or, stranger still, "other"?

These are words that the government came up with out of some kind of taxonomical logic we can only guess at; out of some kind of agenda we should appreciate. They are all, you will note, "Japanese," and so perhaps we can be glad they are unconcerned with those of us not.

At the beginning of E. M. Forster's *A Passage to India*, Dr. Aziz arrives at Hamidullah's house just as he and Mahmoud Ali are debating whether it is possible to be friends with an Englishman. Hamidullah thinks yes, Mahmoud Ali no. Perhaps in their own island country, he suggests, but certainly not here. Aziz will try very hard to prove Hamidullah correct and the reward for his efforts will be a truth for some of us, if not all.

Have I ever really had a Japanese friend? Yes, of course, scores, I want to say. But it is also true that all of these friendships have had a special quality to them: no less genuine, perhaps, but still somehow filtered through a membrane of translation, a distance placed between us that is part of the friendship itself as well as a constant reminder that we are not the same. Our friendship has borders it will not exceed. This is not the indifference with which we foreigners remain uncounted by the Japanese government, but a kind of garbled and distorted, altogether regrettable, talk across a wide chasm I cannot seem to make go away. Even if I wanted.

Tokyo, June 18.

AIDS A TIME BOMB FOR HOMOSEXUALS IN JAPAN

Slowly, insidiously, in men's "saunas" and other gay sex establishments and in private bedrooms, the AIDS virus is spreading among homosexual men in Japan. . . . Yasushi Fujinami, a tanned, muscular man in his 30s, says AIDS has changed his sex life—but not much. Fujinami, who has had some 150 partners and describes himself as much more promiscuous than average, says the AIDS scare which hit the U.S. in the early 1980s prompted him to avoid sexual encounters with foreigners who arrived recently in Japan.[2]

Jean Cocteau remembers his foreign lover. *He was nineteen and everything about him was in the worst possible taste.* Why such contempt? When he gave this Frenchman so much of what he wanted? *He was called Alfred or Alfredo and spoke an odd kind of French, but I didn't worry about his nationality; he seemed to me to belong to the country of prostitution which has its own patri-*

otism, and possibly this was its language.[3] His language: vocabulary and syntax, a land of its own. The foreign lover, it turns out, had an accent.

Why the word "prostitution"? Because it was that simple or easy? Perhaps, there in the infamous Magreb to which Barthes would return to write about his Japan, that was the language—French, but not quite; love, but not quite—that a Frenchman and his Arab lover had to speak.

Ruth Benedict, maybe with her own life as well as those of the enemy in mind, wrote about sexual mores in Japan. *Tetsuji taught me all the words I know.* "The Japanese do not condemn self-gratification." *My accent would make him laugh, and so I would say them often to him.* "They are not Puritans." *Lying in our room, on disheveled bedding, looking up at the ceiling and practicing idioms.* "They consider physical pleasures good and worthy of cultivation." *Language, which is to say my ugly deformation of his, was part of how we lived.* "They are sought and valued." *My corrupt Japanese.* "Nevertheless, they have to be kept in their place." *His corrupt morals.* "They must not intrude upon the serious affairs of life."[4] *Pittari ne.*

> The passwords used by AIDS patients (KS, PCP, CMV, T4/T8) create a sort of secret society within the gay community, an elite corps that demands respect from their peers, from those for whom, in a way, they have taken up arms. A new secret fraternity of signs, a freemasonry of codes, which sometimes unites us even with our doctors.[5]

Barthes wrote from the Magreb: "In Japan—that country I am calling Japan—sexuality is in sex, not elsewhere, not elsewhere; in the United States, it is the contrary; sex is everywhere, except in sexuality."[6] But in that country that I call Japan, sexuality is not only in sex, it is elsewhere, too. It is in the way I flirt in the Japanese language with handsome strangers, using both my fluency and my lack of same to both attract the men in whom I am interested and to mark my difference from them. In the United States, sex for me can never be an effect of my language. There, sexuality is not a thing for which I have words.

> Besides GRID (Gay Related Immune Deficiency), some doctors liked ACIDS, for Acquired Community Immune Deficiency Syndrome, and then others favored CAIDS, for Community Acquired Immune Deficiency Syndrome. The CDC hated GRID and preferred calling it "the epidemic of

immune deficiency." The "community" in other versions, of course, was a polite way of saying gay.[7]

Death in Venice. Auschenbach cannot understand the words that Tadzio speaks, or even get his name right. TadzioTetsujiTadzioTetsujiTadzioTetsuji.

Fielding, soon to be a traitor to his race, learns early upon his arrival in India that he can have the company of Indians or that of Englishwomen, but not both. "The two wouldn't combine," writes Forster. "Useless to blame either party, useless to blame them for blaming one another."[8] And so what happened (in real life, not novels) when we blame each other anyway? For being homosexual, or foreign, or sick, or just not us. Is that a way we can approach, initially with a denial, becoming one another?

AIDS. ARC. HIV. PWA. PCP. KS. STD. VD. CDC. PCB. TB. AZT. These are acronyms everyone uses now in addition to the older ones that, unraveled, tell stories we had wanted to keep to ourselves: FOD for a "Friend of Dorothy," PTM for a "Princess Tiny Meat," and of course, here in Tokyo, HCN.

In a couple of years Ōe Kenzaburō will publish a novel entitled *The Tower of Healing*, an image borrowed from Yeats and his belief in immortality. *The Tower of Healing* is science fiction. It opens ten years after THE GREAT DEPARTURE, which is how those left behind on earth refer to the exodus of a select few to another planet to avoid the terrible nuclear, ecological, and epidemiological disasters that have beset earth.

After the death of her parents in a local nuclear war, Ritsuko, the young woman who is the novel's main character, thought of working as a prostitute despite her fear of AIDS, now rampant around the globe. Raped repeatedly while kept hostage in Europe by a band of renegades, she is sure she is HIV+ (she comforted herself with the thought: everyone who fucks me is also "ending his own life"). Her fears, however, are wholly her own until she begins to have sex with Hajime, one of the Chosen who have inexplicably returned to earth. She insists he wear a condom despite Hajime's insistence that all the Chosen are now immortal. If you're worried, Hajime tells her, why don't you just go get tested?

When did you *seroconvert*? When were you *exposed*? When did you get your *diagnosis*? *Itsugoro byōki ni natta*?

                                        *   *   *

Rudyard Kipling was born in Bombay, the Beautiful Harbor, in 1865. Although most famous for his stories of his native India, he also traveled to
Japan twice, first to Nagasaki for a month in 1889 when he was twenty-three,
and then for two months three years later. In one of his letters to the English
press back in India, he wrote that he "preferred to go to the tea garden and
lie upon a mat studying Japanese, which would be a fine language were it
not for its giggles."[9]

Kipling got that right, if not much else. He viewed Japan through an
Indian lense, and saw little of the grandeur or dignity he, like others of the
Raj, so readily ascribed to India. Why did Japan seem so silly to Kipling?
Why am I so serious about it now? What is it that Kipling did not want to
become here, but that I do?

Barthes' lexicon: "To dream: to know a foreign language and not yet to
understand it."[10] This Frenchman, not the first, had to travel to the Extreme
Orient to dream, to hear sounds and see signs devoid of all meaning but an
aesthetic purity; to find young men for whom he was no celebrity but just a
man who, father-like, doted on their own youthful purity. Japan was more
than anything *not France*, a place where not even the bad French spoken by
Cocteau's Alfred or Alfredo could be heard: happy sex, for Barthes, in a place
where words were everything because they could not mean anything.

> "Hajime, you don't know what those of us left behind on earth for
> the past ten years now do about AIDS, do you? It's the law that anyone
> caught by the authorities and found to be infected has to wear an 'AIDS
> badge' on his or her shirt. And they were about to pass a law that would
> have tattooed our forearms, just like Jews in Germany during the Second
> World War."
> "But that's . . . What about human rights? . . ."
> "Human rights? What about human rights when you and the other
> Chosen left the rest of us behind?"[11]

Time Bomb
> "In my opinion we don't need to worry about 'safe sex' . . . homosexuals in
> Japan are not a high-risk group," says Fujinami, citing the low number of
> reported AIDS patients here . . . They have fewer partners, and practice
> sexual intercourse—the most risky sexual act—less frequently, the com-
> mentators say. Some add that Japanese gay men are protected by the in-

sularity of their society. Japanese who prefer foreign partners do not enjoy sex with Japanese, and vice versa, they say.[12]

Japan was once known as The Third Kingdom of Merry Dreams. It had a profound effect on Kipling, though he misunderstood nearly everything.

The first three chapters of *Kim*, which Edward Said calls "an overwhelmingly male novel,"[13] begin with stanzas from his Japan-inspired poem, "Buddha at Kamakura."

Whether we waltz in Kensington. When Kipling boarded a ship in Calcutta headed for Japan, he was a young and unmarried man. *Whether we dance in Ispahan.* He sailed, however, in the company of a good friend. *London Paris or Timbuctoo, Cairo, Suez or Kalamazoo.* Professor Hill had an American wife, as would Kipling eventually. *Love is as old as Fuji-san!*[14] Rudyard called Mrs. Hill by her nickname, Ted.

It was Forster who was the homosexual and not Kipling, though some have wondered. It is, after all, *A Passage to India* and not *Kim* that is full of women; and not just English women, but the absent Indian one, too.

When is it in *A Passage to India* that Aziz and Fielding make love, as much as love between two men is possible in this novel? In their imperial century? Is it when Aziz lets Fielding see the precious photograph of his late wife? His most valuable possession, his deepest desire? "No woman could ever take her place," Aziz once swore, "a friend would come nearer to her than another woman."[15]

Forster needed his women to make his novel this queer, just as others of us have needed the East or some other direction to make ourselves so as well. Is this a sign of how an Orientalism can be a story about ourselves? Or: a story about other stories.

Unidentified Shadowing Object. "There are all kinds of people in this life," reflects Luchiano. "Rich and poor, sadists and masochists, swindlers and arsonists, royalty and faggots, black people and white people and yellow people and red people. . . . When everyone catches AIDS, they're all the same."[16]

"Although recognized as intelligent and formidable creatures," Lafcadio Hearn wrote, "Occidentals were not generally regarded as quite human; they were thought of as more closely allied to animals than to mankind. They had hairy bodies of queer shape; their teeth were different from those of men;

their internal organs were also peculiar; and their moral ideas were those of goblins."[17]

Kipling called people like himself who traveled the world "the Outside Men."[18] In Japanese the common word for a foreigner is *gaijin*, which can literally mean the same thing. Roland Barthes would not have minded being called this, despite its often derogatory connotations. But more to the point, he did not care what this or any other Japanese word meant, which made him the antithesis of homosexual Orientalists like me, whose work begins with philology, the love of words.

Barthes went to Japan three times in 1966 and 1967. "To live in a country where one doesn't know the language," he learned, "and to live audaciously, outside the tourist tracks, is the most dangerous of adventures."[19] He believed himself to be Kristeva's Insolent Person; he thought himself finally far enough from Paris and his life there to be "himself"—the most exotic thing, to be sure, that he could have encountered in Tokyo.

Years ago Tetsuji and I knew of a little store down an obscure alley in Tokyo that sold poppers, or *kusuri*, "medicine," as we dubbed it in our private patois. Lots of the names we give things are ironic, perhaps none more so than those we apply to ourselves. Uneasy with the intimacy that the sound of our personal names, unadorned, would have made, he was always "Mr. Tetsuji," and I "Mr. John."

Time Bomb. "Nearly one-third of the men reported sexual contact with foreigners. The report concluded that a 'considerable number' of Japanese homosexual men have suppressed immunological functions, and they are therefore susceptible to the AIDS virus."[20]

"I can say that in writing Japan," wrote Barthes, "I carried out the mission of writing, which was the fulfilment of a desire."[21] To this extent, Barthes' Japan was little different from that of foreign men who preceded him. Pierre Loti (whose holy city of Kyoto was found by an admiring reader, Lafcadio Hearn, to be entirely a product of his imagination) was one. Barthes, too, could think that Japanese rooms can be turned upside down and change not at all; or that a city like Tokyo can at its heart harbor a nothingness, when in fact it is full.

Barthes on Japan was a Barthes dismissed as hopelessly ignorant by a famous American scholar of Japanese literature. But my colleague missed the point. Barthes wrote here, in pages purportedly about Japan, finally the book that would be his true autobiography; a kind of book that some famous scholars, certainly not ignorant, avoid writing out of a fear that strangles the very desires they cannot not admit to us, or even themselves.

My time left in Tokyo short, I work hard. I read stacks of novels, short stories, poems and plays about Hiroshima and Nagasaki. I spend my days sitting under an old and barely functional art conditioner. Years in Seattle have made me useless in the heat. The Japanese words I read now are almost always known to me. I no longer use my dictionaries very much. There are only so many ways to describe the undescribable sound, the light, the blast of hot wind. I read about people who have something new to say but no correspondingly new language to say it in. A very modern problem, I think.

"I know you are fond of Japanese things," wrote Oscar Wilde at the height of his fame, which is to say the eve of his downfall. "Now, do you really imagine that the Japanese people, as they are presented to us in art, have any existence? . . . In fact, the whole of Japan is a pure invention. There is no such country, there are no such people."[22]

   Kipling said, "Never believe anything that Mister Oscar Wilde tells you."[23] But on this point, wouldn't he agree? The Japan of his letters back to the Indian press had to have been some personal phantasm. How else could Asian subjects of the Empire have read of that place and not envied it still?

Andrew Holleran, once a promising novelist but now a traumatized survivor of gay men's fate, has written an essay entitled "Ground Zero." "The bomb seems the best metaphor," Holleran says. " 'Oh,' people say when they learn someone left New York in 1983, 'you got out before the bomb fell.' Well, not really, he wants to reply, the bomb fell several years before that. Only we didn't know it."[24]

   Holleran's choice of metaphor annoys me, but I am tempted myself to make the same connection. Holleran, like those in Hiroshima and Nagasaki decades ago, has been unwittingly exposed to an invisible killer that has crawled inside him and now just sits there waiting. The clock is ticking. I hear it on every page I read. Who was it that picked me to write this book about August, 1945? Now, at this time? Who knew that this much irony would be required? This much empathy, this much fear?

Time Bomb

> Takehiko Komiyama, an official at the Infectious Disease Section of the Health and Welfare Ministry, says there have been no government reports on homosexuals in Japan. Though gay men have been tagged as belonging to a high risk group, he said they had no information on the gay population. ... There are yet no plans to investigate this closet community, and therefore no education campaign targeted at homosexuals, Komiyama said, indicating he did not think AIDS among gays was a problem.[25]

"What I am saying here about haiku," writes Barthes, "I might also say about everything which *happens* when one travels in the country I am calling Japan. For there, in the street, in a bar, in a shop, in a train, something always *happens*."[26] He had to have meant: I hear no talking, at least that I can fathom. Therefore I see for the first time in my life bodies in motion rather than mouths, I take notice of *events* that have not been, as he put it, "already written."

Barthes' French for the italicized *happens* is "advient," a word that implies a love affair, too. In his book Barthes will tell us it is Tokyo's red fire hydrants he is enamored of. But those nocturnal wanderings in a city he is glad stays mysterious suggest he is indeed looking for something to happen. Sex with Tetsuji is also often wordless, though we understand each other's language well enough.

Sir Richard, Lafcadio Hearn, and Arthur Waley all shared a mutual passion for languages. Of the twenty-nine he mastered, Burton would, in fact, call Arabic "his most faithful wife." Why are we so drawn to foreign tongues? A place where we pretend to be other than ourselves by virtue of odd verbs and even stranger syntax: a masquerade.

Barthes, a tourist in Tokyo, needed only a simple lexicon. *Rendezvous yaku-soku.* He required only a little help getting around in Tokyo, down the narrow and unlit alleyways, unmarked with signs in any language. *Tous les deux hutari tomo.* A book published in Japan in Japanese, but nowhere else, features scribbled notes that helpful Host Country Nationals had drawn for him in his search for the gay bars where this older foreigner would be welcome. *Où? doko ni?* The question that Kipling asks in *Kim*, according to Edward Said, is: "Isn't it possible in India to do everything, be anything, go anywhere with impunity?"[27] *Quand? itsu?*[28] Barthes thought of Japan: yes.

*   *   *

"In India two roads lead to preferment," wrote Sir Richard, and one of them was the "study of languages."[29]

I first started my study of Japanese twenty-five years ago at college, while the Vietnam War was still going on. I was in a small class made up in equal parts of recent veterans whose lives had been made Asiatic through government fiat, and homosexuals who would choose Asia (its antiques, or its boys, or its very far distance) as a place in which they could refashion themselves. I was a member of both constituencies, and neither: I had been sent to Vietnam, but to its hospitals as a civilian and not to its jungles as a soldier; and I was a homosexual who did not yet know what that would mean. I kept my identity secret from both the veterans and homosexuals, out of a shame that I had not put my life at risk as had the former, and out of a shame that I was putting my life at risk, as were the latter.

We met each weekday morning, early, in a windowless room where we practiced our Chinese characters silently on the blackboard, our verbal inflections out loud. It was, in hindsight, where I rehearsed what I would become. Professor Ozawa, an aspiring jazz critic forced to teach Japanese to support himself, liked me. But I liked someone else.

One day after class, Dale and I went to the student union and ordered coffee. How do you like class? he asks. Oh fine, I answer, and then we lapse into a silence that lasts a long time in order to say a great deal.

Dale and I would have sex together only for a short while. I was not really his type. But both of us continued to study Japanese, its words and its nuances, for years.

Once, back in the days of the empire, Aziz gave Fielding a sign. *"Blast!"* The Indian doctor has been trying to befriend the English official. *"Anything wrong?"* What is, after all, the meaning of friendship between the colonized and the colonizer? *"I've stamped on my last collar stud."* Can affection ameliorate, even erase, the roles that history determines for us? *"Take mine, take mine."* Or, conversely, is the dream of love between races locked in contentious embrace one way it retains its hold? *"Have you a spare one?"* Or perhaps the attractions between us have nothing to do with the nations that spawn us. *"Yes, yes, one minute."* Mr. Fielding was dressing after his bath when Dr. Aziz called on him. *"Not if you're wearing it yourself."* E. M. Forster's Egyptian lover Mohommed el Adl died in 1922, while he was at work on his Indian novel. *"No, no, one in my pocket."* Are insolent foreigners, who cross borders so brazenly, destined to disappoint? *"Come in with it if you don't mind the unconventionality."*[30]

"The Lacanian subject (for instance) never makes him think of Tokyo; but Tokyo makes him think of the Lacanian subject."[31] Why would that be? Because in Japan language is opaque; and Barthes can make no sense of it that is always *their* sense. And so language materializes just because it is such an obstacle to understanding. It produces, for him and out of his desire, a lover: words that take form, stand tall and straight beside him. Words that emerge from his deepest recesses; words that penetrate to his soul.

After Lafcadio Hearn died in 1904, the New York *Sun* published an article about him entitled "A Strange Career":

> It will surprise no one who knew Lafcadio Hearn at all well to hear that a negro woman in Cincinnati now claims recognition as his widow and seeks to obtain as such a share of the American royalties on his remarkable literary work. Hearn spent several years in the Ohio city, and it is sufficiently notorious that in his purely private and domestic relations he consorted with colored people only. Notwithstanding his extraordinary literary attainments, his profound and varied scholarship, and his brilliant and poetic intellectual equipment, Lafcadio Hearn admitted no member of his own race to genuine intimacy.[32]

Lafcadio Hearn was, I am sure, the queerest straight man ever to write about Japan. He was a great admirer of Kipling, but could never have been like him. Kipling, despite his knowledge of an India he was born into, was always English. But Hearn was so many things, and finally none of them.

Were Western readers of *Kim* all meant to identify with the title character? It is of course impossible not to, to a certain extent: the white boy who lives among the brown, speaking their language but always ready to betray them. But I also identify with the Tibetan holy man, whom Kim both serves and learns from. I can even think of myself as Mahbub Ali, the horse trader who teaches Kim how to spy. And I must also think I am in part Colonel Creighton, who "smiled a queer smile" when he saw that Kim's letter to the lama does not mention him.[33] Did Colonel Creighton love Kim? Or simply see him as an opportunity to further the aims of the empire? By becoming its agent? Of course Creighton loved Kim. How could he not, since Kim was "friend of all the world," and indeed all things to all people.

I am all of Kipling's characters, in this most male of his novels. I can be Kim, who passes between the dark and the light, unsure just where he should alight to stay. I can also be Creighton, the lover of boys like Kim. And even the holy man: a foreigner made foreign twice over, dependent on others and saved, time and time again, by that capacity for simple, foolish trust.

The Empire of Signs.   I have never masqueraded as a Japanese, the way Sir Richard did a Moslem pilgrim, or Kim an Indian. But I have felt Japanese, or as close to being so as I will ever, when I met Oda. He was a young Japanese, originally from Okinawa, who had dark masculine good looks. Oda was not his real name, but one he had taken after moving north. We had seen each other several times in Ni-chōme before that one night, when he was bold enough to follow me out of the bar and into the street.

Le rendezvous yakusoku. He suggested we go into a nearby sushi place open all night long to accommodate the homosexuals frequenting the neighborhood. We drank more beer before moving on to one of the cheap inns that dot Ni-chōme. An elderly woman greeted us enthusiastically at the door and showed us to a small tatami room, where Oda and I stood awkwardly in our stocking feet while she laid out the bedding.

Ici koko ni. We looked at each other, smiling as if we were old friends sharing a joke. I suppose we were. Oda was a figure of some repute in Ni-chōme; and I had been around long enough for all the other regulars to have decided if I was to be on their list, and they on mine.

Ce soir komban. The woman backed out of the room, bowing repeatedly as she wished us a good night's rest.

Aujourd'hui kyo. Oda had a long, lean body, sinewy and strong. He was different in many ways from Tetsuji. His face had the cheekbones of someone whose genes were not wholly of here. He was big, bigger than any Japanese I had ever known, and I decided early on that night that I would not play the foreigner this time, which meant I would let him decide who owned the little space, and shorter time, we would have together.

À quelle heure? nan ji ni? I lowered myself onto him, and let his cock go as deep into me as it wanted. It had been a long time since I'd let a Japanese fuck me. It seemed a rule that we were supposed to be on top. "One of ten Japanese men is extremely effeminate in looks and manners when compared to the average male." I rested my hands on his chest, and rocked first back and forth, then up and down. Oda's muscles rippled as he inched

deeper inside me. "But this is as much of a racial-social as a sexual characteristic." As I felt him expanding even more in me, I thought: *this* is how I'll
become Japanese, this is the way I can be what *they* are, and what I am *not*.
He raised his arms to stroke my chest. "And newcomers should not be too
hasty in hanging tags on milksop types."[34] Locked together, Oda and Treat.
Treat and Oda. He would leave a part of him with me, a piece of Japan that
would seep into my guts and, like the sushi and beer, be sucked up into my
flesh and be me. I was, when all was said and done and screwed, still
on top.

Demain ash/ata. He moved faster, and so did I. When done, I asked
him to teach me words that were Japanese, of a sort, but which I did not
know: words from Okinawa, words from *uchinaguchi*, words that, like those
from English or Chinese, both belonged here in Tokyo and did not. Had
something maybe *happened*? Strange syntax. *Quatre heures. yo ji.*[35]

" 'Why can't we be friends now?' said the other, holding him affectionately.
'It's what I want. It's what you want.' "[36]

The neighborhood in Osaka where I lived in the 1970s was near Tennoji,
an easy subway ride on the Midosuji line to my job near Shinsaibashi, but
in other ways a world apart from the glitz of the city's fanciest shopping
district. Tennoji was a sort of a ghetto, filled with foreigners but few of them
white. It was largely Korean, and thus shunned by many Japanese. The rents
were cheap, and the restaurants, too.

There was one other foreigner there, however, who was neither white
nor Korean. An Indian, I would guess. Tall, dark, regal. We never spoke,
only exchanged glances. Glances that went right through each other, like
knives, but not hostile. We could have become lovers. But no, not yet. Not
there.

"Being a White Man," Said says of Kipling, "was therefore an idea and a
reality."[37] That is what Said also says the Orient itself is, an imaginary as well
as an actual place. That much, I am sure, is true. We all imagine: Orientals
too, for whom I am just as sure their own world is just as virtual, just as real.

We all imagine: homosexuals, too. What makes us inhabit, with so much
strangeness but often joy, that little space where what we make up spills over
into where we are. Somewhere over the rainbow, the Ultimate Expatriate
Experience. A person in the mirror not us, but who we are sure we'll be one
day. Is there a word for that place?

*   *   *

Years later, I would hear about Oda's odd death. He left his Swiss lover Peter, a foreigner of many years in Tokyo, to return to Okinawa where he had secretly kept a wife and child. The story is that he got cancer of the tongue, and died horribly even after half his face had been scooped out by doctors. Little pieces of him detached and disposed of in his native place: a fate that now seemed fair, even fortunate, to me. Tokyo is cold and far from the southern islands, and if I were Oda I would not have wanted to die here either. In any case I, like lots of other men in Tokyo, walk about still carrying little pieces of him within us.

The Japanese language is full of foreign words. So many, in fact, that even those words one thinks are native are only borrowed so long ago that their origins have been forgotten. *Matsu* 'pine,' *take* 'bamboo,' *ume* 'plum': three things that seem so thoroughly Japanese are words that had to have crossed water from China before finding their new old home.

All alien words, whatever their vintage, come into Japanese as nouns. English is lucky: any word can be used as a verb, but not so Japanese. Instead, the English and the Chinese that form so much of what Japan can say loom large and solid, things with mass and weight; inertia or momentum, depending on the sentences within which they dwell.

Homo. Gei. Eizu. Pine, bamboo, plum.

My Japanese sentences are especially dense and heavy, belabored by an American accent and handicapped with a small vocabulary used to do too many things. This is the curse of the nonnative to bear, one might put it; or the gift to the one who sees, now so clearly, how language in fact passes through our fingers like sand, a solid thing that nonetheless flows: like love, one might put it, or a virus that goes just as fast, and just as irrevocably lost to life.

JULY

M. Andrew

Pulp novelist Waku Shunzo publishes a new title this month: *Eizu-gai no renzoku satsujin*, or *A Serial Murderer in the City of AIDS*. The first homocide victim is named Ritsuko.

My old friend Ron is in Tokyo for the summer. He lived in Japan with his Japanese lover in the 1950s, when many gay American men, purged from their military or civilian jobs, decided to try to remain in Japan and make their lives there. Eventually Ron left, but he has an endless number of stories about the young days of well-known people who sit on other branches of our family tree; and about a then more furtive homosexuality that retained, as a consolation, the sublime appeal of the illicit.

I am glad to have Ron here. His company is surprisingly welcome just now. I have many friends in Tokyo, but Ron's companionship is special. He is several decades older than me, but that is a distance which makes our presence together in Tokyo so interesting. He tells me about a Japan I never knew, and I show him around a Tokyo that he could not have imagined. Ron is amazed at how many foreigners he sees in Tokyo in the summer of 1987. It did not used to be like that, he says to me. So, I encourage him, tell me what it used to be like. Tell me about Japan when we had no money, but then things were cheaper; when the customs of the people were exotic,

177

but then it was hard to know what was right to do; when the daily risk was the drinking water, when what we feared were only bacteria and not viruses.

Ritsuko, a prostitute, is killed by a customer who blames her for his positive HIV test. He rapes her first because he wants to lodge his infected sperm inside her. Then he strangles her with an electric guitar string and leaves a label with "AIDS" written on it at the foot of her corpse.

What if there *were* a serial murderer? In one of our own cities of AIDS? It's not so far-fetched an idea: ten years from now, America's attention will be briefly riveted by news reports of a half-Filipino, half-white gay man who kills a string of former lovers across America, until finally one of them is famous enough that the authorities care. He will kill himself in a panic. Why will I, ten years later, feel that I knew Andrew Cunanan? Maybe he was Jesusa's American cousin; or maybe some part of his rage and terror is my own.

Maybe it is because we have lived with a serial murderer in our cities for a long time by 1997, which by then will be more than a third of my entire life. There is a stealthy killer whose epidemiological origins are as ambiguous as Andrew's ethnicity. It has killed my former lovers, too. Perhaps I am oddly comforted by the fact that now we have our own serial killer. A terrible thing to think, to be sure, but no worse than the other thoughts we have, some so unbelievable we can never admit them out loud.

The wilful scandal with which foreign gay men led their lives in Tokyo in the late 1970s and early 1980s recalled for some its antecedent in how some Americans lived during the Allied Occupation of Japan from 1945 to 1952. Everyone knows the stories of GIs lumbering into homes with their shoes on (at one end of the arrogance) and of jeeps that did not care to stop after running over small children (at the other). Then there are the stories a few of us have heard, like how some of us profited here not by husbanding our Army salaries, as claimed, but by using our PX privileges to deal in penicillin and those other things that the Japanese desperately needed, but could not purchase themselves.

Then there are the stories that only Ron and his friends knew, and that I learn of in the summer of 1987. In the purge of homosexuals from the U.S. military that occurred late in the Occupation, a list of names was compiled and handed over to the Japanese government in a gesture of international homophobic solidarity. To be on this list meant subtle but incessant harassment. One American Ron introduces me to this month is a successful publisher who has never been allowed more than a six-month visa, which he must renew twice each year by flying abroad and submitting his papers to some consular offical to peruse indifferently and, if lucky, have stamped with the Emperor's government seal of approval. Why stay on? I ask him. My work is here, he answers. So is yours, Ron reminds me, and you are here, too.

Pierre Loti, né Louis Marie Julien Viaud, was born in 1850 and died in 1923. He was a writer, a naval officer, an adventurer, an artist, a member of the Académie Français, and an acrobat. He was the subject of a cult in his own lifetime. In a sense his entire adulthood would be a disguise, as Viaud disappeared and Loti, not only his pen name but the name of his novels' most important hero, came to be him.

    Thus Loti/Viaud would go to many far places and tell all of France about them: Tahiti, Senegal, the Middle East. He made his first trip to the Extreme Orient in the early summer of 1883 when he left for Annam. He had become a sailor because, he wrote, he was in love with "the far-off shores of the *colonies*."

The second victim was Dorothy, a model. She was also found with an "AIDS" tag attached to her lower body. She was killed, however, with a knife stuck deep in her vagina. Dorothy had a foreign name because, Waku writes, her father was Haitian.

> Oh, what magic and mental turmoil there was during my childhood in the simple word "the colonies," which, at that time, denoted in my mind every far-off tropical land with its palm trees, enormous flowers, Negroes, animals and adventures.[1]

My first trip to Asia was to Vietnam as well. Loti, too, went on account of a war. Annam, a province of French Indochine, had dared to revolt and needed to be taught a lesson. But neither Loti nor I took up arms. He was a journalist, I a hospital worker. Loti's grisly reports to the home front undermined public support of the war; I was there in Annam too because I objected to my own nation's penetration. But we were both witnesses to Asian wars that would largely define the modern West's petulant relationship with the East. The Annam War would secure French control over Indochina, and the one I attended would lose America its own interregnum. Other than that, perhaps our national histories are similar.

    Ron's first trip to Asia was, like mine and Loti's, the result of a war that our country chose to fight in. His trip, however, was to Japan in the aftermath of America's greatest twentieth-century victory: total victory over the Empire of Japan following the bombings of Hiroshima and Nagasaki. We did not write books, at least at first, for readers back home eager to hear of our adventures. Ron was in the intelligence service; I worked with civilian amputees. Young men from America ripped away from what they knew and put where they would have to learn; and learn what later would become the thing we dedicated our lives to. Loti's life was different, then, if not entirely. Ron's and mine are the same, minus the differences.

Twenty-eight year-old Chieko, like Ritsuko, is killed with a guitar string. She lived in Kobe with her husband, who is currently on assignment for his company in Manila.

Shimada Masahiko says:

> I guess that in the fifties and sixties the gays were still underground. It wasn't long after the war that economic growth had things hopping in Japan, but think about it from the point of view of homosexual foreigners who came to Tokyo in those days. Back in America they were still underground, but for ten dollars in Japan they could have a young man as handsome as a movie star. Now *that* is a real sado-masochist relationship.[2]

Ōe's Ritsuko decides to go for her AIDS test. Her desire to marry Hajime and have his child is greater than her fear. But there are risks. If she is discovered to have infected Hajime, she will receive the death penalty.

> The AIDS Testing Center was an unexpectedly small and dreary building. On one side of the entrance was a police office, and I could see someone wearing a uniform inside. Sometimes people would try to run away when they were told they were HIV+, they didn't want to wear the AIDS badge or be arrested for their crimes, and so the police were of course always on guard.
>
> Everything went well until they drew my blood. The nurse carried the test tube away as if it were filled with an explosive. A man dressed in white, with a broad forehead and scrunched-up eyes and nose asked me a series of hostile questions at his desk next to the testing room. "Why do you think you're infected?" . . . "If you think you've been positive for ten years, then you're a carrier and we'll have to conduct follow-up tests on all the men you've been with." . . .

When I left the Testing Center, I walked defiantly past the police waiting there to take care of suspected AIDS carriers. I started down a sidewalk with so many puddles and so much dog shit there was hardly room to walk.[3]

After yet another sensational murder, the police finally close in on Okinaka Tomoshige and arrest him. He is a rock guitarist with AIDS. He is not homosexual or a drug user, but very promiscuous. He is called a *fukushū no oni*, or "Avenging Monster."[4]

Ron once showed me a photograph of himself taken in the 1950s. Much younger, yes, but also less handsome than he is now. He was heavier and his face showed clear and unbecoming signs of worry. All that is gone now. Was it a stressful life in Japan that made him look older than his years? Or was it the other way around, and he stayed on in Japan for so long precisely because, though a plain-looking man in America, here was a country that found him beautiful?

There is a children's game sold in Japan called "Bacteria Panic." You know you're the loser when you're left holding the single card marked "AIDS." There is also a game, this one for adults, called "Human Trash." Its cards, which players "buy" and "sell," contain forty-eight photographs of women with information including their past sexual experiences and blood types. An AIDS card, depicting two men embracing, serves as a joker to allow a player to change a desired woman's blood type at will. A more offensive version of this game, called "Human Trash . . . Snicker, Snicker" sold 18,000 sets before the manufacturer took it off the market.[5]

I played games myself as a child in the 1950s. There was an amusement park near where we lived. Decades later, when I returned to live near there as a graduate student, all that would be gone. It had been replaced by blocks of seaside condominiums that left no trace of the ferris wheels and roller coasters that had thrilled us, no sign of the hot dog stands or game arcades that we made our parents take us to.

What is still there, however, is one stretch of the long boardwalk along the beach. As boys we could crawl underneath it and watch the people strolling above through the wooden slats that cast cool shadows onto the sand below. Sometimes we smoked cigarettes, or tried to catch anonymous glimpses of the adult women's undergarments by looking straight up. Then there was my favorite game, which was comparing my penis with the other boys' and watching them get hard as I touched them.

Ron, I would learn years later, lived in this same neighborhood for a while when I was a boy playing these games beneath the boardwalk. I never told him about what we little boys did down there, because it was such an ordinary anecdote and because our lives before we met as grown adults was not often a topic of our conversation. Ron, I guessed, had things he did not want to share with me.

The man Ron would love was the one he found, as Kishida himself put it, "in the gutter." It is Tokyo, the mid-1950s, and enter stage-right a fallen actor-slash-gigolo. It could have been a movie starring Marlon Brando. But it was not.

They lived, in part on remittances from Ron's family back in Minnesota, in a drafty little house on the outskirts of Tokyo. They socialized with other ex-military men and their Japanese lovers who had settled more or less permanently in Japan despite the purge that had ended their service careers. Via an intergovernmental courtesy, the United States gave the Japanese authorities important information that would be used to harass these American homosexuals for the rest of their "time" in Japan.

Kishida would eventually follow Ron to America, though he would never be happy there. That is where I met them both, and spent evenings listening to Kishida play his koto for us after dinner: baneful melodies, probably poorly executed, but part of the story that Ron did want me to hear and that I was pleased to listen to. Kishida was none too fond of me since I recalled for him the youth he no longer had, but he was always polite. Still more years later, Ron did in fact leave Kishida for a younger man, but by then the real hurt would be that the younger man was American.

It was not long after I was born that my parents took us to the little town by the sea that my mother had come from. I still remember watching my father build our first real house from my stroller. His brothers came down to help him pour the concrete for the foundation, and another came down again to help with the electrical wiring. I always watched, which means only watched, even when I was old enough to help my father. I felt from a very early age that I was different, not really his son and maybe even an alien from another world sent to earth to infiltrate the population. I had all the usual boyhood friends, but those friendships were already more intense than would have been normal, and my relationship to them already oddly introspective. I was a typical kid, a bit on the bright side if a little less athletic than the others, but Rockwellesque in my earnestness and mischief. I played my role perfectly. My superiors back on Mars were surely pleased with me.

One of my two best friends was Jackie, the more sensitive of the many sons of the local big businessman, a boy himself much bigger than I but cursed with a girl's name nickname (the same as mine, and also the same of the President's wife, to our undying shame). The other was Gary, also sensitive, the prettiest of the many sons of Sonny, who owned the local septic tank company and whose family had been the town's most important black family for generations. Sonny's older sister had been my mother's own best friend in school, and she would walk her home to prevent her from being bullied by other girls. Jackie would no doubt grow up to inherit the family business and spawn many more Jackies; Gary actually did grow up to marry briefly, and have a daughter, but even then kept a husband on the side. And what would they have come to say of me, if they had lived long enough? That I grew up, went off for adventure in the Far East, disappeared? Went west, vanished? If people don't hear from you for a few years, everyone assumes you are dead.

Loti was not excited about Japan when he went there in the summer of 1885. His destination aboard the *Triomphante* out of Ma-Kung was Nagasaki, one of the three treaty ports agreed upon at the beginning of Japan's opening to the West. Asia, he said, was "a real land of exile where nothing attracts or charms me."[6]

Why is it so common, and thus so apparently important, for Westerners who go to Asia to insist upon their indifference? What kind of prelude is just this disavowal? What dangers are thereby hopefully avoided? The truth is: if everything attracts, and if everything charms, then everything can betray you.

Ron and Kishida must have been an unusual couple in Japan back then. Did the neighbors think the one was the other's houseboy? *At Eyoub I became rather the spoilt child of the neighborhood.* Or did they, true to custom, simply pretend not to notice? *Samuel, too, is very popular.* One wonders, just as one wonders what Miss Chrysanthemum really thought and really knew. *Suspicious at first, my neighbors have now decided to overwhelm with kindness the charming stranger of Allah's sending whose domestic affairs puzzle them so hopelessly.*

Ron made the money, such as it was. Kishida did the shopping, such as was required. A scant decade after the war two men, both veterans from enemy sides, were living in a discreet and efficient balance. *In my loneliness*

I have come to depend upon Samuel, that vagabond friend of mine, whom I picked up on the quay at Salonica.[7] It would last for years, but no longer than one American man's passion for things Japanese did.

Jackie and Gary never were really good friends themselves. There was too much bad history between their fathers and their rival businesses for that to be. But the three of us, in the basement of my father's hand-built house, spent the better part of an early adolescent summer learning to be the very best of friends. Amid the tools and the workbenches and the piles of leftover lumber and metal piping I was never allowed to help my father with, three boys from all sides of the tracks played a new game whose rules we quickly improvised. A couple of years later, we would reconvene in the same place to smoke dope. Jackie would by then be running the weekend crews in his father's dairy, and Gary would by then have discovered his blackness and made his necessary new friends. But in the basement, where my father never initiated me into his own male rites, memories remained of the excitement of a past summer (but not too past) when Jackie, Gary and I made ourselves young men despite the chasms of money and color between us.

Roland Barthes, like Loti, at moments claimed to be immune from the romance of the Orient. Barthes tells us that Loti believed "Whether Turkish or Magrebi, the Orient is merely a square on the board, the emphatic term of an alternative: the Occident or *something else*";[8] and for Barthes himself, "the Orient is a matter of indifference."[9] But Barthes was not indifferent to Loti himself. "Loti, a traveler specializing in the East," as he described him, was "the bard of Istanbul" among other things.[10] Like me, Barthes has his family tree, too—collateral branches of the same great clan.

Jackie leaned back against the pile of old tires in the basement. He had already taken off his pants and had a little, fat erection that stood straight up out of the wispy beginnings of his pubic hair. His breathing was heavy and he had an almost pained look on his face as Gary and I started to play with him and take turns jerking him off. I got down between his legs, my knees on the cold concrete floor, and studied the way his cock and testicles grew out of his lower belly. I examined Jackie's sex as carefully as he and I would soon be dissecting a frog together in Mr. Adam's biology class. An alien species taken apart by two boys, Jackie and me, with a knowledge of anatomy that the seventh grade's Mr. Adams was not to teach.

*   *   *

Loti writes in his novel, *Madame Chrysanthème*:

> These customs, these symbols, these masks, all that tradition and atavism have jumbled together in the Japanese brain, proceed from sources utterly dark and unknown to us; even the oldest records fail to explain them to us in anything but a superficial and cursory manner, *simply because we have absolutely nothing in common with this people.* We pass on in the midst of their mirth and their laughter without understanding the wherefore, so totally does it differ from our own.[11]

Unidentified Shadowing Object

October 1, 1994. Friday. A small package is delivered to Dr. Sasakawa's home. The sender is the Pathology Department in the H University Medical School. A short letter is enclosed.

"As directed by the will of Mr. Osamu Takamado, who committed suicide by drowning on August 18 of this year in Rika Township, Reiha Country, Toyama Prefecture, this is to be delivered to Dr. Ken'ichi Sasakawa as a remembrance of the deceased. These were extracted from the body of the deceased, but there is no need for concern as they have been sterilized."

The doctor carefully opened the box that had been packed with so much care. Inside were two lumps made of a clear gel side by side each other. Dr. Sasakawa, an obstetrician, immediately realized that these were silicon sacs used in breast-augmentation surgery.[12]

In Loti's first novel, *Aziyadé*, a young French naval officer—also named Loti—is dispatched to Istanbul ("old Stamboul") by Europe's empires intent on disciplining the Turks for their impunities. But he falls in love with the beautiful Circassian harem girl Aziyadé when he glimpses her through a barred window. In order to meet her, Loti must dress as an Oriental to escape detection. *Behold your friend Loti in the middle of the room with three old Jewesses silently busying themselves about him.* The ruse works; Loti successfully woos his Aziyadé. *They have hooked noses and are picturesquely garbed in flowing, spangled tunics, with necklaces of threaded sequins, and catogans of green silk.* But he must also have enjoyed his colorful subterfuge. *Swiftly they divest him of his uniform and set to work to array him in Turkish dress, beginning with the garters and gilded gaiters, which they kneel down to adjust.* Back in Paris, Loti would frequently show up at parties dressed in the flowing robes of the Orient. *Loti preserves the brooding and sombre demeanor befitting a hero of melodrama.* The vestments of a Turk, but also the seductiveness of a woman's finery. *Two or three daggers, with silver, coral-studded handles and blades damascened with gold, are thrust into his belt.* Did Loti's costume make him feel Oriental? And more or less masculine? *A gold-embroidered tunic with flowing sleeves is slipped over his head, and a tarboosh adds the finishing touch.*[13] Or something altogether different?

So Loti becomes Arlif, not just that day but every day. He uses the trunk he keeps stashed away at a disreputable café to change from his white man's clothing to his Oriental's. Usually he is happy to be Arlif, which is to say *both* Arlif and Loti, though there are days when he despairs over his chances in making the masquerade complete; and there are also the days when he hates the Turk he has become, or wishes to be.

When Loti wrote his first novel, he gave his hero his own name but changed his nationality. The real French Loti became the false English Loti. Was that the original reason why this had to be a novel about death? And masquerade?

Jackie died in South Vietnam, three months after I arrived there myself. I did not learn this until several years later, and then only via the casual remark of a relative. By that time, Jackie and I had drifted far apart, as he had become a heterosexual and I a homosexual.

As was the custom for the European traveler of his day, Loti did not allow his disdain for the Oriental, so wholly unlike himself, to interfere with his usual practice of heterosexuality, which after all is the attraction of opposites. In Turkey, he was incensed when a local Jew tries to please him by offering him boys in lieu of the more expensive women; but in Japan, there are no such obstacles. Japan proves especially amenable in this regard, or so Loti reports: "No matter where one goes, in houses one enters for the first time, one is quite at liberty to kiss any mousmé who may be present, without any notice being taken of it."[14]

Lafcadio Hearn liked Loti's novel about Turkey. "Constantinople and the romantic Golden Horn," he said of it, "have never been portrayed with such elegance." But Roland Barthes saw more elegance in *Madame Chrysanthème*, just as he did in Japan itself. "Loti's Orient," wrote his admirer Barthes, "includes moments of winter, of fog, of cold: it is the extremity of our Orient."[15]

Aziyadé consents to become Loti's mistress, though she knows full well he will almost certainly abandon her to return to Europe and marry. Once her fears are realized, she begs him: make me your sister.

Marriages in port cities like Nagasaki were brief, expedient affairs: easily arranged and even more easily dissolved. Loti called on the services of a Japanese go-between dressed in a bowler hat and white gloves and known as M. Kangourou, and whom Loti described as a "confidential agent for the intercourse of races."

> Yves stood near me on the bridge, and we were talking of the country, so utterly unknown to us both, to which the chances of our destiny were now wafting us. As we were to cast anchor the following day, we enjoyed the state of expectation, and formed a thousand plans.
> "As for me," I said, "I shall at once marry."[16]

One opinion of the Japanese is that a calling like Miss Chrysanthemum's was largely tolerated in old Japan because it was, as one scholar put it "designed to control homosexuality, which had apparently grown beyond tolerable limits over the centuries of war."[17]

Was it a war that allowed Ron and me, and so many others, to be homosexuals? Or that made us so? *At Salonica I met a young woman of extraordinary charm, Aziyadé by name, who helped me while away some months of exile.* Transported away from family and friends, taken to our port cities or those of foreign, even enemy, countries, how was this the prize freedom we were granted? *Also a ragamuffin called Samuel, who has become my friend.*[18] Samuel, only the first of the many handsome young men in Loti's novels, pilots the little boat in which Loti and his Aziyadé spend their passionate hours, under a sky filled with the stars of the eastern Mediterranean.

Was Jackie still a heterosexual when a Vietnamese bullet shattered his chest? Or had he, too, met his Samuel, someone who became his friend?

"Oliver's prolonged and futile suffering," writes Emmanuel Dreuihle of his lover dead of AIDS, "was as heart rendering as that of a young soldier gut-shot and abandoned by his comrades out of the battlefield. He would writhe in agony, livid, gripping his belly, his torment dragging on like that of Americans mortally wounded in the jungles of Vietnam, who would finally close their eyes, alone with death, convinced that the world had forgotten them, that they were dying for nothing."[19]

Through Mr. Kangaroo's good offices, it is Miss Chrysanthemum who comes to be Loti's wife. "Chrysanthème," he writes, "has brought but few things with her, knowing that our married life would be of short duration."[20] He calls her his "fairy."

Tetsuji never made my apartment his. *I took you to have a fling.* I suppose he must have left a toothbrush by the bathroom sink, and at least sometimes a change of clothes in my closet. *Perhaps you weren't very successful, but you gave what you could, your little person, your curtsies, and your little music.* But unlike the boyfriends other foreigners often had, mine was either entirely respectable of my own privacy, or hesitant to make our arrangement seem any more permanent than it was destined to be. *In sum, you were dainty enough in your nippon way.* Unlike Loti and Miss Chrysanthemum, Tetsuji and I actually conversed, and shared intimacies. But what we did not share between us will always be more than what we did. *And who knows, perhaps I will think of you sometimes, indirectly, when I remember this beautiful summer, these pretty gardens, and the concert of all these crickets.*[21]

> I announce our departure, and a tearful pout suddenly contracts her childish face. After all, does this news grieve her? Is she going to shed tears over it? No! It turns to a fit of laughter, a little nervous perhaps, but unexpected and disconcerting—dry and clear, pealing through the silence and warmth of the narrow paths, like a cascade of little mock pearls.[22]

Ōe's Ritsuko got left behind too, by a man who did not need her any longer. He abandoned her to go to Mars. Ritsuko, stranded on earth, had to face the great epidemic alone without him. The Chosen were celebrated as great heroes, modern-day Jasons; as a consequence, the Unchosen began to think of themselves as decadent, suicidal, worthless. Ritsuko would have gone to Mars too, had she been one of the Chosen. But she was not included among their number. Hajime did not offer to take her along. Even after his return, just as when Pinkerton returned to Madame Butterfly, that betrayal changes everything.

Just how different is Ritsuko from Aziyadé, from Miss Chrysanthemum, from Tetsuji, from Andrew? Hajime is petrified of AIDS, but he resists wearing a condom when he starts to have sex with Ritusko—he is a hero, after all, and immortal. But Ritsuko was warned by the doctor at the testing center that she, a so-called "Left Behind," will never be allowed to marry one of the Chosen. Hajime's relationship with Ritsuko will not last long.

In time, if a very long time, Gary met another black man, also named Gary. They settled in Baltimore, where my Gary had gone to study pottery. They bought a row house, moved in together, and filled it with African-American folk art and crafts. A living room decorated with quilts; a kitchen with tempera paintings of little boys sitting on fences and eating watermelon; upstairs, in the bedroom, carved figures of African gods on the top of the dresser next to framed photographs of both their grandmothers.

The second Gary died first, and my Gary six months later. Both men had had ex-wives, and I spent a weekend with them in the row house sorting out personal belongings. They got all the art: a white man cannot have posters of Aunt Jemima hanging in his house, however much he'd like to. But I got Gary's clothing, all of which fit me, and which I wear when I feel like remembering him, or being him.

Aziyadé, whose name Loti had had tatooed onto his chest ("this tatooing, like every other mark or blemish upon my earthly body, would accompany me into eternity"[23]), was no happier than Miss Chrysanthemum upon hearing the news of her own lover's imminent departure. Aziyadé reacts with somewhat less stoicism than Chrysanthemum will, however, and she shatters a small blue and gold Turkish coffee cup with her hand. Cut, she nearly bleeds to death. Her blood spills from her hand onto her clothing, her chair, the floor: blood that might well be the portent of her rage and anger more than her sadness, slowly oozes to form a pool of thick liquid at her feet.

Loti always enjoyed his special diplomatic immunity. He never, even for a moment, thought of himself as someone who shared the same firmament, much less the same gods, as the Japanese among whom he walked and made love to. *But it is a soul which more than ever appears to me of a different species to my own.* If there is a villain in my story, I suppose it is he: a totally contemptuous user of women and foreigners and therefore a perfect icon for both unbridled "patriarchal hetereosexuality" and "a racist Orientalism." *I feel my thoughts to be as far removed from theirs, as from the flitting conceptions of a bird.* Some people now say that Loti must really have been a homosexual, so strident is his literary heterosexuality. Does that make him better for the purposes of my story, or worse? But that simple lesson is what my life, and this little book, wants to confound, because there are no heroes, only this candidate of a villain. *Or the dreams of a monkey.* They say that Loti's obsession with the exotic—his house had "Chinese rooms" and "Arab rooms"—was his attempt to recapture the simple joy of his happy youth in the bosom of a loving family. They say that our youths were not happy and that is why we are what we are. I say that it was my desire not to flee back to my family, but away from the life it augured, that launched me on my own travels eastward.

Loti was the author of the novel that led to the play that led to the opera that became for many gay men part of the great gay mythological repertoire. *I feel there is betwixt them and myself a great gulf, mysterious and awful.*[24] If Loti's little story of sad Miss Chrysanthemum is part of what we are, what part of us still remains to struggle against that patrimony?

Aziyadé was such a success back home in France that it became popular to throw "Aziyadé parties," where all the guests would come dressed as their favorite character from the novel.

Madame Butterfly's entrance onto the stage has been called one of the great gay moments in opera. Not so much an entrance, actually, but the *threat* of her entrance, because that means she will indeed desert us and go to her undeserving Lieutenant Pinkerton. *Opera kills the things it loves.* Maybe that is why I have never liked opera, or why I prefer the word "gay" to "queer." *Like Butterfly, if I enter opera, I will die, so I linger on its border to prolong and never complete my moment of entrance.* Why does being homosexual mean tragedy for so many of us? Why can't Butterfly get what she wants, just as we should be able to, too? *I long to remain outside the frame of opera, immune to its dangerous charms.* Puccini's Japanese opera: the ultimate safe sex. *But I also feel narrative's seduction: I want to enter the story and I want the plot to proceed.*[25] What you need, in other words, is a goddamned good fuck.

Roland Barthes identified not only with Loti's novels (*Aziyadé*, he wrote, "is not altogether a novel for well-brought-up girls, it is also a minor Sodomite epic, studded with allusions to *something unheard-of and shadowy*"[26]), but with Loti himself. "The lieutenant nobly dispatched, the author will go describing cities, in Japan, in Persia, in Morocco, i.e., will go on designating and searchlighting (by emblems of discourse) the space of his desire."[27] Finally, Barthes and Loti are two Europeans more than they are either one man who likes men or another who does not.

It is not Aziyadé who is taken back to Europe, but Achmet, the second of the lieutenant's beloved manservants. "I promised," writes Loti, "to give Achmet a home beneath my roof and to entrust my children to his care."[28] And when his ship leaves Nagasaki harbor, Loti throws Miss Chrysanthemum's farewell bouquet of fading white lotus flowers out a porthole.

Let us imagine as Andrew Cunanan would a century later, that Miss Chrysanthemum and the green-eyed Aziyadé do not accept their fate, do not fall into sorrow and do not mourn their losses when their lovers leave them. Or even commit suicide. Let us imagine that instead of hurling themselves in a displaced act of rage, that instead of *dying themselves*, that like our half-Oriental Andrew these two women decide to avenge their hurt and murder Lieutenant Loti ?

Aziyadé might use poison, Chrysanthemum a well-placed cut at the throat as Loti sleeps. Or they might not resort to stealth. Maybe, like Andrew, they will stand in clear view, on a public street early one summer morning and shoot their lovers dead with perfectly aimed shots.

Our murderesses (if not our murderer) might well be celebrated as heroines who redressed the arrogance of the West and its men. *" 'Come, Loti,' she said at last."* They say now that Andrew was not dying of a virus, just dying to be loved by men who promised everything that their civilization dangled before them. *" 'I understand. This is the end. Tell me the truth.' "*[29]

Ritsuko: join your sisters Chrysanthemum, Aziyadé, Andrew: do the needful, strike the blow, let them know how angry you are, how ignoble you feel this fate to be. I beg you: Make me your sister.

The French lieutenant is already aboard his ship and ready to leave Nagasaki when Mr. Kangaroo shows up unexpectedly with tatooers in tow. Our Frenchman chooses among the designs a dragon.

As it is being carefully etched into the flesh of his right breast, he bleeds. "One of the artists hastens to staunch it with his lips, and I make no objection," Loti writes, "knowing that this is the Japanese manner, the method used by their doctors for the wounds of both man and beast."[30] And so our tasty little Frenchman, covorter with whores, shares his blood with an anonymous Japanese man and invites a penalty that even his diplomatic immunity might not, were he one of us today, spare him.

It is Luchiano finally, and not Andrew, who has the perfect revenge. She bites her former lover on the arm, infects him, lets her body live on, for a while, in his.

Luchiano understands the logic of cannibalism that Ruth Benedict celebrated. To feed on another who is also oneself, is an act that announces the love we feel for our own kind, as well as the bloody sacrifice that such love demands. Anthropologists since Benedict and Mead may argue whether cannibalism has ever really occurred in human history, but Luchiano is our living proof of how one man (at least, once a man) can lose himself and gain another (still a man) by devouring his flesh. For me cannibalism is not only my sexual encounters with other men, but the scholarly pursuits of my sabbatical year. A late-twentieth century Orientalist (and homosexual), I look for what is the same in Japan as well as what is different; and my discoveries, once made part of my thoughts and ideas and imagination, let my own body live on in this country, at least for a while.

Predictably enough for a novel as formulaic as *A Serial Murderer in the City of AIDS*, Okinaka Tomoshige is found innocent. (Still, we do not know his fate.) The serial murderer turns out to be another virus-infected member of Okinaka's rock band, Nagasawa Tetsuo. A newspaper in Florida reports that an autopsy performed on Andrew Cunanan's body proves that he was not HIV+ after all. Does this make Tetsuo's murders logical and Andrew's merely tragic? Does the presence or absence of a virus make all our stories real or fantastic?

At the end of another novel, *Unidentified Shadowing Object*, we learn that it was never Luchiano who infected Dr. Sasakawa with HIV but his very own wife.

"But two days are short enough," Loti writes, "when they are the last in life and all that is left to two lovers, who have speedily to make the most of each other, as if they were doomed to death."[31] In this novel more about death than love, it is Aziyadé who is dead by its artless end, not Loti: of grief, he writes with no remorse. But in the the last pages of the novel we read the newspaper obituary of a young officer who, having joined the Turkish Army under an Oriental masquerade, has been killed in the last battle of the war and buried with other martyrs of Islam. Jackie dead, Gary dead, many men's lovers dead. Loti dead, Luchiano dead, Barthes dead, Andrew dead, everyone dead.

AUGUST

The Great Sympathetic
Paradox

I have to write a report this month for the Japan Foundation and tell them how I have spent my sabbatical. It is now only weeks before I pack up and leave. But I procrastinate. Maybe it is the heat, but more likely it is because I am still so far from being done with my work. I devote all of the sixth to writing my report, except for watching the early-morning memorial ceremonies in Hiroshima on television. The sixth is also one of the days I take my pill. I pour them out of their plastic vial and count: just enough until I get back to America.

Daniel has come from Takayama to crash at our house for all of this month and the next. His English teaching contract is up and he's got an interview for a new job at Tokyo Disneyland in Chiba. To do what? I ask. Dunno, he says. Anything. Daniel wants to stay in Japan and he will do what it takes to pay his rent and guarantee him a visa. He is just at the beginning of his love affair with Japan, and although I am ever nearer the end of mine, I keep my mouth shut. He is young and my perspective is different. Perhaps Daniel will stay in Japan for years, even forever. More than a few of us do. But if not he should find out why he doesn't belong here for himself. This is a pedagogy best not shared, if only because I suspect my own tutorial here has not been entirely reliable: the isolation of the expatriate means we dwell as much upon ourselves as we do our new countries.

Daniel looks even more handsome than he did last spring. His excitement about being in Japan, his joy at being a center of attention, seem the precise measure of his youth. But at the same time a Japanese diet has made him leaner, more mature-looking and masculine. Ben is back in California for a long vacation, so I could offer him the bedroom upstairs. But instead I invite Daniel to spread out the bedding in the living room, just underneath the air conditioner, and just outside the sliding doors to my own room.

A few days later Ritsuko goes back to the Center for her results. She finds out she is negative, as was everyone tested that day except for two, a foreign woman and a Japanese man who had traveled abroad. Ritsuko goes home feeling euphoric, though home is only a makeshift shelter scavenged from the trash of a destroyed Japan. She is now ready to have Hajime's baby.

We do not read anything further of Ritsuko's less fortunate testees. Let me guess. The Insolent Persons are branded, doomed to be harassed by the AIDS police until they die, while Ritsuko will go home to breed, be a post-apocalyptic Harriet for her interplanetary Ozzie. This plot must make some sort of crazy sense to someone, I suppose. To me it is a morality tale of whose moral I am positive. This is one novel I will not read again. Or teach to my classroom of students, of whom two or three prefer, as do I, other stories. We would write a different conclusion to this novel.

Shoko and her husband Aki are driving the three of us back to Tokyo after a weekend at the Hakone Prince Hotel. Shoko is complaining how the Prime Minster ruined our stay by showing up with an immense entourage to play golf; Aki is lecturing me never to buy a Jaguar because it will always be in the garage. I ask them when they will finally come to visit me in America. Shoko says she would, if she didn't have an infant daughter now. "You know, AIDS and all." Don't be ridiculous, I snap at her. After a moment of silence in the very silent car, Shoko tells me that once you're a parent, you think differently about things.

Here's one way we might end Ōe's novel. On their way out of the Center the HIV-positive foreign woman (let's call her Jesusa) and the Japanese man

(Tacite?) strike up a conversation, have a cup of coffee together, go to a movie and fall in love. Suddenly a cure for AIDS is discovered and they live happily ever after. Meanwhile Ritsuko and Hajime give birth to a baby who is terribly deformed because of his parents' irradiated genes. For a lack of courage they let him die by refusing to feed him, and for the rest of their miserable lives Ritsuko and Hajime are haunted each night by a ghost who never permits them a moment of peace.

Rumor. In the summer of 1992, novelist Nakagami Kenji is dying from a reported liver condition in a Tokyo hospital. A year later a Japanese friend tells me that at the very end of his life Nakagami confessed to friends that he is a homosexual—and that so are many Japanese writers. Among others, he names Ōe Kenzaburo.

Was it Komagome Hospital? Nakagami, a celebrity, would have had a private room and therefore no one to watch him die, or help.

"In a society that institutionalizes homosexuality," Ruth Benedict ruled, "they will be homosexual."[1]

Sarah Schulman, another American lesbian, went to Japan in the early 1990s on a five-day trip. There she met Japanese homosexuals and brought her readers back home a fresh ethnographic report:

> Like most homosexuals in the world, these people just wanted to find a boyfriend and be happy. But they live in such a state of invisibility and deprivation that they could not even imagine the basics of gay life. Furthermore, living in a prescribed society like Japan, these gay people just wanted to know the rules for being homosexual.[2]

What *are* "the basics of gay life"? Schulman seems to know. I wonder what it is that my Japanese gay friends and ex-lovers are missing out on. It is odd to read about them described as invisible and deprived when I see them everywhere—and sometimes even happy at that. Schulman's report sounds like an American missionary's fundraising appeal for an orphanage in the third world. Rules for Being a Japanese Homosexual, Number One: Prepare to be saved from yourselves.

* * *

An American expert on Japan writes:

> For although it is seldom noted in scholarly books about Japan, it is an interesting fact that since the war Japan has had a strong attraction for male homosexuals. It is difficult to say precisely why this should be so. The psychologically trained anthropologist George De Vos suggested it is merely because homosexuality in Japan is less of a taboo and therefore the homosexual is less stigmatized and his life is less compartmentalized. A good many Japanese homosexuals also have stable marriages and children, and their homosexual affairs are treated much as liaisons with bar girls or geisha might be. According to one American homosexual living in Japan, some Japanese wives accept a homosexual lover for their husbands more easily than a relationship with a bar hostess because there is less chance of losing her own position or of having her home broken up.[3]

Rules for Being a Japanese Homosexual: Number Two. Remember that you are at least better than a bar hostess. Keep in mind that your lover's wife is actually glad it's you. You matter so little and can do no damage. Like a ghost, you may haunt homes at night but will never appear in the light of day.

Shoko and I talk over dessert while Aki goes to take care of the bill. Have you seen Jimmie? she asks. I have to stop and think about whom she is talking. Then I remember: oh yeah, motor scooter, American, young, magazine editor, gay, the friend of a friend of a friend. Haven't seen him in years, I reply. Moved to Hawaii, Shoko suggests. Then I think: Shoko believes that all foreign homosexuals here know each other. I am beginning to become irritated when I realize she may be right.

We fall into a silence at the table as a waiter stops by to refill our water glasses. Shoko is still beautiful like a boy and I can still imagine her and me together without Aki. We are on the patio of the restaurant, looking out over the tall pines that circle the blue mountain lake.

Edward Said published *Orientalism* in the late 1970s, when I was a graduate student. I read it with excitement, almost overnight. Here was the book that talked about *us*, what *we* were training to become: Western experts on the East. The book was critical in ways we younger experts-in-training welcomed. Simply to be spoken of served our narcissistic vanity. Our Orientalist fathers were indeed culpable, we nodded in the smug knowing way that intellectual

sons, eager to throw off father's authority, like to do. Orientalism, Said instructed, is a discourse in which the West's knowledge about the Orient is inextricably bound up with its domination over it. *Discourse*. We, of course, could see this now and would be different. *Knowledge*. But "we" were different already, and always had been: different in ways that Said's angry book ignored. *Domination*.

The idea that "we" homosexuals, whether American lesbians or Japanese gay men, share a community because we "share" a lifestyle may be an entirely American and parochial idea. Perhaps jet-setting radicals can export this idea to other places, but it may not be so radical, or useful, from the point of view of the people who live there. Rules for Being a Japanese Homosexual: Number Three. Five Japanese friends go to a bar in Ni-chōme for a drink while three hundred strangers show up at an Act-Up meeting in San Francisco. You are not a community while we are. What's wrong with you? Why are you having a good time? Why do you care for each other, rather than for us?

Shoko, Aki, and I make a odd threesome. They are very stylish, upper-class Japanese, while I am a typically rough-hewn American, awkward in expensive hotels and fancy restaurants. Why do they take me along on their excursions? Don't I risk embarrassing them? What is it that I do for them? They must tire of having to explain things to me twice. Why do they care so much for me?

Many of the Orientalists Said takes up were homosexual, or rumored to be. But that is a circumstance that intrudes on Said's argument only at its edges. Sexuality, in Said's view, was not one of the prizes to be won in Europe's expansion. "The Oriental-European relationship," he writes, "was determined by an unstoppable European expansion in search of markets, resources, and colonies." "Once we begin," Said assures us, "to think of Orientalism as a kind of Western projection onto and will to govern over the Orient, we will encounter few surprises."[4] Even Said, later in his book, cannot be sure of this. He speaks, for instance, of "some deeply felt and urgent project" as why some Europeans go to the Orient; and when he suggests at the same time that "to be a European in the Orient *always* involves a consciousness set apart from, and unequal with, its surroundings," he leaves open the question of just what politics are imposed on and by his generic "Oriental-European relationship." "The main thing to note," Said concedes, "is the intention of this consciousness: what is it in the Orient for?"[5]

* * *

"It is this which I shall call: Japan."[6] Rules for Being a Japanese Homosexual:
Number Four. You live a country that others will always invent for themselves
and for you. Roland Barthes did it, and this year I am doing it, too. Roland
and I may do it because neither of us is quite sure who we are ourselves, and
a foreign country gives us the opportunity to ask the important questions. But
you invent Japan for yourselves as well, not because you are foreigners (like
us), but because you are (like us) homosexuals. Late at night, haunting some
little bar, five of us (Japanese and foreign alike) sit in a row at the counter
and tell each other amusing stories not quite true, but always truthful.

The cover to Edward Said's *Orientalism* is a painting entitled *The Snake
Charmer*. Although the book itself makes no mention of homosexuality, this
is a painting of a boy naked save for the huge snake wrapped about him.
Accompanied by a musician who presumably tames the venomous reptile,
they entertain a row of older men resting against the interior wall of a sump-
tuous Oriental palace. The boy's back is to us, and we are offered an unob-
structed view of his youthful buttocks, which like the rich turquoise tiles of
the palace wall are warmly, wonderfully illuminated by a source of light em-
anating from beyond the border of the picture.

Some of the assembled older men lean forward, clearly expressing
delight in what they see: be it the snake, or the boy, or more likely the
tantalizing fantasy of the two entwined together. Others appear less charmed;
no doubt this is a fantasy some enjoy more than others. But all are dressed
in the flowing robes and turbans of the Ottoman Orient.

And what about us, the real intended audience for this painting? Its
artist, Jean-Léon Gérôme, was both one of late nineteenth-century France's
more popular painters and, not coincidentally, the noted portrayer of Europe's
lascivious desires for the Orient. Gérôme himself made two trips to Egypt,
the artistic results of which now hang in famous museums everywhere. Boys
embracing snakes were apparently a favored theme, since he returned to it in
a later painting.

What are we meant to appreciate, to enjoy? The entranced snake, or the
entertainers endangered by it? The leering men away at a safe distance? Or
the two bright moons of a young boy's ass, as vulnerable as their nudity can
make them? Said's book may make no mention of homosexuality and Europe's discovery of what it is not, but the paperback's cover says plenty.

* * *

Our American expert on Japan continues:

> Like their British counterparts in certain Arab countries, a number of Amer-
> ican homosexuals who fell in love with Japan for personal reasons stayed
> on to become experts on the language and the culture. Some became trans-
> lators of Japanese poetry and novels, others became experts on Kabuki or
> *Noh* or the Japanese film. Over the years they have performed an enormously
> valuable service in introducing Japanese arts and aesthetics to Americans.
> It is fair to say, however, that in doing so they have been guided by their
> own tastes and have often emphasized the subtle, the hypersensitive, the
> perverse, so that many Americans have absorbed vaguely homosexual con-
> notations from Japanese culture.[7]

Homophobia such as this is the common sense of my profession. Hypersen-
sitive and perverse, we have conspired to make America think Japan is our
own homosexual paradise. (And who are these "many Americans" who are
absorbing our connotations?) While the truth, of course, is that Japan is not
homosexual at all. Japan, the unwitting victim of our sordid predilections, is
a place that should be understood as just as *heterosexual* as *us*, were it not
for the self-interested promotions of a certain anonymous community: too
cowardly to name names, this expert's slander belongs to her own very curious
panic.

Shoko and I were briefly lovers in the late 1970s, while Aki was living in
Paris and having, she told me, adventures of his own. Her taut, slim body
lay naked atop her Chinese bed in the warm afternoon light that came through
the thin shades. Smooth and light brown skin; large dark nipples atop tiny
breasts. Her apartment was in a building whose first floor was home to a
professional Noh theater, and we would hear the slow, seductive sounds of
the rehearsing drums waft up to where, exhausted, we rested and talked.
Discourse. Once, she pulled a book out from a drawer in the night table, and
made me read it out loud. *Knowledge*. She laughed every time I mispro-
nounced a Japanese word, which was often. So your Japanese really isn't that
good after all, she concluded triumphantly. *Domination*.

Said declines to pursue one answer in particular to his question: Why is the
Orientalist in the Orient? He has to admit on the basis of an overwhelming
archive that "Every European traveler or resident in the Orient has had to

protect himself from its unsettling influences. . . . the Orient seemed to have offended sexual propriety; everything about the Orient . . . exuded dangerous sex, threatened hygiene and domestic seemliness with an excessive 'freedom of intercourse.' "[8] But that is as far as Said will go. "Why the Orient seems still to suggest not only fecundity but sexual promise (and threat), untiring sensuality, unlimited desire, deep generative energies, is something on which one could speculate: it is not the province of my analysis here, alas, despite its frequently noted appearance."[9] Perhaps Said's Victorian "alas" is accompanied by a Victorian modesty, but his readers are not similarly restrained. While we might let ourselves think Said is referring only to the heterosexual potential of a masculinized empire dominating a feminized East, in another chapter ("Latent and Manifest Orientalism") he reminds us that "Orientalism also encouraged a peculiarly (not to say invidiously) male conception of the world. . . . The Oriental male was considered in isolation from the total community in which he lived and which many Orientalists . . . have viewed with something resembling contempt and fear. Orientalism itself, furthermore, was an exclusively male province."[10] So can we believe Said is right in every case when he rules "An Oriental man was first an Oriental and only second a man"?[11]

My experience, and that of at least a few of my fellow travelers, teaches lessons other than those implied in Said's history of us. "He wanted to go to the East; and his fancy was rich with pictures of Bangkok and Shanghai and the ports of Japan," writes Maugham in *Of Human Bondage*, a work that Said might well have cited as an example of the predatory Western, male imagination, had he been that interested in us. But we can take away an alternative reading if we think that the Orient is in fact that different, if sexuality assumes surprising forms in places other than our own, and if we are mistaken in thinking that a Barthes or a Burton is only projecting his Western desires rather than having them quite matter-of-factly satisfied.

"Each Orientalist," writes Said, "recreated his own Orient according to the fundamental epistemological rules of loss and gain."[12]

1980.   Shoko demands to know if I really do like boys. We are in her kitchen, it is several hours after one of our encounters, and she is preparing a French supper for us. I laugh, probably a bit too loudly. If I say yes, I risk having the conversation that will lose her as a lover; if I say no, she will know I am lying. Her question, in any case, was rhetorical. Whatever I risk to gain, or lose, has already been calculated.

*   *   *

"Hence the goal of transvestitism," wrote Barthes, "is *finally* (once the illusion of being is exhausted), to transform oneself into a describable object—and not into an introspectible subject."[13] When Barthes went to Japan, a place he would later dream of, it was as a transvestite himself. He was what he could not be in France: finally a *man*, no longer a celebrity but just another older and eager white gentleman. An eminently describable object. And why shouldn't we allow him that moment? When others, too, find pleasure in the charade?

One evening when I return home to our house from a day in the library, I see that Daniel has left a note for me on the kitchen table. Scribbled quickly, it says he is going to cook dinner for the two of us tonight and that we have a reason to celebrate. He signs it "love, D." It is written in his half-boyish, half-mannish scrawl. Half-serious, it is also half of what he thinks he is expected to write.

He makes baked chicken, and we have it with the best bottle of champagne he could find in Mejiro. When he first burst in he told me the news: he's been hired to work at Tokyo Disneyland. As what? I ask. Peter Pan, he says. I'm going to walk around the park dressed up as Peter Pan and welcome kids in English. Let their parents take pictures of them with me. Perfect, I think. I don't want him to grow up anyway.

We talk about a lot of things, like the joy of living here and the exacting price, too. Would making love with him tonight make any of this clearer, or more certain, or *true*? Yes, in fact, it most certainly would. But we were meant to be lovers only briefly, on his way to somewhere else in life; just as he will have his one and only encounter with Japan now. He will, in fact, grow up one day and hardly believe he was ever here.

Ruth Benedict never did travel to Japan. But her wartime study *The Chrysanthemum and the Sword*, though much maligned today for its simple ideas, is still the classic American study of that country and its different ways. In 1934, ten years before turning her attention to Japan, she wrote an essay entitled "Anthropology and the Abnormal."

> As a matter of fact, one of the most striking facts that emerge from a study of widely varying cultures is the ease with which our abnormals function in other cultures. It does not matter which kind of "abnormality" we choose for illustration, those which indicate extreme instability, or those which are

more in the nature of character traits like sadism or delusions of grandeur or of persecution, there are well-described cultures in which these abnormals function at ease and with honor, and apparently without danger or difficulty to the society.[14]

This was not likely the view Benedict's colleagues and mentors at Columbia shared at the time. Edward Said was not a professor there yet. Was it her own lesbianism that inspired this liberal defense? But my point is: it may well be our present enthusiasm for rectifying the Western penchant for construing non-Western cultures as exotically "other," and doing so for purely Western imperatives, that makes us lose sight of Benedict's anthropological insight, inspired by its own local (even personal) imperatives, that they *are* different.

That is a truth any traveler heterosexual, homosexual, or whatever, can realize. What is specific to the homosexual abroad, however, might be an exception to the rule that encounters across borders are always encounters of self and other. "I have often spoken in this book," says Said, "of the sense of estrangement experienced by Orientalists as they dealt with or lived in a culture so profoundly different from their own."[15] But I would counter, there is also intense and frequent identification on the part of the gay Western man in the gay Eastern world: that sometimes the Oriental man is, in fact, a man first and only an Oriental second.

> Someday we must write the history of our own obscurity—manifest the density of our narcissism, tally down through the centuries the several appeals to difference we may have occasionally heard. [16]

1980. After dinner Shoko showed me a letter Aki had sent her. I could have managed, with effort, to read his difficult scrawl, but I pretended otherwise because I knew my clumsy failures amused Shoko. He's been in the Loire Valley, she summarizes for me, with Funaki-*san*. Lucky Aki, I think. Funaki had been a classmate of Aki and Shoko's in college and was without a doubt the sexiest man they had ever introduced me to. One Sunday years ago Aki and Funaki and I went to a hot springs together in Izu. On our return, Funaki reported to Shoko (not intending to be funny) that inspection revealed my body had all of its required parts. *Chanto shita karada yo.* Shoko laughed, but I began to wonder why this woman had so many male friends, and one male husband, so ambiguous in their sexuality.

Why is Funaki in France too? I ask. Oh, just *une petite vacance*, she says. To see Aki. To get away from Tokyo. And, in the middle of Europe, she might have added, to cross borders like any other Insolent Person. Who will write the book, I wonder, about gay Eastern men in the Western world?

"What can I do to live?" a number of Schulman's Japanese hosts, concerned about AIDS, ask. "I tried to sound confident as I answered. *These guys don't have a chance.*"[17]

Schulman misunderstood the question, of course. Rather than write off the male homosexual population of Japan in a thought she thinks to herself (and then shares out loud with us back home), Schulman's more intelligent response would have been: You tell me. How *do* you live? How *have* you survived? What do *you* know that we may not? Teach *me* something.

Rules for Being a Japanese Homosexual, Number Five: we look at you and see a Japanese first, and only a while later a homosexual. Orientalism is a practice not only of empires, but of some quite queer novelists and critics, too. *You guys don't have a chance.*

Tetsuji walked in around ten, an hour after he closed up the art framing shop in Nakano. I already had a drink in my hand, and poured one for him as he unlaced his running shoes in the entryway. Tuesdays I always made dinner for him, which is to say Tuesdays he had to suffer through my experiments in Japanese cuisine. Wednesday was his day off and he could sleep over this one night of the week.

He sat at the table and listened to me as I put the food on the plates and told him about my day. Later, he would do the dishes while I lay out the futon in my room. He has news, he says. We have to celebrate. What is it? I ask. *I liked to undress him, playing with each part of his body as it came into view.* Well, I'll tell you later. *I put his penis into my mouth, breathed in the smell of his crotch, made him hard.* Let's make love now. *I ran my hands over his chest.* I've been thinking about you all day. *I rubbed his forearms, used my tongue to fill his navel with my saliva.* A customer came into the shop who reminded me of you. *I gently nibbled on his scrotum, licked the underside of his purple head.* I want to really have you tonight. *I looked into eyes, looking for the sign.* I wanna fuck you. *He used his strong thighs legs to spread my legs further apart.* Nah? Aw you're frisky tonight, aren't you. *I wrapped my arms around him when he wrapped his around me.* Why is it that sometimes I even believe we are becoming the same person? *I kissed his neck and shoulders furiously.* Do you ever fantasize that we'll be together forever? *He lowers his belly to spread my sperm around, letting it glue us together.* Does that hurt? *I consumed him whole.* Don't stop, that's great. *The borders of our selves bleed into each other.* Do it again. *He gave me a part of him, just as I will give him part of me.* No, I won't stop. I love you too.

My sabbatical year is not only the year of Japan's AIDS panic, but the year of its frantic efforts to "internationalize." The newspapers are full of articles and editorials about Japan's need to end its insularity and join the world as fearless equals. Learn more English, the citizenry is exhorted; take more trips abroad, the consumer is advised. And buy more English biscuits. Even an American car if you can. The steering wheel may be on the wrong side, but doing anything different in Japan, as long as it is with something American, is so very stylish.

Japanese exports and now Japanese capital, too, flood markets everywhere. Japan is increasingly regarded with suspicion as a selfish country, one unwilling to play by the rules everyone else observes. Japan responds with characteristic hype. *Kokusaika.* Internationalization. Use our riches to do good. Bring down the borders that separate us from our fellow human beings everywhere. Open the door to foreigners. But beware of the ones already among us. Who know as much of us as we do of them. They may even be dangerous. *Infected. Contagious. Strange.* Some American things are not so stylish, after all. *The strangeness of the world.*

Sir Richard had Spekes by his side in Africa. *He wanted to go to the East.* Lieutenant Loti survived his exile in Turkey only with the friendship of his sidekick Samuel. *And his fancy was rich with pictures of Bangkok and Shanghai, and the ports of Japan.* And then Loti, again an exile, this time in Nagasaki, with that of his best friend Yves. *He pictured to himself palm-trees and skies blue and hot, and dark-skinned people and pagodas.* Why are our stories of the Oriental adventurers so often the stories of their close friendships with other men? *The scents of the Orient intoxicated his nostrils.* William and Ichirō, Ron and Kishida, John and Tetsuji. *His heart beat with passionate desire for the beauty and the strangeness of the world.*[18]

"We who are non-Japanese students of Japan," wrote one of us who is an American historian of Hiroshima and Nagasaki, "form a culture of our own."[19] There are good reasons why. When Roland Barthes traveled to Tokyo, it was with the absurd need of the modern homosexual in mind. "Desire always proceeds toward an extreme archaism, where the greatest historical distance assures the greatest unreality, there where desire finds its pure form: that of an impossible return, that of the Impossible (but in writing it, this regression will disappear)."[20] I wonder if Barthes understood how needful these words tell us he was, or just how absurd. Could the nineteenth century see things more clearly? Or the homosexual a little less absurd? Pierre Loti wrote: "Axiom: It is always one's own self that one loves in the person of another." The narcissism that drove both Barthes and the West into Asia is not hard to figure. "Whenever I come across such an *alter ego*, I am conscious of an accession of strength." What remains to be pondered is whether this narcissism is good or bad. "It would seem that the corresponding qualities in two persons combine, and that sympathy is nothing but a yearning, an impulse, towards this amalgamation of forces, which, to my mind, is synonymous with happiness." I think: why not good? But is this amalgamation of forces, too, a way of having our way? "With your permission I will call this phenomenon the great sympathetic paradox."[21]

Daniel is my own sidekick this month. We hardly go out during the day, given the heat and humidity. But at night we take turns leading the other to some new place in Tokyo we can explore together.

One of these adventures is to the Suehirotei in Shinjuku, halfway between the station and the bars. The Suehirotei is one of the few traditional vaudeville halls left in the city, and we are there to listen to a succession of storytellers and comedians entertain us with both famous and improvised routines far beyond our fluency to understand. I have been here before, if only because this *yose*, too, is a kind of Japanese literature that I must master. But for Daniel it is a first. He has hardly seen any theater, anywhere, and tonight at the Suehirotei he has a good time watching Japanese raconteurs on stage hurling across the room to us words that, like bits of gossamer, are gone before we can catch them.

Later that evening, the Japanese language we hear at a favorite gay bar of mine is easier to fathom. We get into an enthusiastic conversation with the three men seated next to us about Japanese theater. None of them has ever been to hear *yose*, but the oldest one used to go to the Kabuki frequently when he was a student. He tells Daniel all about the great actors he once saw, and while the names mean nothing to this American, he nonetheless understands that acting is part of what all we five gay men, in a tiny little room in a corner of Asia, share.

*   *   *

If, as according to Said, the Orient is a theatrical "stage" for the West, it is also at root homosexual. Actors, like gay people, rely on others—the audience, or people of the same sex—to let us know we exist. Our ontology is dependent on that reflection, that narcissism; that confirmation, even if only by the sound of applause, or furtive touch, of people we cannot see for the sake of a darkened hall, or dark bar, that we exist. And here in Japan, where our bodies and our accents put us on stage wherever we go, it makes all of us, male or female or homosexual or heterosexual, gayer than we would ever guess.

> Sexually exiled from the repressiveness of the home culture . . . homosexuals have searched instead for fulfilment in the realm of the foreign. Not necessarily as second best: over and again in the culture of homosexuality, differences of race and class are intensely cathected. That this has also occurred in exploitative, sentimental, and/or racist forms does not diminish its significance; if anything it increases it. Those who move too hastily to denounce homosexuality across race and class as essentially or only exploitative, sentimental or racist betray their own homophobic ignorance.[22]

Schulman's hosts take her to a bar. But she is irritated at what she finds. *A long stark corridor featured thirty or so doors, lined up next to each other like entrances to nuns' cells.* Nuns' cells: severe, solitary, and sexless. *Behind each door was a cubicle containing a bar, about five stools with the wall directly behind the stools and a bartender.* A cubicle, which is to say a featureless box devoid of style or space. *The same five friends will go to their bar every night after work. It is like a second living room.* The same five friends. Always the same. No imagination. *As we sat there with our umpteenth round of drinks I realized that this was yet another phenomenon I would never understand.* An umpteenth round, and *still* inscrutable. What is one to make of these sorry people? *Why would hundreds of gay people choose to come to the same building night after night and then divide up into privatized units of friends thereby ignoring the possibility of community contained within those walls?* Why indeed. Could it be that they like each other? Or, just maybe, that five people is already a "community"? *The next morning, bewildered and exhausted, I boarded the plane for home.*[23]

Sarah Schulman is a disappointed missionary. *Discourse.* Her religion won her no converts, her fervor no followers. *Knowledge.* Like the Jesuits before her, she can only marvel at how this race lives so far from truth. *Domination.*

Death in Venice

Desire projected itself visually: his fancy, not quite lulled since morning, imagined the marvels and terrors of the manifold earth. He saw. He beheld a landscape, a tropical marshland, beneath a reeking sky, steaming, monstrous, rank—a kind of primeval wilderness-world of islands, morasses, and alluvial channels. Hairy palm-trunks rose near and far out of lush brakes of ferns, out of bottoms of crass vegetation, fat, swollen, thick with incredible bloom. There were trees, mis-shapened as a dream, that dropped their naked roots straight through the air into the ground or into water that was stagnant and shadowy and glassy-green, where mammoth milk-white blossoms floated, and strange high-shouldered birds with curious bills stood gazing sidewise without sound or stir. Among the knotted joints of a bamboo thicket the eyes of a crouching tiger gleamed—and he felt his heart throb with terror, yet with a longing inexplicable. Then the vision vanished.[24]

"The geopolitical realities of the Arabic Orient," declares an American professor of English, "become a psychic screen on which to project fantasies of illicit sexuality and unbridled excess . . . This appropriation of the so-called East in order to project it upon an otherness that mirrors Western psychosexual needs only confirms the phenomenon that Said calls 'Orientalism.' "[25]

Western men, this scholar is sure, enjoy "fantasies of a decadent and lawless East, where their "encounters put into crisis assumptions about male sexual desire, masculinity, and heterosexuality specific to Western culture." But just how does he know that what is "specific to Western culture" is not also specific to other cultures? What kind of an "othering" is going on here? He may claim that his goal is to extend the boundaries of "gay and lesbian studies" "by showing how contingent and Western its conception of 'homosexuality' " is. But to do so, he needs exactly the expertise of the Orientalists he considers suspect in the first place. Just because the reputation of an unbridled homosexuality in the non-Western world is "one firmly wedged in the dominant Western imaginary," it does not necessarily make that reputation false.[26] *Discourse.* The more important question is: Why do we want so much to think it is? *Knowledge.* Because we are still, even after all that has been said, missionaries of a scandalized West; or of a homosexuality at profound odds with itself. *Domination.*

"The allure of Japan has, over the ages, proved especially irresistible to homosexual men. Truman Capote, during a trip to Tokyo, declared himself to be in heaven."[27]

*　　*　　*

One bottle of champagne was not enough, so we start in on Ben's supply of real whiskey. Later that night, when as a result I have to get up to go to the bathroom, I slide the bedroom door open, only to remember that Daniel is sleeping there at my feet. He is snoring gently, despite his youth. It is a sign that he drank too much too, or that he is not as young as I would like to think.

The air conditioner is on high, but he has kicked his sheets away and is lying almost entirely naked on the thin bottom futon. I can see him clearly in the glow from the alleyway streetlight shining in through the frosted glass of the front window. He lies on his stomach, his strong arms crossed underneath his head, which is turned in the direction away from me. His back is broad and perfectly free of blemishes and birthmarks. His buttocks are smooth and firm. The body slowly rises and falls in rhythm with his breathing and the small sounds he makes.

I step over him to go to the bathroom at the other end of the house, but on the way back to my bed I stop and squat low to examine his body more closely. I think I can smell his perspiration. The hairs on the back of his legs look slightly damp, pressed flat against his long hamstrings. I kiss the small of his back just where the strength of his dorsals end and the curve of ass begins. His body is the amalgam of the boy now a man, but a man whose body remembers the boy. He lives here in Japan, in my house, trying to be both a child and an adult at the same time. Why does he attract me so much? Is he what I was, or what I never was? I do not touch him again. Some people say that homosexuality is always a case of arrested development, that we are just folks caught in the narcissistic phase. And I sometimes think that my interest in Japan can also be explained by the childishness it celebrates as a nation. Daniel: my very own Peter Pan. My very own Japan.

Arriving in Tunis, Gide notes: "I had of course expected to see camels, but I had never succeeded in imagining them so queer."[28]

"Gradually, almost unconsciously" admits Lieutenant Loti in *Aziyadé*, "I am becoming a Turk. I am perfectly at home in these surroundings," he claims, "which have lost all trace of strangeness."[29] Are such moments a colonial delusion, or something more inevitable? Freud says that our sexual object-choice goes either one of two ways: the anaclitic or the narcissistic, the latter in which our ego has to be replaced by one as similar to our own as possible. "A strong libidinal fixation to the narcissistic type of object-choice is to be included in the predisposition to manifest homosexuality."[30] Loti becomes a Turk. Sometimes I wonder if I am not becoming Japanese. But most often of all I think: I am that man whom I love.

Sir Francis "Dirty Dick" Burton was famous for impersonating Orientals; I could use first-person pronouns in Tokyo gay bars to believe that I, too, was "passing"—as *one of you* (fellow homosexuals), our racial differences here if nowhere else suspended for the moment. To the extent that homosexual desire is narcissistic, then might not the Western homosexual gone-East have the experience of encountering the "Oriental" as same rather than different?

"He looked across at Tadzio," Thomas Mann writes in his novel about a German and a Pole with the telltale Oriental eyes of a Slav, "and saw that the lovely boy returned his gaze with a seriousness that seemed the copy of his own."[31]

One American homosexual goes to Japan and, knowing nothing, writes: "There are few gay commercial establishments, compared to the American network of bathhouses, bars, restaurants and hotels. . . . even the trendy Shinjuku district of Tokyo is no gay mecca."[32] But another American, one of those "translators of Japanese poetry and novels" who has lived in Japan on and off for years since the war, writes that Shinjuku is, in fact, "in the running for the designation homosexual capital of the world."[33] Why does one say one thing, and another its opposite? Because the latter is not only gay, but an Orientalist.

    Roland Barthes famously described Tokyo as having, unlike any other city, an Empty Center. He, too, saw nothing where there is in fact a great deal. Why? While in Japan in the summer of 1997, I count the number of gay bars and sex clubs that have chosen to be listed in a directory. There are close to a thousand. Why do so many of us think otherwise? An empty Japan is proof of our own fullness.

It used to be that men from the West condemned the East, above all else, for its lewd perversions. *In China there are those who reject normal sex and indulge in depravity, they abandon sex with women and instead they corrupt young males.* When William of Adam condemned the catamites of Islam, it was doubtlessly in part to make sure that Christians were not, could not be, Muslims. *This kind of filthiness is not even discussed by wise men in the West, for fear of defiling their own mouths.* The whole distinction of being Christian, which is to say European, was built on this original rejection of homosexuality. *Even the wild animals only make their bonds between female and male, none of them overturn the nature heaven gave them.* When Mateo Ricci and Francis Xavier went to the Far East, it was also with the purpose of discovering, and then excising, the endemic native populations of sodomites, and worse. *Men who are like this never blush for shame; how sinful these men have become.* Well, the missionaries succeeded beyond their wildest dreams apparently. *The members of my humble society retain all their seed, and do not plant it out in the fields.* Because when foreigners go East nowadays they may find *no homosexuals at all.* No community. Not many places to go. *"These guys don't have a chance."* Few commercial establishments. No gay mecca here. *If you doubt the wisdom of this, how much more should you question throwing it away into a ditch or a gutter.*[34]

There is a Primal Scene for Orientalists, too: when we stumble into a place that is not ours and witness in the dimmed light before us two people who love each other locked, it would appear, in violent struggle. We do not know how to react. Should we go to rescue the part of the Orient we have always wanted to defend, even against our own side? Or join that other part, the one that seeks to dominate, win its own pleasure, make *known* what was *not known*. But then we see, as our eyes grow more accustomed to the dimness, a smile on mother's face even as father intensifies his attacks, his passion.

AIDS is a "disease" that trespasses all of our boundaries. It works its way into cells that no cure can reach, lets us think we are fine when, for years, we are already dying; and then launches its attack on all fronts at once, making our bodies revolt in a panic that makes life all the more intense, even as it deserts us. AIDS is, like the libido, a power before which we eventually must give in, but perhaps not without our own victories.

Why shouldn't it be homosexuals who die of AIDS? When our sexuality, born of powerful but never understood urges, evolves into the fine arts we practice and polish in late-twentieth rituals the Greeks could not have imagined. *He asked me to use my hand.* What boundaries *there* are not also trespassed? Homosexuality is, like human will and creativity, the chance to be more than what we have thought we could be.

And why shouldn't it be an *Orientalist* homosexual who lives in dread of AIDS? When the cultivation of the very knowledge he has always sought, even as it is the source of his intellectual pleasures, is a knowledge secured only by transgressing yet other borders: between continents, across oceans, among the exotic men and women he finds he loves, but cannot conceive of without remembering: *they are not you . . . they can never be you . . . how else am I to know you?* Orientalism is, like other kinds of passion, the gamble we take whenever we seek to learn.

"This is where I should have been born. I should be one of these men, speak their language, and have a name as one of them. I should have a low, broad nose like theirs, the earthy colour of their skin, the blackness of their straight hair and oval eyes."[35]

Yet another gay foreign visitor to Japan in the 1980s writes: "Japan has neither a significant gay rights movement nor a very visible gay community, not even in Tokyo. Few people would identify themselves as gay, particularly women, who in Japanese culture are defined by their fathers, husbands and sons."[36] Why, over and over again, do our pronouncements about gay people in Japan decline the very possibilities we award ourselves so routinely?

Edward Said speaks of a "structural irony" produced whenever we look at "an" Oriental both as an individual and as a type.[37] Do we look at the sex to which we are attracted any differently? Is a woman not also: women? The men I fall in love with endowed both with something theirs and no one else's: but also everything that all men are, and without which there is no passion possible.

If Orientalism is inherently ironic, and therefore fatally flawed, then so too is Eros. Perhaps the flaw is in fact an irony we learn to live with, given the alternatives. No, I've got it backwards. It is that irony that we live *for*.

By the middle of next month Daniel will have found an apartment to share with an Austrian who is also beginning work at Tokyo Disneyland. As what? I'll ask. He'll be a Peter Pan, too, but at the other end of the park. He's a twenty-three year-old named Hans. A bit jealous, I dub him Tokyu Hans in a bad pun that only expatriates would understand. Everything here is some kind of inside joke for us, anything so easily rendered a camp witticism. It is a way of *being* in this place we only clumsily come to inhabit. Daniel will stay on here for a few months beyond me, but he will spend that time with another foreigner who, unable to understand himself enough, goes abroad in search of that difference in his race, his nationality, his gender, and most likely his sexuality, too. Rules for Being Any Kind of Homosexual: Number Five. Don't ever think: this is what I was, and this is what I am not any more. Don't ever forget: it is that irony that we live for.

*   *   *

In time Shoko and I lost touch with each other. Needing more space for their child, she and Aki sold the apartment above the Noh theater and bought a house in some inconvenient suburb. Both their careers took up more and more of their time. Aki's architectural firm expanded abroad and he followed. Shoko stayed behind, and I read in the papers one day that she was even thinking of running for the Diet with the patronage of her powerful father. Funaki was transferred to Nagoya, and I moved in with Dan. I don't know what happened to Daniel, but I presume he grew up. We all grew up.

SEPTEMBER

My Tokyo

The heat broke a little early this year, and some days I enjoy going outside again. Tokyo summers can make you feel like an invalid, a shut-in. Crippled by the temperature and handicapped by the humidity only a few weeks ago, now that I feel my strength and energy return. I feel great in September 1987. A miracle cure. Lazarus. I should go to the Yakushi temple in my old neighborhood of Nakano and offer up thanks. A sabbatical year that started badly may end well yet.

A Headline

AIDS CARRIERS TOTAL 298, UP 43 SINCE MAY

Now there are more of us, a government committee reports. "Of them," I will soon be able to say, since this is the month I leave. Give up on the things I never really meant to do, squeeze into cardboard boxes the things I mean to save and take home. *The committee said that AIDS virus carriers and those with AIDS symptoms are now spread out in 34 prefectures*. It has been a good year, all considered, and my book about people whose two cities were destroyed is that much closer to being finished. *Of the 50 with AIDS symptoms, 28 are already dead*. Others things are close to being finished, as well, in this

My Year of AIDS Hysteria, My Year in Japan, My Year on Sabbatical, My Year of the A-Bomb. *Of the seven new cases with AIDS symptoms, three were infected through the use of imported blood products contaminated with the AIDS virus.* I think: okay, I've had twelve months to consider the pluses and minuses of my life so far, to tally up the *son* and *toku* and make a number of decisions about the future, including what is to come after my silly infatuation with this place. *Of the remaining four, three were male homosexuals—one of them a Japanese man in his thirties, another a Japanese man in his forties and a third a foreigner in his thirties.* It's time to rethink both what binds me to Japan and what holds me away at a distance. I'm in my thirties, not young anymore but not old yet, and I can still make a change if I need to. *The fourth is a Japanese woman in her forties married to a foreigner.* This year in Japan has focused my thoughts on where I belong, who I think I am, just when it is I can believe I have found any answers at all. I can take what I have been given here this year and mold it in my hands into whatever friendly gift or deadly weapon I desire. I can hand or hurl it back with the conviction of a person who knows he was, after all, *really here. She was infected through heterosexual intercourse.* Forget what they say about you, in whatever language or with whatever fears that govern them. You know better now. *All of these four people are living in Tokyo.*[1] Living in Tokyo. Why does that seem so important to me just now, so real? Why am I worrying about leaving this place that often wants to reject me? *I do not love you anymore, but I am afraid of being alone.*

Partly it is the lingering heat, partly it is my finances, but I seldom go to Nichōme anymore. I am winding down my year here. No, that's not quite honest. I can't bear the looks, the indifference I meet after so many years of attention. Yes, I'm older now, in my thirties and no new face. Is *that* the truth? I wear an invisible little badge on my shirt, an "AIDS mark" told by my pale white face and paler blue eyes and that speaks as plainly as any yellow star. No, that's not quite honest either. What I can't bear is the beautiful fact of how passion survives all this, how it compels us to meet and even fall in love despite all warnings; how my own desires will still have me cross borders, become Kristeva's Insolent Person: simply be, whatever the consequences. When did you get out? When did you know? What? Why not?

From a pamphlet entitled "AIDS ABCs" published and distributed by the Ministry of Health and Welfare:

Q: What kind of people are at high risk of becoming AIDS carriers?
A: . . . Male homosexual sex behavior is thought to easily lead to infection by the AIDS virus. Moreover, male homosexuals in Europe and North America tend to have sex with an indiscriminate number of partners. (In this they resemble prostitutes.) For these two reasons the virus spread rapidly within the gay male community.[2]

In 1992 the Ministry will prepare a new pamphlet entitled "AIDS Roars with Laughter" that, through the use of cartoons, seeks to educate the public. It teaches that AIDS "declares a war of genocide against human beings" and instructs that "Germany has been infested with homosexuals from ancient times."[3]

Lafcadio Hearn worked piecemeal on an autobiography, but in time abandoned the project. Pierre Loti told the Duchesse de Richelieu that *Madame Chrysanthème*, his most autobiographical work, was "the diary of a summer of my life, in which I have changed nothing, not even the dates. . . . The three principal personages are *myself*, *Japan*, and the *effect* produced on me by that country."[4]

My memoir of this sabbatical year has those same characters plus one more: a viral shadow that pursues me and haunts Japan, and which makes the effect produced on me by that country impossible now to imagine without it. What narrates the history of this one body in this one place speaks through us both, like a ventriloquist through his puppets. One day there will be a cure, I am sure, but the many lessons taught us by this invisible strand of primitive, uncanny proteins will remain.

Dan called one night. He tells me that Brandon left a message on our answering machine. It was long, rambling, hysterical, and manic. "It's all been a mistake," a stratchy voice shouted from the tiny cassette. "I don't have AIDS at all, I'm going to be fine, Steve and I will be able to go to France after all. Isn't that great? Those fuckin' doctors, they don't know shit. Give me a call, we want to hear from you guys, and when are you coming to New York anyway?"

Like Ritsuko, I want to go home too. *"He's losing it. It's got to be dementia."* I am tired of Japan. I miss Dan. *"What are you going to do? Call him back?"* Although I came here a year ago in part to get away from the bad news in

America, it is just as bad here now. *"I mean, you guys were good friends, weren't you?"* I might as well face my fears where I belong, rather than where I do not.

> Meanwhile, a pack of queens were on the move that summer in Europe. Some lived by their wits, others on remittances from home. In 1948 they converged on Rome and Paris and Tangier. In the next decade, it would be Athens and Istanbul; later Tokyo, where life was cheap in the seventies and Americans honored. Then Tokyo excluded them and the survivors fled the setting sun for San Francisco.[5]

In a few years, a major Japanese intellectual journal will devote an entire issue to the theme of "Gay Culture." They mean by that English writers like Isherwood, French philosophers like Foucault, and American artists like Mapplethorpe. All of them are spoken of knowingly by Japanese experts. But not a single word, anywhere in the journal, is expended on Japan or on a Japanese person. The voyeurism of Japan is not complicated by narcissism.

Otori Hidenaga, a theater critic, writes to Japan's readers: "It is difficult for anyone in Tokyo to imagine, but New York is completely 'contaminated' by gay culture. . . . At first it struck me at very odd, but eventually it became commonplace to me—that's how much New York is saturated with gay men."[6]

An unexpected encounter this month: sex with a black man, French, a functionary in his country's embassy. He lives in Azabu, in a building that his government owns.

Guy has a fondness for candles. He lights them all over the bedroom, some on the dresser, some on a small antique Thai table beneath the windowsill—a souvenir of some earlier posting. His English is perfect. I can guess that Guy has lived many places. *Un bac de la monde*. But our sex, like Barthes', is silent, save for the rustle of sheets and the muted rush of late-night traffic two stories below.

Above his bed, in the flickering light of the candles, a scroll hangs with a chain of dancing Chinese characters. In cursive script, I could not have deciphered them even were I looking right-side up. From this low, indecorous angle, they look all the more mysterious still. Hearn's first day in the Orient, and closer and closer to my last: but, almost a century apart, the same fascination with meanings always just beyond our grasp, a truth best realized amid the messy ardor of other, equally foreign, truths.

*   *   *

"When I thought about it," theater critic Otori continues, "I realized nearly all my friends in New York are gay. You could say that I am 'contaminated' by gay culture myself."[7]

   The theater critic tells Japan about a gay party he went in New York. No sex, he tells us. Imagine: a gay party with no sex! In America! *"Nyū Yōku wa mō sekkusu nanka shinai,"* he writes. "There's no *sekkusu* anymore in New York."[8] But there is Brandon, alone with his nightmares and the telephone beside him.

I decide to give my own party. In Tokyo. *"Nan no party?"* Shoko asks. I shrug. Nothing special. A party for myself. *"Ah, wakatta wa yo. Sōbetsukai."* *"De mo nai,"* I retort: not exactly a going-away party either. A party. Just a party. Shoko promises to bring friends. What about Aki? she asks. Of course bring Aki. She gives me an odd look. That was a long time ago, I want to say to her. But in fact, it was only five or six years in the past. Only five or six: but now, how could I think of having sex with this woman? Who would not be expecting me to worry about her health?

"Is it because I am about to leave this country, because I have no longer any link to bind me to it, any resting-place on its soil, and that my spirit is already on the wing?"

   Pierre Loti's Frenchman is about to leave Nagasaki and his little Chrysanthemum. "I know not, but it seems to me that I have never as clearly seen and comprehended it as to-day. And more than ever, do I find it little, aged, with worn-out blood and worn-out sap; I feel more fully its antediluvian antiquity, its centuries of mummification, which will soon degenerate into hopeless and grotesque buffoonery, as it comes into contact with Western novelties."[9]

But I cannot go home. I can only "go back." America ceased being "home" for me a very long time ago—my imaginary communities have not been nations since, at age eighteen, I saw Vietnam. (But that is another story, and not this one.) This latest Asian journey of mine is the one that has shown me how gossamer my fantasy of a place apart was, how real my life in the midst of these trials is. I am eager to return to Seattle, by which I mean to Dan. I know it is inevitable that we will want to retreat into our house and make it the whole of the world—"home" is him, and I am grateful the equation still works—but now I also know that into our house and into the private space we define between us I will carry the weight of all the history we dream we can escape. My own Unidentified Shadowing Object.

I decide to give the party on the Saturday night before my return to America. Many of my friends, both Japanese and foreign, gay and straight, have entertained me frequently this past year. I need to do something for them, throw a real party for all of them. I want to end my year here with an evening that declares: I really did live here. I want a party with many guests with whom I trade inside jokes, references to past intimacies and other things particular to the native. On the eve of my departure I want to give a party that announces: we are here, too, even if not for much longer.

Rumor. A number of Japanese women exchange students at Boston University are sent home to Japan after they test positive.

I start out by calling the people who are the least likely to come without a great deal of notice. Nels, the sometimes-gay newspaper correspondent; Jerry and Jaime, very apt to be away in Hawaii at this still hot time of year; Steven and Joshua, new arrivals from New York here to trade bonds and make a fortune, and for whom I can do the favor of making all the right introductions. And of course, I need to contact the world travelers Sir Richard Burton and Pierre Loti; the always busy scholars Arthur Waley and Roland Barthes; and don't forget Kipling and Benedict, too. I hope they are free.

September 1997. Japan, which in the late 1980s assumed the way to spare itself from AIDS was to exclude foreigners, is today near the end of the 1990s a more sophisticated and placid place. At least it is for me, and in those places I still frequent. It is a country where safer sex and its logic have apparently succeeded far better than in the United States. Japan now acts rationally, not irrationally; and it is people in Seattle, not Tokyo, who are currently witnessing the great (if in hindsight thoroughly predictable) second wave of new infections. How *I've* changed in the past ten years has been to realize how invested I was, and still am, in a kind of global homosexual fraternity that legitimizes my work, even while I have had to face up to how I managed to privilege myself as an Insolent Person within that subculture. I am as convinced as ever that my desires (my perfectly phrased "sexual orientation") govern every moment of how I live my life as a student and teacher of Japan, and likewise other things both of and not of myself .

My visit to Tokyo ten years after I left Tokyo's Mejiro for Seattle's

Fremont is the best in some time. The yen is cheaper than in quite a while, and there are new friends eager to see me. The many little comforts and inevitable surprises of this country impress me all over again. But Ben's house is gone, torn down by its owner to build a more modern building, and my favorite gay bar has closed it doors. I am glad to have lived long enough to know this nostalgia, which is yet one more sure-fire strategy I have of making myself feel I really do belong in Japan.

There are the other guests who I can be sure will show up. Shoko has already said yes, as have Shigeo and Ayako. They all know each other from the early eighties, when we frequently socialized together. Should I invite Chan? Of course. Denny, an antique-dealer friend of mine through Jerry, accepts at once when I call him at the gallery. Barbara can come, but she doesn't know about her husband Nakazato. Babette will be happy for the excuse to flee Kyoto for a weekend. I'll ask her to bring Ravi and Bo along, too. Daniel will be there all day to help me clean the house and run errands. I'll put him in charge of making sure everything is ready for Aziyadé, Chrysanthemum, Ritsuko, Butterfly, and Andrew.

"The almost Oriental politeness of the West Coast," writes Edmund White in his book about gay America, "is one of its most distinctive regional features."[10]

Long ago, before AIDS would give White his only theme, he traveled America and wrote about places like where I am going back to this month. Reading his travelogue now, almost two decades after it was published, it is as if he too were a Western traveler going to foreign, exotic countries. At the time what made Seattle foreign was White's deep attachment to New York, the place where the smartest gay men thought it was natural for them to congregate. *1982. I leave New York, my old home, for my new home.* Now, in the late 1990s, what makes White's description of Seattle so exotic on a second read is that there is no disease, no death or dying, anywhere in it. *I came to Casablanca for the waters. I was misinformed.* My Seattle, not so long after I arrived there and more so now, is a place that AIDS has turned into a miniature version of Edmund White's New York, and his later Paris, too. They have no problems in no places that we do not have here. And what about Tokyo? My Tokyo.

But if my point is that the homosexual Orientalist, like the female one, or those who are "Oriental" themselves, will relate to his or her object of study in ways that complicate and confound the "objectifying" distortion that Said predicts, I must also confess that the gay-Oriental identification across national and racial lines is a very fragile thing, and is itself often complicated and confounded by the quirks of history. In my own case, in this year of my sabbatical, it was Japanese AIDS hysteria (and my own) that questioned the smug exception I had imagined for myself as someone who had a *right* to be in Gay Japan because I was gay, if not Japanese. The cover story I had worked out for myself as an American scholar in the Asian studies business was blown for good. Now it was time to start over, from scratch, and build my rationale on firmer and less conceited grounds.

I suppose that in some sense I am one of Loti's "Western novelties" responsible for Japan's descent into "buffoonery." What have I been doing here this year anyway? Reading a few books, which is something I could have done just as easily back home. Spread my fellowship yen around the local economy. Added a little exoticism and levity to the scene. Isn't the entire scenario ludicrous? An American homosexual in Japan: it's an old story, and always droll. But like Puccini did to Chrysanthemum in making her Butterfly, this is a comedy easily recast as tragedy.

"At the moment of my departure, I can only find within myself a smile of careless mockery for the swarming crowd of this Lilliputian curtseying people,—laborious, industrious, greedy of gain, tainted with a constitutional affection, hereditary insignificance, and incurable monkeyishness."[11] Loti had to say such things, and he would have even if he had not been a racist. This is how one separates oneself from those he loves, by finding myriad faults where yesterday there were none. Each day now I am especially irritated by Tokyo's sheepish crowds, by the climate and the steep cost of everything. My Tokyo: a lover whose left ear one morning suddenly appears misshapen, or whose way of giggling has gotten under my skin. Any excuse will suffice to desert now.

1992.   I am back in Japan briefly, and the Ministry of Education has a large banner hanging outside its building: **AIDS Prevention Begins with Education**. Just what does that mean? What am I missing in this message? If no gay man I meet in Japan engages in unsafe sex, it is hardly thanks to a government that still prefers to speak in riddles over plain truth.

*   *   *

"Now let us have done with that region," says Marco Polo of Japan, "which is very inaccessible and out of the way. Moreover, Messer Marco Polo never was there. And let me tell you the Great Kaan has nothing to do with them, nor do they render him any tribute or service."[12]

But was it so easy for Loti's hero to leave Nagasaki? The last Japanese whom he sees is a relative of Chrysanthemum's, a man described as a "poor cousin, twice removed, who is a djin," which is to say a lowly rickshaw driver. We never learn his name, perhaps he had none: instead, we know him only by the number of his carriage, 415.

> Poor cousin 415, how right I was to have held him in high esteem; he is by far the best and most disinterested of my Japanese family. When all my commissions are finished, he puts up his little vehicle under a tree, and much touched by my departure, insists upon escorting me on board the *Triomphante*, to watch over my final purchases in the sampan which conveys me to the ship, and to see them himself safely into my cabin.
> His, indeed, is the only hand I clasp with a really friendly feeling, without a suppressed smile on quitting this Japan.[13]

Maybe our French lieutenant is a homosexual after all. Not all of us who have come to this country have liked it. But sometimes hate is a way of refusing love, if only because it is a passion of equal pitch.

"The difference between myself and other writers on Japan," wrote Lafcadio Hearn, "is that I have become practically a Japanese."[14] "Practically," he carefully qualified, but what can that mean? That he performed a role all those years, but that it was still a role. Hearn, too, was a transvestite after all. Can any of us go East, not effect a charade, and still be taken seriously? What a problem: we must fake to be real, and we must be real in order to fake.

"There are ways and ways," Rudyard Kipling wrote in 1892, "of entering Japan."[15] Ways and ways of leaving it too, one might add. I start to say good-bye, first by taking some of my academic colleagues out to lunch, giving others small tokens of my appreciation. How do I leave this place? If even only for a while, since I will be back again and again. A year apart at the most, and then something inside me starts yearning for the same city I am now so pleased to disparage. An erotic desire really; a lover whom one demands, even as one wishes all the passion to be over and even forgotten.

So just how dirty was Dirty Dick? As dirty as anyone who cruised the boy brothels of Karachi in the name of the Empire might be. But also as clean as anyone who, by virtue of his desire for people other than his own, could also see how human they are, too. Dirty Dick is my hero, my older brother, my lover. I want him to go discover things with him, find the origin of the Nile by his side, explore those dens of inequity together. Is my own interest in the Orient really a desire to *be* the Orient, or instead its conqueror? Do I want to be Sir Richard, or his submissive servant? My Tokyo.

"Skin Cancer Is On the Rise," reports this month's *Japan Times*, and as proof they offer the news of Ronald Reagan's "cancerous lesion" that had to be removed last month. *But medical science has left many questions unanswered.* All of America' attention is riveted on a little bump on our leader's nose. We are also treated to pictures of polyps in his rectum. Blow by blow descriptions of the Army doctors' deft scalpels. *Why, for example, do many people with fair skin who spend all their lives in the sun not get skin cancer?* God forbid he be taken from us, much less because of a skin lesion. *Why do others with little exposure in the sun develop a malignancy of the skin?* Why indeed? Why *are* some of us taken for such seemingly little cause; and others, the wildest among us, go on forever? Who made up these rules, anyway? *Can a cancer be prevented from recurring?*[16] Such luxurious and enviable questions for our president's doctors to ponder. When *will* I test positive? When *will* I know just who I am?

Today I pack the last of my notes. Two cardboard boxes of little lined cards and sheets of yellow legal-pad paper covered with scribbles, with my crude understanding of what happened decades ago in Hiroshima and Nagasaki. *I think to myself: when I packed to come here, it was with the idea that leaving Dan for a year would be good for the both of us.* Why did I dare to attempt this? An American, and one too young to have anything but a borrowed view of that time? *Now I know better. I should not have come here without him.* Years later, the book will be published, and well received: but I could not let this story of the incineration of two cities out without coupling it to my own story. To how I came, despite everything, to think of this story as mine to tell. *I think to myself: I will not be able to survive this another time without him.*

I return again and again, even a decade later, to the story of Keiko and Asada. Two Nagasaki lovers, one Japanese but married, the other single but Chinese. Why does this particular novel, out of the many from Hiroshima and Nagasaki, affect me so much? In part, yes, because of Asada's cowardice before his death, which reminds me of my own. But there is also my attraction to Keiko, the doomed foreigner in Japan, irradiated by a weapon that I (I: that part of me that is American) assembled and dropped. But the truth also has to be: this illicit affair, wrong for many reasons, is the queerest one I read in my sabbatical year.

Something deep and powerful, not far from a troubling passion, made me write a book about August 1945. I will dedicate it to my friends both real and imagined who did not survive: Japanese in two cities whom I never knew, and to Americans in several more whom I did.

September. The *Japan Times* reports: "No Sign of Cancer in Emperor: Doctor." All of Japan reads of the emperor's recent surgery. Like the American president he is old and susceptible to cancer, if not our other popular modern diseases. *Cancer.* The word strikes even more terror in Japan than it does in America. *Gan.* But the newspapers reassure us. *He consumed 450 cc of a thick soup Tuesday morning.* Hirohito's body, like Reagan's, is better known to us than our own. *And he began walking exercises in the afternoon.* Thousands of us are dead already, and yet even this Emperor's body is more real than our own. *As of Tuesday at noon, the Emperor's temperature was 36.5° C (97.7° F).* In time, it will be the cancerous Reagan who outlives the reportedly cancer-free emperor. *His pulse rate 90 per minute, blood pressure 154 over 78, and respiration 15.* Old men, teetering between life and death, sanity and madness: men who made their careers denying the least bit of truth, but their own blood and bone and muscle and breath are now subjected to more sublime punishments. *The Emperor took 1,000 calories through an intravenous drip of glucose and 200 hundred from food.*[17] I would be happier to die of our own diseases, at home and among friends, than in public with the precise volume of my piss and shit reported to a morbidly curious public.

There will be a second AIDS panic in Japan. In 1991 and lasting into 1992, the Japanese media will once again take cognizance of the virus, but only because a report is released asserting that a large percentage of the foreign sex workers in the Tokyo metropolitan region are HIV+. *Jesusa, how are you doing?* The media, true to form, is ruthless in tracking down the reportedly infected—if they are foreign. The emperor's cancer, the president's nose; and now the Thai or Chinese or Filipina prostitute, left nameless but otherwise as scrutinized as any of our leaders. *Jesusa, we still read all about you!* The rationale was: who can speak of civil rights, of privacy, when all *our* lives are at stake? Surely we know! *Jesusa, listen up*. Remembering Aziyadé, I say: let me be your sister. My final drag. My Tokyo. Your Tokyo. Our Tokyo.

The day of the party is very hot, and the air conditioner has been running all day. The house is still warm, however, and Daniel is sitting in the living room in his underwear drinking a beer when I come back from my last trip to the supermarket. Slightly embarrassed to be this nearly naked in front of me, he goes upstairs to put clothes on.

Shigeo and Ayako are the first to arrive. Daniel is not even back downstairs yet. They leave their shoes in the entrance and stand about awkwardly, not sure if they are entitled to sit on the few chairs I have.

Barbara and Nakazato arrive at the same time Denny does. They are sharing a joke when I open the door for them. I had not realized that they know each other, but am hardly surprised. Soon I have enough guests that the party actually starts. For a while I am free to watch them talk to each other. I lean against the wall in the kitchen, sipping my own drink, and stare out into the living room at a dozen people chat about things other than me and my imminent departure. I catch Daniel's eye as Denny is talking to him, the latter applying the full body press. Now I am the one who is slightly embarrassed.

"Denny, have you met Daniel before?"

"Yes, sure. We all went with Jerry and Jaime to go see, what was it, that movie about, you know, two guys who . . ."

"Oh yeah, a few months ago, right. What has Denny been talking to you about, Daniel?"

"John, it's really a coincidence. Denny here says he knows the guy who's just hired me at Chiba. Denny, do you know this Austrian guy named Hans?"

Suddenly everyone seems to show up at once. Behind Shoko and Aki is Roland Barthes, who's brought Julia Kristeva. Others pile in while Shoko explains to me in unwelcome detail how she's been wearing her new Jurgen Lehl designer jumpsuit everyday for two weeks, including tonight, to break it in properly. When I see that Arthur Waley is by himself in the corner, I take her over to him in order to break away. Meanwhile, Lafcadio is lecturing Sir Richard on penises of the West Indies; and Ruth Benedict is hearing Babette talk about the differences between people in Tokyo and Kyoto. Over by the stereo, Chan is trying to get Empty Sea to talk about his years in China over the din of the music.

I go back into the kitchen to get some more food and bump into Pierre Loti, who is scrounging in the refrigerator looking for something non-alcoholic to drink. When I offer to help, he interrupts to say to me that Brandon is a really sweet guy—have I known him long? But before I can answer, Daniel comes in to tell me that Hank called from the station to ask directions and will be here soon. I ask Ōta Dōkan to pick up the phone and tell him the way.

Shoko comes in to ask for a piece of paper so she can give Sarah her phone number. Kewpie, who's standing nearby with Mr. Kangeroo, lends her a pencil. The room is getting more and more crowded, so I go back out into the living room.

Brandon has cornered Sarah. She looks uncomfortable, so I go over to join them.

"Do you have a good doctor here in Tokyo?"

"Yes, Brandon, you should go to this Nakamura who's at Komagome. He's part of a team that is trying out the experimental trials here in Tokyo. What's your T-count anyway?"

Before I hear Brandon's answer, Daniel grabs me by the arm and leads me to the door. Andrew and Shōgun Tsunayoshi have chipped in to bring a big tray of sushi, and a number of my guests are sitting cross-legged on the floor eating it. Jaime tells me he's thinking of moving back to America, too, but Jerry's work is keeping them here. Fine, I tell him, that way I'll have a place to stay when I come back to visit. Jaime says sure, and now you can return the favor by introducing him to that big blond standing over there talking to Daniel. I turn around to see who he means: it's Stephen. I am struck at just how much he and Daniel look alike.

Arthur comes over and asks me what I'm going to do back in America. Write a book, I answer. Any plans to translate? he asks. Maybe, I answer, but my English is not much better than my Japanese. Arthur waves his hand in the air and says: English is your native country, really now, don't forget it. It is the only language you will ever feel at home in. It's your Japanese you should be worrying about. Okay, Arthur, coming from you, that means something. But how did you ever do it? Arthur just smiles, and excuses himself by saying he has something to ask Roland.

Aziyadé shows up very late, and is in a bad mood until Pinkerton cheers her up. Jackie and Gary light up a joint and pass it around. Aziyadé takes a deep toke and tells Kewpie some joke I don't catch. My party is a complete success. All my friends are here.

There will doubtlessly be more AIDS panics in Japan, or the equivalent. It is the panic that seems to matter here, not the affliction. In 1973 it was a run on sugar and toilet paper that had the nation in a panic. Now, with equal hyperbole, it is a safe blood supply. The Japanese will for a long time yet to come find reasons for doubting they share anything with us, the other peoples of the earth; when in fact, it is their knowledge of how similar we are that inspires their hysteria.

And how do we respond? Some of us embrace the Japanese as we might ourselves, either out of love or the desire to render them immobile by our grasp. Alternatively some of us want to be made like them, by them. That too can be either an honest act of love or one of discreet domination. We are here after all, to assert our own claims to truth, to learn why and how we have come just this far.

It's late now, and I begin to wish my guests would start heading home. But others are still arriving. Scott shows up in a very loud kimono and carrying a Mr. Junko clutch. He tells everyone he's quit graduate school and now has a full-time job as a *urikko* at the Issey Miyake Men's boutique in Aoyama. He vows to stay in Japan until Chiyonofuji marries him.

Miss A is already passed out on the sofa, her head on Jesusa's lap. Daniel has asked Darron to help pick up some of the dirty glasses, and Gaetan is mopping up something that Saikaku spilt in the hallway. The party has moved into its not-pretty phase.

I go into the bathroom, but before I close the door I notice in the mirror over the sink that I can see the reflections of some of my guests in the living room. Nothing, I note, but the queer hardcore. When Glen takes couple of steps to tell Scott something, Luchiano can suddenly see me staring straight at him, and he mouths something silently for me to understand. I give him a big smile in return, and he comes over to join me before the mirror. He tells me I'm looking very good tonight and that he's always thought that he and I should get together. Maybe next time, I tease, when I'm back living in Japan again.

Luchiano fakes a pout, puts one hand over his right breast and then runs a finger from the other up a hairline crack in the mirror that has been there since I moved in. He draws blood. He pretends to be hurt. Whimpering in pain, he raises his bloodied fingertip to my lips. Kiss it and make it better, he says. It's your last chance, he whispers in my ear. Make a Japanese girl happy, he pleads.

It is beautiful weather on Monday, my last day in Tokyo. *Dan calls at seven in the morning to say hello.* All my friends are at work and there is no one to see me off. *He says he's got the whole house ready for me.* But I enjoy being alone today. *"I'll be at the airport gate waiting for you."* I mail boxes of books at the post office, I spend the yen I no longer need in neighborhood stores. *"I want to make love with you, too."* I go today to places I have pleasant memories, and it is Shinjuku where I find myself at noon, in front of the My City department store where I think, no, Their City. *I ask him: "Do you forgive me?"* Soon to be Used-to-be My City. With just a handful of My People in it. *Luchiano, get your damned finger out of my mouth.* My Tokyo.

I don't remember who was the last to leave the party on Saturday. Daniel walked out to the main street and flagged down taxis for everyone. I go through the house picking up leftover drinks and soiled napkins. That done, I start upstairs to check on Ben's room only to come across Asada and Keiko sitting on the staircase and sharing a cigarette. Great party, Asada says. I really liked your friends, adds Keiko. Especially Guy, she says. Asada is looking much better than the last time I saw him, and I tell him so. There is a long moment of an almost awkward silence between us on the staircase, interrupted only by the sound of Daniel coming back into the house after seeing off the last guests.

"So what will you do when you get back to Seattle?"

I tell Asada about how I have to start teaching again, but the first thing will be to find a place to live. Daniel comes over and sits down on a stair, too.

"What are you going to do, Daniel?"

Daniel tells us about Hans, their apartment, and the jobs they'll have at Tokyo Disneyland.

"Well, we'll miss you, John. Maybe one day Keiko and I will make it to America. The doctors say I'll be okay for at least another couple of years." Keiko looks right into my eyes as her lover tells me this.

Nagasaki is a long way from my house, so I tell Asada and Keiko to spend the night upstairs in Ben's room. I hear them opening the closet and rolling out the futon while Daniel and I finish cleaning up. When we're done, we have a nightcap together in the living room, and Daniel asks me about all the guests he he hadn't met before tonight. Denny's going to take him surfing near Fujisawa tomorrow, he says. And that older woman, Shoko, has invited him to come over for dinner soon.

Later that night, Daniel already asleep in his futon on the living room floor, I am tossing and turning. The room is hot, and I think about all the things I need to do before getting on the plane. For some reason I suddenly decide I should take that cracked mirror down off the bathroom wall. I am probably thinking I'll replace it tomorrow with a new one. I need to leave Ben's house having made at least some improvement to it. But as I am wrestling with the glass, trying not to wake anyone up, it shatters neatly along the crack and falls in pieces to the floor. The Great Mirror Shattered. I say to hell with it and go back to bed. By the time I get up late Sunday morning, someone has swept up all the shards for me.

A bit earlier than I have to, I hail a cab Monday afternoon to take me and my luggage from Ben's house to the downtown airport terminal. As I pass through emigration, I surrender my Japanese identity card and get my passport stamped with the state's permission to leave. Just before boarding I make one last phone call with the last of my Japanese coins. I call Tetsuji, who by luck is at home teaching some private students. I don't tell him that I wish he had come to the party. I know he had his reasons. Instead, I just tell him I am leaving today. He wishes me well, as I do him.

NOTES

Certain Details

1. Abe Takeshi, quoted in James W. Dearing, "Foreign Blood and Domestic Politics: The Issue of AIDS in Japan," in Elizabeth Fee and Daniel M. Fox, eds., *AIDS: The Making of a Chronic Disease* (Berkeley and Los Angeles: University of California Press, 1992), 331–32.

2. Randy Shilts, *And the Band Played On: Politics, People, and the AIDS Epidemic* (New York: St. Martin's Press, 1987), 156.

3. Nicholas Bornoff, *Pink Samurai: Love, Marriage and Sex in Contemporary Japan* (New York: Pocket Books, 1991), 424.

4. Okado Tetsuo, "Sei to ai no ijōsei: eizu shokku no naka de," *Gendai esupuri*, no. 239 (June 1987), 13.

5. Matsudo Jūzo, quoted in Ishii Shinji, ed., *Eizu no bunka jinruigaku: "Eizu genshō" o dō yomu ka* (Tokyo: JICC Shuppankyoku, 1987), 41.

6. "Japanese Hemophiliacs Unhappy with Doctors' Handling of AIDS Crisis," Japan Economic Newswire, Kyodo News Service, March 23, 1987.

7. Kohama Itsurō, "Eizu no erosu-teki sonzai," in Ishii, 133.

8. Boye De Mente, *Bachelor's Japan* (Rutland, VT: Charles E. Tuttle Co., 1989), 89.

9. "Five More AIDS Victims Reported," *Japan Times*, September 27, 1986.

10. Hadley Cantril, *The Invasion from Mars* (Princeton, NJ: Princeton University Press, 1947), 9.

11. Ihara Saikaku, *The Great Mirror of Male Love*, trans. Paul Gordon Schalow (Stanford, CA: Stanford University Press, 1990), 189.

12. Kogawa Tetsuo, "Eizu to 'densen' media no shūen," *Gendai shisō*, vol. 14, no. 9 (September 1986), 180.

13. George Hughes, "Lafcadio Hearn and the Fin de Siècle," in Sukehiro Hirakawa, ed., *Rediscovering Lafcadio Hearn: Japanese Legends, Life and Culture* (Kent, UK: Global Oriental, 1997), 88.

Stray Dogs, Ready Cash

1. Marco Polo, "Marco Polo's Account of Japan and Java," in *Old South Leaflets, Volume II* (Boston: Directors of the Old South Work, undated), 17.

2. Ihara Saikaku, 197.

3. Basil Hall Chamberlain, *Things Japanese: Being Notes on Various Subjects Connected with Japan, for the Use of Travellers and Others* (London: K. Paul, Trench, Trubner & Co., 1927), 4.

4. Marco Polo, ibid.

5. Hadley Cantrel, 6.

6. Ibid., 22.

7. Ibid., 32.

8. Ibid., 16.

9. Ibid., 41.

10. Julia Kristeva, *Strangers to Ourselves*, trans. Leon S. Roudiez (New York: Columbia University Press, 1991), 30.

11. Boye De Mente, 26.

12. Ōshima Kiyoshi, *Seikimatsu no yamai* (Tokyo: Kōbunsha, 1986), 40.

13. Julia Kristeva, 31.

14. Ibid.

15. E. M. Forster, *A Passage to India* (San Diego, CA: Harcourt Brace Jovanovich, 1984), 322.

16. *Sannō gaiki*, quoted by Donald H. Shively in "Tokugawa Tsunayoshi, the Genroku Shogun," in Albert M. Craig and Donald H. Shively, *Personality in Japanese History* (Berkeley and Los Angeles: University of California Press, 1970), 98.

17. Ibid., 99.

18. Ibid., 110–11.

New Words

1. Thomas Mann, "Death in Venice," in *Death in Venice and Seven Other Stories*, trans. by H. T. Lowe-Porter (New York: Knopf, 1954), 53.

2. Akasaka Norio, "Eizu ni okeru kyōkai to kōtsū," in Ishii, 95.

3. Thomas Mann, 64.

4. "Teachers, Students Want to Keep Out Foreigners with AIDS," *Japan Times*, April 30, 1987.

5. " 'Shiitake' Substance Might Deter AIDS," *Japan Times*, March, 26 1989.

6. Hadley Cantril, 42.

7. Kent Ashford, *The Singalong Tribe* (London: GMP, 1986), 84–85.

8. Thomas Mann, 64.

9. Ibid., 6–7.

10. Jean-Paul Sartre, *Saint Genet: Actor and Martyr*, trans. Barnard Fretchman (New York: New American Library, 1964), 91.

11. Ruth Benedict, *The Chrysanthemum and the Sword: Patterns of Japanese Culture* (Boston: Houghton Mifflin Co., 1946), iii.

12. "No Minorities in Japan, Government Declares," *Japan Times*, November 22, 1986.

The Common Good

1. Thomas Mann, 67.

2. E. M. Forster, *Howard's End* (Cutchogue, NY: Buccaneer Books, Inc., 1984), 224.

3. Emiko Ohnuki-Tierney, *Illness and Culture in Contemporary Japan* (Cambridge: Cambridge University Press, 1984), 42.

4. Thomas Mann, 65.

5. Pierre Loti, *Madame Chrysanthème*, trans. Laura Ensor (London: Routledge, 1985), 11.

6. Lafcadio Hearn, *Writings from Japan: An Anthology*, edited with an introduction by Francis King (London: Penguin Books, 1984), 38.

7. Peter Katel, "Choosing to Die," *Newsweek*, May 16, 1994.

8. Pierre Loti, 95.

9. "AIDS Virus Found in Blood Samples," *Japan Times*, December 6, 1986.

The Theory of the Japanese People

1. Rudyard Kipling, *Kipling's Japan: Collected Writings*, eds. Hugh Cortazzi and George Webb (London and Atlantic Highlands, NJ: The Athlone Press, 1988), 77–78.

2. Ibid.

3. Thomas Mann, 57.

4. "Ministry Reports First Diagnosis of Female AIDS Patients Here," *Japan Times*, January 18, 1987.

5. Eric A. Feldman and Shohei Yonemoto, "Japan: AIDS as a 'Non-Issue," in *AIDS in the Industrialized Democracies: Passions, Politics, and Policies*, eds. David L. Kirp and Ronald Bayer (New Brunswick, NJ: Rutgers University Press, 1992), 344–45.

6. Cindy Patton, *Inventing AIDS* (New York and London: Routledge, 1990), 39.

7. "Thirty-three Tokyo Residents Test Positive for AIDS Antibody," *Japan Times*, January 24, 1987.

8. Edward Said, *Orientalism* (New York: Vintage Books, 1979), 125.

9. Edward Said, 190.

10. Ibid.

11. Sir Richard Francis Burton, *A Plain and Literal Translation of the Arabian Nights Entertainments, Now Entitled The Book of the Thousand Nights and a Night, With Introduction, Explanatory Notes on the Manners and Customs*

of Moslem Men and a Terminal Essay Upon the History of The Nights by Richard F. Burton (Benares: The Kamashastra Society, 1885–86), vol. I, 316.

12. Alex Shoumatoff, "In Search of the Source of AIDS," *Vanity Fair*, vol. 57, no. 7 (July 1988), 96, 117.

13. Shimada Masahiko with Larry McCaffery, "Avant-Pop, Aprés-Pop," *Yuriika*, vol. 26, no. 6 (June 1994), 136.

14. Thomas Mann, 63.

15. Akasaka Norio, 91.

16. Hadley Cantril, 41–2.

17. Eric Feldman and Shohei Yonemoto, 351.

18. Shimada Masahiko with Larry McCaffery, 137.

Morals Business

1. Hadley Cantril, 23.

2. "Law Considered to Bar Entry of AIDS Carriers," *Japan Times*, February 4, 1987.

3. Emmanuel Dreuilhe, *Mortal Embrace: Living with AIDS*, trans. Linda Coverdale (New York: Hill and Wang, 1988), 113–4.

4. J. E. De Becker, *The Nightless City . . . or the "History of the Yoshiwara Yukwaku"* (Yokohama: M. Nossler & Co., 1905), 367–68.

5. Ibid., 368.

6. Ihara Saikaku, 304.

7. Jocelyn Ford, "Fear of AIDS Sparks Stringent Gov't Reaction," Japan Economic Newswire, Kyodo News Service, February 25, 1987.

8. J. E. De Becker, 371.

9. Englebert Kaempfer, quoted in Oliver Statler, *The Japanese Inn* (New York: Random House, 1961), 158.

10. "Eizu no hisshi kamoku," *Asahi jānaru*, vol. 29, no. 5 (February 6, 1987), 92.

11. Shimada Masahiko, *Mikakunin bikō buttai* (Tokyo: Bungei Shunjū, 1991), 68.

12. Rudyard Kipling, *Kim* (London: Penquin Books, 1989), 174.

13. Ibid., 331.

14. Richard O'Brien, "The Rocky Horror Picture Show" (Http://faq. rhps.org/faqtext/t-ttrhs.txt: August 21, 1997), 24–25.

15. Yozo Narita, "Taking Stock," *Japan Times*, August 27, 1991.

16. Shimada Masahiko, *Mikakunin bikō buttai*, 33–34.

17. Jean Pearce, "Getting Things Done," *Japan Times*, October 18, 1992.

18. Shimada Masahiko, *Mikakunin bikō buttai*, 34–35.

19. Roland Barthes, *Empire of Signs*, trans. Richard Howard (New York: Hill and Wang, 1982), 53.

20. Karatano Kōjin with Watanabe Yūji, "Metafā to shite no eizu: Jinrui no yamai ni obieru tan'itsu minzoku kokka no men'ekikei," *Asahi jānaru*, vol. 29, no. 6 (February 13, 1987), 88.

21. Shimada Masahiko, *Mikakunin bikō buttai*, 109.

22. Barthes, "Pierre Loti," in *Critical Essays*, trans. Richard Howard (New York: Hill and Wang, 1980), 116.

23. Asada Akira, "AIDS no/AIDS ni yoru datsukochiku," in Shimada Masahiko, *Mikakunin bikō buttai*, 187.

24. Shimada Masahiko, *Mikakunin bikō buttai*, 130.

25. Ibid., 183.

26. Roland Barthes, *Roland Barthes by Roland Barthes*, trans. Richard Howard (New York: Hill and Wang, 1977), 184.

27. Shimada Masahiko, *Mikakunin bikō buttai*, 43–44.

28. Roland Barthes, quoted in Louis Jean Calvet, *Roland Barthes: A Biography*, trans. Sarah Wykes (Bloomington: Indiana University Press, 1995), 68.

29. Asada Akira, 184–5.

30. Shimada Masahiko, *Mikakunin bikō buttai*, 148.

31. J. Hillis Miller, "The Critic as Host," in Harold Bloom et al., *Deconstruction and Criticism* (New York: The Seabury Press, 1979), 221–22.

32. Ibid., 222.

33. Ibid., 253.

34. Asada Akira, 186.

The Social Situation

1. "Law Would Bar Aliens with AIDS," *Japan Times*, March 27, 1987.

2. Tacite Eiji, quoted in Philippa Bourke, "Bad Blood," *Tokyo Journal*, vol. 13, no.4 (April 1994), 33.

3. "Japanese Hemophiliacs Unhappy with Doctors' Handling of AIDS Crisis," Japan Economic Newswire, Kyodo News Service, March 23, 1987.

4. Emmanuel Dreuihle, 128.

5. Philippa Bourke, 34.

6. Ueno Teruaki, "Ostracism, Hysteria Plagues Japan's AIDS Patients," Reuter Library Report, May 17, 1992.

7. Ruth Benedict, *Patterns of Culture* (Boston and New York: Houghton Mifflin, 1934), 262.

8. Margaret Mead, quoted in Margaret M. Caffrey, *Ruth Benedict: Stranger in This Land* (Austin: University of Texas Press, 1989), 329.

9. Padre Gaspar Vilela, quoted in C. R. Boxer, *The Christian Century in Japan 1549–1650* (Berkeley: University of California Press, 1967), 69.

10. Ruth Benedict, "Sex in Primitive Society," in *An Anthropologist at Work: Writings of Ruth Benedict*, ed. Margaret Mead (Westport, CT: Greenwood Press, 1977), 572–73.

11. Ruth Benedict, "Anthropology and the Abnormal," in *An Anthropologist at Work*, 267–68.

12. Margaret M. Caffrey, 301.

13. Sir Richard Francis Burton, vol. X, 312–18.

14. Ruth Benedict, "Sex in Primitive Society," 572.

15. Shimada Masahiko, *Mikakunin bikō buttai*, 107–8.

16. Sata Ineko, *Juei*, in *Nihon no genbaku bungaku*, ed. Kaku-sensō no kiken o uttaeru bungakusha (Tokyo: Horupu Shuppan, 1984), vol. IV, 144.

17. Susan Baur, *Hypochondria: Woeful Imaginations* (Berkeley: University of California Press, 1988), 153.

18. Ruth Benedict, *The Chrysanthemum and the Sword*, 187–89.

Special Friends

1. Matsuda Jūzo, quoted in Ishii, 42.

2. Christopher John Farley, "Grapevine," *Time* (April 19, 1993), 15.

3. Matsuda Jūzo, quoted in Ishii, 43.

4. Yonemoto Shōhei, "Eizu-gaku genron," *Chūō kōron*, vol. 102, no. 5 (April, 1987), 197.

5. Ibid., 200.

6. Renée Sabatier, *Blaming Others: Prejudices, Race and Worldwide AIDS* (Philadelphia: New Society Publishers, 1988), 114.

7. Fawn McKay Brodie, *The Devil Drives: A Life of Sir Richard Burton* (New York: W. W. Norton, 1967), 34.

8. "Aiding the Stock Market with a Rumor of AIDS," *Japan Times*, May 7, 1987.

9. Shaykh Nafzawi, *The Glory of the Perfumed Garden: The Missing Flowers* (London: Neville Spearman, 1975), 39–40.

10. Richard Burton, vol. X, 88.

11. Shaykh Nafzawi, 57.

12. Lafcadio Hearn, *Writings from Japan: An Anthology*, 147.

13. Sir Rutherford Alcock, *The Capital of the Tycoon: A Narrative of a Three Years' Residence in Japan* (New York: Harper & Brothers, 1863), II, 189–90.

14. Lee Edelman, "The Plague of Discourse: Politics, Literary Theory, and AIDS," *South Atlantic Quarterly* vol. 88, no.1 (Winter 1989), 310.

15. Basil Hall Chamberlain, 360.

16. Fawn McKay Brodie, 108.

17. Ibid., 143.

18. Ibid., 321.

19. W. G. Archer, quoted in Brodie, 77.

20. Isabel Burton, quoted in Alexander Maitland, *Speke* (London: Constable, 1971), 202.

A Play of Muscles

1. William M. Hoffman, *As Is* (New York: Random House, 1985), 94.

2. Lafcadio Hearn, *Writings from Japan: An Anthology*, 147–48.

3. "AIDS Carriers Similar to Cockroaches, Expert Says," *Japan Times*, September 5, 1987.

4. William M. Hoffman, 94.

5. Ueda Akinari, "The Blue Cowl," in *Partings at Dawn: An Anthology of Japanese Gay Literature*, ed. Stephen D. Miller (San Francisco: Gay Sunshine Press, 1966), 128.

6. *Shūkan Asahi*, vol. 42, no. 19 (May 8, 1987), 1.

7. Ruth Benedict, "The Uses of Cannibalism," *An Anthropologist at Work*, 44.

8. Shimada Masahiko, *Mikakunin bikō buttai*, 122.

9. Hadley Cantril, 147.

10. Lafcadio Hearn, ibid., 338.

11. Marco Polo, 4.

12. Lafcadio Hearn, *Letters from the Raven*, ed. Milton Bronner (New York: Boni Books, 1907), 133.

13. Emmanuel Dreuihle, 20.

14. Lafcadio Hearn, *Glimpses of Unfamiliar Japan* (Rutland, VT: Charles. E. Tuttle Co., 1976), 69.

15. Lafcadio Hearn, *The Writings of Lafcadio Hearn* (Boston: Houghton Mifflin, 1923), XIII, 10.

16. Lafcadio Hearn, *Writings from Japan*, 47.

17. Paul Murray, *A Fantastic Journey: The Life and Literature of Lafcadio Hearn* (Sandgate: Japan Library, 1993), 218.

18. William M. Hoffman, 95.

19. Thomas Mann, 64.

20. Emmanuel Dreuilhe, 20.

21. Lafcadio Hearn, *Writings from Japan*, 140.

22. "A Strange Career," *New York Sun*, July 27, 1906.

23. Shimada Masahiko, *Mikakunin bikō buttai*, 156–57.

24. Quoted in Ivan Morris, ed., *Madly Singing in the Mountains* (New York: Walker and Co., 1970), 196.

25. George Orwell, *Shooting an Elephant, and Other Essays* (New York: Harcourt, Brace, 1950), 2.

26. Lafcadio Hearn, *Two Years in the French West Indies* (New York and London: Harper, 1923), 40.

27. Ibid., 38–39.

28. William M. Hoffman, 94.

Syntax, Et Cetera

1. Michel Foucault, *The Order of Things: An Archaelogy of the Human Sciences* (New York: Random House, 1990), xv.

2. Jocelyn Ford, "AIDS a Timebomb for Homosexuals in Japan," Japan Economic Newswire, Kyodo News Service, June 18, 1987.

3. Jean Cocteau, *Le livre blanc*, trans. Margaret Crosland (London: Peter Owen Limited, 1969), 38.

4. Ruth Benedict, *The Chrysanthemum and the Sword*, 177.

5. Emmanuel Dreuihle, 133.

6. Roland Barthes, *Empire of Signs*, 28–29.

7. Randy Shilts, 158.

8. E. M. Forster, 63.

9. Rudyard Kipling, *Kipling's Japan*, 84.

10. Roland Barthes, ibid., 6.

11. Ōe Kenzaburō, *Chiryōtō* (Tokyo: Iwanami Shoten, 1990), 92–93.

12. Jocelyn Ford.

13. Edward Said, *Culture and Imperialism*, 136.

14. Rudyard Kipling, ibid., 242.

15. E. M. Forster, 55.

16. Shimada Masahiko, *Mikakunin bikō buttai*, 83.

17. Lafcadio Hearn, *Writings from Japan*, 296.

18. Rudyard Kipling, ibid., 210.

19. Roland Barthes, quoted in Calvet, 153.

20. Jocelyn Ford.

21. Roland Barthes, quoted in Calvet, 181.

22. Oscar Wilde, quoted in Kipling, ibid., 45–46.

23. Rudyard Kipling, ibid., 35.

24. Andrew Holleran, *Ground Zero* (New York: New American Library, 1988), 22.

25. Jocelyn Ford.

26. Roland Barthes, ibid., 79.

27. Edward Said, "Introduction," in Kipling, *Kim*, 42.

28. Roland Barthes, ibid., 17.

29. Fawn McKay Brodie, 48.

30. E. M. Forster, *A Passage to India* (New York and London: Harcourt Brace Jovanovich, 1952), 64–65.

31. Roland Barthes, ibid., 99.

32. "A Strange Career," New York *Sun*, July 27, 1906.

33. Rudyard Kipling, *Kim*, 164.

34. Boye De Mente, 112.

35. Roland Barthes, ibid., 23.

36. E. M. Forster, 322.

37. Edward Said, *Culture and Imperialism*, 227.

M. Andrew

1. Pierre Loti, quoted in Alec G. Hargreaves, *The Colonial Experience in French Fiction: A Study of Pierre Loti, Ernest Psichari and Pierre Mille* (London and Basingstoke: 1981), 23.

2. Shimada Masahiko with Larry McCaffery, 137.

3. Ōe Kenzaburō, 114–18.

4. Waku Shunzo, *Eizu-gai no renzoku satsujin* (Tokyo: Kōdansha, 1987), 162.

5. "Women Protest 'Human Trash' Game," *Japan Times*, September 4, 1991.

6. Michael G. Lerner, *Pierre Loti* (New York: Twayne Publishers, 1974), 65.

7. Pierre Loti, *Aziyadé*, trans. Marjorie Laurie (London: Kegan Paul International, 1989), 48, 52.

8. Roland Barthes, "Pierre Loti: *Aziyadé*," in *New Critical Essays*, trans. Richard Howard (New York: Hill and Wang, 1980), 116.

9. Roland Barthes, *Empire of Signs*, 3.

10. Roland Barthes, "Pierre Loti," 105.

11. Pierre Loti, *Madame Chrysanthème*, 184.

12. Shimada Masahiko, *Mikakunin bikō buttai*, 97.

13. Pierre Loti, *Aziyadé*, 12.

14. Pierre Loti, *Aziyadé*, 273–4.

15. Roland Barthes, "Pierre Loti," 116.

16. Pierre Loti, *Madame Chrysanthème*, 7.

17. Cecilia Segawa Siegle, *Yoshiwara: The Glittering World of the Japanese Courtesan* (Honolulu: University of Hawai'i Press, 1993), 23.

18. Pierre Loti, *Aziyadé*, 38.

19. Emmanuel Dreuilhe, 51.

20. Pierre Loti, *Madame Chrysanthème*, 149.

21. Ibid., 317.

22. Ibid., 294–95.

23. Pierre Loti, *Aziyadé*, 130.

24. Ibid., 290–91.

25. Wayne Koestenbaum, *The Queen's Throat: Opera, Homosexuality, and the Mystery of Desire* (New York, Poseidon Press, 1993), 199–200.

26. Roland Barthes, "Pierre Loti," 111.

27. Ibid., 114.

28. Pierre Loti, *Aziyadé*, 101.

29. Ibid., 144.

30. Ibid., 316.

31. Ibid., 150–51.

The Great Sympathetic Paradox

1. Ruth Benedict, "Anthropology and the Abnormal," 278.

2. Sarah Schulman, *My American History: Lesbian and Gay Life During the Reagan/Bush Years* (New York: Routledge, 1994), 243.

3. Sheila K. Johnson, *The Japanese Through American Eyes* (Stanford: Stanford University Press, 1988), 88.

4. Edward Said, *Orientalism*, 95.

5. Ibid., 158, 157.

6. Roland Barthes, *Empire of Signs*, 3.

7. Sheila K. Johnson, 89.

8. Edward Said, ibid., 166–67.

9. Ibid., 188.

10. Ibid., 207.

11. Ibid., 231.

12. Ibid., 130.

13. Roland Barthes, "Pierre Loti," 115.

14. Ruth Benedict, ibid., 263.

15. Edward Said, ibid., 260.

16. Roland Barthes, *Empire of Signs*, 4.

17. Sarah Schulman, 244.

18. Somerset Maugham, *Of Human Bondage* (New York: The Modern Library, 1942), 537.

19. Richard H. Minear, "Orientalism and the Study of Japan," *Journal of Asian Studies*, vol. 39, no. 3 (May 1980), 507.

20. Roland Barthes, "Pierre Loti," 117.

21. Pierre Loti, *Aziyadé*, 102.

22. Jonathan Dollimore, *Sexual Dissidence: Augustine to Wilde, Freud to Foucault* (Oxford and New York: Oxford University Press, 1991), 250.

23. Sarah Schulman, 246.

24. Thomas Mann, 5–6.

25. Joseph A. Boone, "Vacation Cruises; or, The Homoerotics of Orientalism," *PMLA*, vol. 110, no. 1 (January 1995), 89.

26. Ibid., 90–91.

27. Ian Buruma, *The Missionary and the Libertine: Love and War in East and West* (London and Boston: Faber and Faber, 1996), 40.

28. André Gide, *If It Die*, trans. Dorothy Bussy (London: Secker and Warburg, 1951), 259.

29. Pierre Loti, ibid., 43, 78.

30. Sigmund Freud, "Libido Theory and Narcissism," *The Standard Edition of the Complete Psychological Works of Sigmund Freud*, trans. James Strachey (London: Hogarth Press, 1966–74), XVI, 427.

31. Thomas Mann, 62.

32. Merv Haddad, "The Discreet Charm of Gay Life in Japan in the Early 1980s," in Stephen O. Murray, ed., *Oceanic Homosexualities* (New York and London: Garland Publishing, Inc., 1992), 373.

33. Edward Seidensticker, quoted in Buruma, ibid.

34. Matteo Ricci, quoted in Jonathan Spence, *The Memory Palace of Matteo Ricci* (New York: Viking, 1984), 229.

35. Peter A. Jackson, *The Intrinsic Quality of Skin* (Bangkok: Floating Lotus Books, 1994), 31.

36. Merv Haddad, 371.

37. Edward Said, ibid., 234.

My Tokyo

1. "AIDS Carriers Total 298, Up 43 Since May," *Japan Times*, September 25, 1997.

2. Shoseishō kansen taisakushitsu, ed., *Eizu ABC*, no date, 3.

3. "Protest Forces Sponsors to Cancel AIDS Booklet," *Japan Times*, November 30, 1992.

4. Pierre Loti, *Madame Chrysanthème*, 4.

5. Gore Vidal, *Palimpsest: A Memoir* (New York: Random House, 1995), 176.

6. Ōtori Hidenaga, "Eizu no shintai," *Yuriika*, vol. 25, no. 5 (May 1993), 128.

7. Ibid.

8. Ibid., 129.

9. Pierre Loti, ibid., 327–28.

10. Edmund White, *States of Desire: Travels in Gay America* (New York: E. P. Dutton, 1980), 1.

11. Pierre Loti, ibid., 328.

12. Marco Polo, "Marco Polo's Account of Japan and Java," 5.

13. Pierre Loti, ibid., 329.

14. Lafcadio Hearn, quoted in Paul Murray, *A Fantastic Journey* (Folkestone: Japan Library, 1993), 186.

15. Rudyard Kipling, *Kipling's Japan*, 195.

16. "Skin Cancer Is on the Rise," *Japan Times*, September 16, 1987.

17. "No Signs of Cancer in Emperor: Doctor," *Japan Times*, September 30, 1987.